Towards Universality
Le Corbusier, Mies and De Stijl

D0537795

The central theme of this book is the striving for universality as opposed to the individual and the particular. The foundation manifesto of De Stijl begins: *There exist an old and a new consciousness of the age. The old is directed towards the individual. The new is directed towards the universal* (1918). This first opposition is intersected, however, by a second one: that between the open and the closed. The universality aimed at by De Stijl artists like Van Doesburg and Mondrian resembled that of the universe itself: it was boundless. Their paintings continued, in theory, beyond the limits of the canvas; their architecture sought to abolish the wall as the boundary between interior and exterior space. But each of Le Corbusier's buildings and paintings was itself a self-contained universe, held within a clear frame. Mies fluctuated between two ideals; in the 1920s, in such designs as the brick country house and the Barcelona Pavilion, he outdid even the De Stijl architects in openness, but in his later work in America he reverted to the closed neo-classical box.

Richard Padovan has worked as an architect in various European countries and published extensively. He is the author of *Proportion: Science, Philosophy, Architecture* (1999) and *Dom Hans van der Laan, Modern Primitive* (1994), and his translation of Van der Laan's *Architectonic Space* appeared in 1983.

First Manifesto of *De Stijl*, 1918

1 There exist an old and a new consciousness of the age.
   The old is directed towards the individual.
   The new is directed towards the universal.
   The struggle of the individual against the universal shows itself in the world war as well as in today's art.

2 The war is destroying the old world together with its content: the dominance of the individual in every field.

3 The new art has brought to the fore the content of the new consciousness: equilibrium between the universal and the individual.

4 The new consciousness is ready to realize itself in every field, including exterior life.

5 Tradition, dogma and the dominance of the individual (the natural) stand in the way of that realization.

6 We, the founders of the New Representation,* therefore call upon all those who believe in the reform of art and culture to destroy whatever impedes this development, just as we have destroyed it by abolishing naturalistic form in the new representational art. For naturalism hampers that pure expression which is the ultimate consequence of every true artistic conception.

7 Throughout the world, today's artists, driven by a shared consciousness, engage in a world war fought out on the spiritual plane against the dominance of individualism and arbitrariness. We therefore identify ourselves with all those who struggle, either spiritually or materially, for the creation of international unity in Life, Art and Culture.

8 For this purpose we have set up the journal *De Stijl*, the aim of which is to bring to light the new philosophy of life. Everyone can participate by:

9.1 Sending your (full) name, address and profession to the editors as a token of support.

9.2 Contributing material (critical, philosophical, architectural, scientific, literary, musical, etc., as well as illustrative) to the monthly *De Stijl*.

9.3 Distributing and translating into other languages the ideas published in *De Stijl*.

Signatures of the contributors: ANTONY KOK, poet
THEO VAN DOESBURG, painter   PIET MONDRIAAN, painter
ROBERT VAN'T HOFF, architect   G. VANTONGERLOO, sculptor
VILMOS HUSZAR, painter   JAN WILS, architect

---

* In Dutch, *Nieuwe Beelding*, literally 'new imaging'. Although the published English version gives 'new plastic art', hence the generally adopted term 'Neo-Plasticism', the author argues in Chapter 2 that 'new representation' is preferable.

Towards Universality
Le Corbusier, Mies and De Stijl

Richard Padovan

London and New York

*This edition includes no reproduction of artists' original drawings.
The reproductions which are herein are the subject of the
author's interpretation.*

First published 2002 by Routledge
11 New Fetter Lane, London EC4P 4EE

Simultaneously published in the USA and Canada by Routledge
29 West 35th Street, New York, NY 10001

Routledge is an imprint of the Taylor & Francis Group

Typeset in Gill Sans by Bookcraft Ltd, Stroud, Gloucestershire
Printed in Malta by Gutenberg Press

British Library Cataloguing in Publication Data
A catalogue record for this book is available from the British Library

Library of Congress Cataloging in Publication Data
Padovan, Richard.
  Towards universality: Le Corbusier, Mies, and De Stijl/Richard Padovan.
    p. cm.
  includes bibliographical references and index.
  1. De Stijl (Art movement) – Influence. 2. Modern movement
  (Architecture). 3. Le Corbusier, 1897–1965 – Criticism and interpretation.
  4. Mies van de Rohe, Ludwig, 1886–1969 – Criticism and interpretation.
  I. Title.
NA1148.5.D42 P33 2001
7241'.6–dc21   2001019119

ISBN 0–415–25962–2 (hbk)
ISBN 0–419–24030–6 (pbk)

Contents

Figures

This edition includes no reproduction of artists' original drawings. The reproductions which are herein have been redrawn by the author and are the subject of the author's interpretation.

Preface

The main protagonists of this book are Le Corbusier, Mies van der Rohe and the De Stijl group. Its purpose is not to add to the already vast literature on these three separate subjects; rather, it aims to explore the relations *between* them, and especially the influence that De Stijl exerted on Le Corbusier and Mies – as well as on several other figures, such as Donald Judd. But while the relation of Le Corbusier and Mies to De Stijl may reveal new aspects of these individuals, my principal objective is the converse: to locate De Stijl more precisely through its relation to Le Corbusier, Mies and other artists. For the De Stijl phenomenon is notoriously elusive. As soon as you think you have finally managed to pin it down you discover that it has changed its form, slipped from your grasp and reappeared in another corner of the field.

In his book *Painting as Model* Yve-Alain Bois puts forward three distinct though mutually overlapping definitions of the phenomenon 'De Stijl': as a journal, as a group of artists and as an idea. None of these definitions is entirely satisfactory. The first is undermined, as he points out, by the eclectic policy of the journal's editor, Theo van Doesburg, who in 1927 not only listed among the 'main collaborators' of De Stijl the dadaists Hugo Ball, Hans Arp and Hans Richter, the futurist Gino Severini, the constructivist El Lissitzky and the sculptor Constantin Brancusi, but added to them his own dadaist and futurist aliases, I.K. Bonset and Aldo Camini. The second, more common, identification of De Stijl with the original signatories of the foundation manifesto is only slightly more accurate, however. Apart from the fact that it leaves out three important architect members of the group (J.J.P. Oud, Gerrit Rietveld and Cor van Eesteren) who either refused or joined too late to sign, Bois points out that it fails to take account of such things as 'van der Leck's defection from the movement during its first year, or Wils's and van't Hoff's during the second, Oud's during the fourth, Huszar's and Vantongerloo's during the fifth, and finally that of Mondrian in 1925.'[1] He therefore favours the third definition, which was that adopted by Van Doesburg himself. Reviewing the first ten years of De Stijl in 1927, Van Doesburg wrote: 'De Stijl as a movement developed gradually out of De Stijl as an idea.'[2]

Not even this third definition will quite do, however. 'De Stijl as an idea' is the vaguest of the three definitions, as Bois admits, and moreover there turn out to be as many 'De Stijl ideas' as there were participants in the movement. Although he argues that the conceptual nature of this definition makes it 'the most restrictive', and thus

1. Y.-A. Bois, *Painting as Model*, MIT Press, Cambridge, Mass., 1993, p. 102.
2. T. van Doesburg, '10 jaren Stijl', in *De Stijl*, vol. VII, nos. 79/84, 1927, p. 5.

the most exact, Mondrian's, Van der Leck's and Oud's concepts of the De Stijl idea differed fundamentally from Van Doesburg's. If Rietveld, unlike these others, never found it necessary to distance himself from the movement, it is only because he was not by nature inclined to ideological dispute. Therefore, while the main concern of this book is the ideology of De Stijl, I do not claim to be able to give this a final definition.

It seems to me that the best way to approach the moving target of De Stijl is not to try to locate it definitively – to fix it, so to speak, 'in one place' – but to delimit a wider territory within which it can occupy various positions. I have attempted to stake out this territory by approaching it from several different, more or less independent directions. Each of the eight chapters can be read as a separate essay, and although a common thread of argument runs through them they can be read in any order the reader prefers. They are intended as a ring of marker posts; hidden somewhere between them the shy animal known as De Stijl may be found moving around.

There is, however, one theme that is central to the whole book, and which unites in my opinion all its protagonists: the striving for the universal and the general, as opposed to the individual and the particular. This was, I believe, not only the essential 'De Stijl idea', but also the 'Miesian idea' and (at least in the 1920s) the 'Corbusian idea'. It was the glory, but ultimately also the downfall, of 1920s modernism. So the final message of the book, contained in the last chapter, is that a balance must be found between universality and individuality, between permanence and change. At the end of that chapter I quote Plato's remark from 'The Sophist' that the philosopher 'must refuse to accept from the champions either of the One or the many Forms the doctrine that all Reality is changeless; and he must turn a deaf ear to the other party who represent Reality as everywhere changing. Like a child begging for "both", he must declare that Reality or the sum of things is both at once – all that is unchangeable and all that is in change.'[3]

Cutting across this first theme, however, there is a second opposition: that between the open and the closed. The universality aimed at by De Stijl artists like Van Doesburg and Mondrian resembled that of the universe itself: it was boundless. Their paintings continued, in theory, beyond the limits of the canvas; their architecture sought to abolish the wall as the boundary between interior and exterior space. But each of Le Corbusier's buildings and paintings was a self-contained universe, held within a clear frame; in reaction to De Stijl, he advocated 'the pure envelope which covers abundance with a mask of simplicity'. Mies fluctuated between the two ideals: in the

3.   Plato, 'The Sophist', in F.M. Cornford, *Plato's Theory of Knowledge*, Routledge and Kegan Paul, London, 1960, p. 242.

1920s, in such designs as the brick country house and the Barcelona Pavilion, he outdid even the De Stijl architects in openness, but in his later work in America he reverted to the closed neoclassical box.

I am very grateful to my commissioning editor, Caroline Mallinder, who has remained faithful to the project through five years of delay in delivering the manuscript. I wish to thank the editors of *The Architectural Review* and to the College of Architecture, Illinois Institute of Technology, the original publishers of essays that I have incorporated into chapters four and six. Finally, I am indebted to the late Bruno Zevi, whose pioneering book *Poetica dell'architettura neoplastica*[4] first opened my eyes to the fundamental importance of De Stijl in modern architecture.

Richard Padovan
December 2000

4.   B Zevi, *Poetica dell'architettura neoplastica*, Libreria Editrice Politecnica Tamburini, Milan, 1953; revised edition, Giulio Einaudi, Turin, 1974.

The Open or the Closed
De Stijl and Le Corbusier

1.1 De Stijl and architecture

The phenomenon we call 'De Stijl' was not an organized movement but a frequently changing collection of artists who rarely if ever met each other and never exhibited together. What connected them and gave them the semblance of a common direction was the magazine *De Stijl* and the driving personality of its founder and editor, the painter and writer Theo van Doesburg (1883–1931). Although the group's greatest achievements were in the field of painting – above all the work of Piet Mondrian (1872–1944) – Van Doesburg believed that its ultimate field of activity must be architecture. Two years before he died, looking back over the thirteen-year 'Struggle for the New Style' in the pages of the Swiss journal *Neuer Schweizer Rundschau*, he wrote:

> It is unquestionably the *architectonic* character of the works of the most radical painters that finally convinced the public of the seriousness of their struggle, not merely to 'influence' architecture, but to dictate its development towards a collective construction. Although in 1917 there was as yet no question of such a collective construction, certain painters attempted, in collaboration with architects (van der Leck with Berlage, I with Oud, etc.) to transfer systematically and coherently into architecture and into three dimensional space the ideas they had developed through painting on canvas. The germ of a universal style-idea was already latent in this struggle to combine architecture with painting in an organic whole.[1]

Consequently Van Doesburg was keen to involve architects as well as painters in De Stijl, and three members of the founding group were architects: Robert van't Hoff (1887–1979), J.J.P. Oud (1890–1963) and Jan Wils (1891–1972). The furniture designer and architect Gerrit Rietveld (1888–1964) joined about a year later. Other original members were the painters Bart van der Leck (1876–1958) and Vilmos Huszar (1884–1960) and the sculptor Georges Vantongerloo (1886–1965).

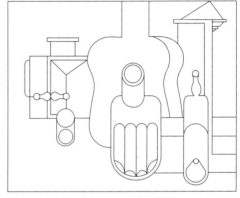

Figure 1.1 C.-E. Jeanneret (Le Corbusier), *Composition à la guitare et à la lanterne*, 1920

---

1. T. van Doesburg, 'Der Kampf um den neuen Stil', in *Neuer Schweizer Rundschau*, 1929, 41–631; reproduced in Dutch and English translation in *De Stijl: De Nieuwe Beelding in de Architectuur/ Neo-Plasticism in Architecture*, Delft University Press, Delft, 1983.

Despite the inclusion of architects, De Stijl's direct impact on architecture did not get much further than the sporadic collaborations between painters and architects which Van Doesburg mentions. If one excludes sculpture, the movement's total realization in three-dimensional space was pitifully small: some furniture, one or two small houses and a handful of short-lived interiors; the rest remained on paper, as unrealized projects and manifestos. The gulf between this minimal concrete achievement and the movement's revolutionary aims – nothing less than the creation of a new life, a new man and a new world – is either comical or tragic, according to one's point of view. Certainly Van Doesburg, towards the end of his life, saw it as tragic. Reacting to the public's rejection of his interiors for the Café Aubette, Strasbourg, which he had struggled so hard to create during 1926–8, he writes despairingly to Adolf Behne:

> when the aubette was just finished, before its inauguration, it was really good and significant as the first realization of a programme which we had cherished for years: the total artistic design [gesamtkunstwerk]. yet ... the public cannot leave its 'brown' world, and it stubbornly rejects the new 'white' world. the public wants to live in mire and shall perish in mire. let the architect create for the public ... the artist creates beyond the public and demands new conditions diametrically opposed to the old conventions, and therefore every work of art contains a destructive power.[2]

1.2 An art of destruction

The claim that the aim of art is destruction occurs frequently in De Stijl literature. But what was to be destroyed? In an article which appeared in De Stijl in 1927, Van Doesburg calls for

> the total destruction of traditional absolutism in any form (the nonsense about a rigid opposition as between man and woman, man and god, good and evil, etc.) The elementarist sees life as a vast expanse in which there is a constant interchange between these life factors.[3]

√ De Stijl's central goal was the abolition of all conventional boundaries, whether in painting, in architecture or in life. The world was seen as a continuum in which all the usually discrete categories merged together: male and female, human and divine, good and evil, inside and outside. In painting, the frame, conceived as the limit of the

2. T. van Doesburg, letter to Adolf Behne, November 7, 1928, quoted in translation in N. Troy, The De Stijl Environment, MIT Press, Cambridge, Mass., 1983, p. 176.
3. T. van Doesburg, 'Schilderkunst en plastiek', in De Stijl, vol. VII, no. 7, 1927, p. 87.

composition, was abolished. What appeared on the canvas was merely a fragment of a boundless continuity. Applying the same principle to architecture, Van Doesburg declares in the eighth point of his architectural manifesto (1924) that 'The new architecture has *broken through the wall*, thus destroying the *separateness of inside and outside* ... This gives rise to a new, open plan, totally different from the classical one, in that interior and exterior spaces interpenetrate.'[4]

The problems arising from De Stijl's aim of replacing the structurally contained, enclosed spaces of traditional architecture with a continuously flowing space in which there was no longer any fixed boundary between inside and outside, or between one room and another, will be explored further in Chapter 4. The purpose of all this destruction – of categories, of confines, of walls – was to help bring about the realization of what was seen as man's future (and inevitable) destiny: the absorption of the individual into the universal. This aim, coupled with the necessity of destruction, appears most famously in the opening words of the 'First Manifesto of "De Stijl", 1918:

1   There exist an old and a new consciousness of the age.
     The old is directed towards the individual.
     The new is directed towards the universal.
     The struggle of the individual against the universal shows itself in the world war as well as in today's art.

2   The war is destroying the old world together with its content: the dominance of the individual in every field.[5]

It is important to realize, however, that when the De Stijl artists talk about 'the individual' they do not only mean 'the individual personality', still less 'the individual artist'. They sometimes mean both of those, but they also mean 'the individual thing' in the sense of 'the particular thing'. The opposition that they speak of between the individual and the universal is really that between the *particular* and the universal, which is a fundamental concept in classical philosophy. For some philosophers, particulars are primary, and universals are purely mental derivations from particular instances (we derive the general idea of 'red' from the experience of particular red things). But for Plato, in contrast, the real world is the world of universal Ideas or Forms, of which the particular things that we experience with our senses are only the imperfect reflections. The latter concept is central to De Stijl theory, where it stems not only from Plato but also from eastern thought (from theosophy in Mondrian's case) and from nineteenth century German philosophy, particularly G.W.F. Hegel

4.   T. van Doesburg, 'Tot een beeldende architectuur', in *De Stijl*, vol. VI, no. 6/7, 1924, p. 80.
5.   'Manifest I van "De Stijl", 1918', in *De Stijl*, vol. II, no. 1, November 1918, pp. 2–5, signed by Theo van Doesburg, Robt. van't Hoff, Vilmos Huszar, Anthony Kok, Piet Mondrian, Georges Vantongerloo and Jan Wils.

(1770–1831), whose influence was absorbed primarily from the leading Dutch Hegelian of the time, G.J.P.J. Bolland. The opposition of particulars and universals will recur throughout this book and is the main subject of Chapters 2 and 3.

1.3 Mondrian: evolution from the individual-natural to the universal-abstract

Humanity's need to transcend the individual in order to evolve towards the universal is a constant theme of Mondrian's writings, where the individual (i.e. the particular) is identified with the natural, and the universal with the abstract. In this context Carel Blotkamp's assessment of the centrality of the concept of evolution in Mondrian's art and thought cannot be improved upon:

> To Mondrian evolution was 'everything'. Not only are his theoret-ical articles imbued with evolutionary thinking, this concept also generated the process of change that characterized his work to the very end of his life. In order to understand this, we must take into account that in Mondrian's thinking evolution was closely bound up with destruction. He did not view this as a negative concept: on the contrary, the destruction of old forms was a condition for the creation of new, higher forms. Initially this was expressed in his choice of subject-matter, exemplified in the paint-ings and drawings of flowers in states of decay. Later, in his Cubist period, he came to the realization that abstraction, which implies the destruction of the incidental, outward image of reality, could be used to portray a purer image of that reality, and to represent a higher stage in evolution. And finally, the principle of destruction was applied to the means of expression themselves: his Neo-Plastic work is, in effect, the result of a whole series of destructive actions.[6]

The most evident characteristics of De Stijl as *style* are a direct consequence of this opposition of the universal-abstract to the indi-vidual-natural: the straight line replaced the curve, the rectangular plane replaced the solid form, and the six 'abstract' colours (red, blue, yellow, white, grey and black) replaced 'natural' colour. Mondrian's essay 'Neoplasticism in Painting' (*De nieuwe beelding in de schilderkunst*), serialized in the first twelve issues of *De Stijl*, is the first, and arguably the most complete, exposition of De Stijl theory. The implications of the Dutch term *nieuwe beelding* (literally 'new imag-ing'), and the inadequacy of the usual translation 'neoplasticism',

6. C. Blotkamp, *Mondrian: The Art of Destruction*, Reaktion Books, London, 1994, p. 15.

which Mondrian himself introduced, will be discussed more fully in Chapter 2. Meanwhile, except where 'plastic' occurs in a title too well known in English translation to be altered, *beelding* will generally be translated here as 'representation' or 'plastic representation'. For instance, instead of the now familiar 'Neoplasticism in Painting', the meaning of 'De nieuwe beelding in de schilderkunst' might be better conveyed by 'New Representation in Painting'. In the essay Mondrian argues that

> If we see human consciousness – in time – *growing* towards defini-tion, if we see it – in time – *developing* from individual to universal, then it is for us logical that the new plastic representation can never return to form – or to natural colour ... The new plastic representation can be called abstract not only because it is the direct representation of the universal, but also because that repre-sentation excludes the individual (the natural-concrete)[7] ... Abstract-real painting can represent both aesthetically and mathe-matically because it has an *exact mathematical means of represen-tation.* The means to achieve this is *colour brought to definition.* To make colour definite involves: first, *reducing natural colour to primary colour*, second, *reducing colour to the flat plane*, and third, *delimiting colour – so that it appears as a unity of rectangular planes.*[8]

It might appear that the delimited coloured rectangle itself consti-tutes a bounded figure, and thereby contradicts the De Stijl principle of *destroying* all boundaries. But odd as it may seem, in Mondrian's view it would be wrong to consider a rectangular plane as bounded in the same sense as a solid 'corporeal' form contained within its 'rounded' surface:

> Ordinary vision does not perceive colour in nature as plane; it perceives things (colour) as *corporeality*, as *roundness* ... Extension – an exteriorization of the active primal force – brings corporeal form into being through growth, attachment, construction, etc. Form results when extension is bounded ... [Now] if the time is ripe, this *boundedness of the individual in the representation of exten-sion must be given up*, for only then can extension be represented in all its purity. If the bounding of form comes about through the *closed line* (contour), then this must be tautened into the *straight line* ... so that extension is realized *without individual delimitation*, except insofar as this arises from the colour-differences of the planes and through rectangular relations of lines or coloured

7. P. Mondrian, 'De nieuwe beelding in de schilderkunst', in *De Stijl*, vol. I, no. I, 1917, p. 5.
8. Mondrian, 'De nieuwe beelding', in *De Stijl*, vol. I, no. 3, 1918, p. 29.

planes. By means of rectangularity, colour is delimited without being *enclosed.*[9]

Underlying all this striving for the most abstract possible form of representation (for a *nieuwe beelding*) is a metaphysical – and in the case of Mondrian, an avowedly theosophist and thus religious – belief that history is moving inexorably towards a higher, supra-natural and more spiritual level of human consciousness:

> *In abstract-real representation man has a contrast to the natural. By* ✓
> *opposing nature he can learn to know it, and so come to knowledge of*
> *the spirit.* In this way art becomes truly *religious.*[10]

The natural, earth-bound self-consciousness of the individual is increasingly giving way to a universal spiritual awareness. In fact, for Mondrian, a radically new kind of human being is in the process of evolving out of the old with the help of the machine – a being who by liberating himself from the external bonds of the material can turn his attention increasingly inwards to the spiritual:

> The new man must indeed be entirely 'different' from the old ...
> He ... uses his physical being as a perfect machine ... without
> *himself* becoming a machine. The difference lies precisely in this:
> formerly man was *himself a machine*; now he *uses* the machine,
> whether his own body or a machine of his own making. To the
> latter he leaves so far as possible the heavy work, *himself* concen-
> trating on the inward ... I posit this new man as a 'type' that is as
> yet only partially realized ... but it *is* beginning to appear! And it is
> quite logical that they who represent this new type are alien to the
> former man, alien to his expression, to his art, and so on.[11]

It is the task of the new art to represent and give expression to the new universality, the new inwardness, the new spirituality. Only when the entire human environment has been transformed by the new art – that is, when the new art is no longer confined to the artist's studio and the separate canvas but has permeated architecture – will the new human type feel at home in the world. For:

> why must universal beauty remain hidden in art, while in science
> for instance we strive for the greatest possible clarity? ... *It is*
> *architecture's great task to make universal beauty clearly visible to*
> *us, and to that end work together as one whole with sculpture and*
> *painting* ... Architecture has only to realize tangibly what painting

9.   Mondrian, 'De nieuwe beelding', in *De Stijl*, vol. I, no. 4, 1918, pp. 42–3.
10.   Mondrian, 'De nieuwe beelding', in *De Stijl*, vol. I, no. 8, 1918, p. 89.
11.   P. Mondrian, 'Natuurlijke en abstracte realiteit', in *De Stijl*, vol. III, no. 3, 1920, p. 28.

has demonstrated abstractly through the New Representation
[*Nieuwe Beelding*] ... For the present, we still live in the midst of
the old! ... We live as strangers in another man's house, with
another man's furniture, carpets, utensils, paintings! If we go out
into the streets, they too are alien to us. If we go to the theatre,
the same. The cinema? With its antiquated morality and its
'nature'? Not even that is of our time.[12]

1.4 Van Doesburg: the goal of history, and four-dimensionality

The equivalent inspiration for Van Doesburg's thought came not
from religion as such but, as has been said, from the nineteenth
century German philosophers, in particular from Hegel. Hegel argues
in his *Philosophy of Art* that the highest goal of fine art must be to
become, together with religion and philosophy, a means for the liberation and self-realization of the spirit, an inevitable evolution towards
an ever higher and more spiritual consciousness. *The Philosophy of
History* portrays history, not as merely a record of events and the
cross-connections between events, but as something that has a
purpose, a goal; and that goal is the evolution of the Spirit towards a
fuller consciousness of itself:

> The History of the world is none other than the progress of the
> consciousness of Freedom ... The destiny of the spiritual World,
> and – since this is the *substantial World*, while the physical remains
> subordinate to it, or, in the language of speculation, has no truth *as
> against* the spiritual – *the final cause of the World at large*, we allege
> to be the *consciousness* of its own freedom on the part of Spirit,
> and *ipso facto*, the *reality* of that freedom.[13]

The broad parallels between this and Mondrian's theosophically
inspired concept of evolution are evident, and it is interesting that
Hegel's principal Dutch interpreter, G.J.P.J. Bolland, placed theosophy
in a direct line of descent from Hegel in his book *Schelling, Hegel,
Fechner en de nieuwere theosophie* (1910).[14]

A second important ingredient of Van Doesburg's thought was
the idea of four-dimensionality. The time dimension, combined with
the three dimensions of Euclidian space, formed a new concept:
'space–time'. Pseudo-scientific, mystical or occultist theories about
the possibilities of non-Euclidian space were much in vogue in the late
nineteenth and early twentieth century: an example is Edwin E.
Abbott's fantasy *Flatland* (1884). The Dutch journal *Eenheid*, to which

---

12. *Ibid.*, pp. 29–30.
13. G.W.F. Hegel, *The Philosophy of History*, Dover Publications, New York, 1956, p. 19.
14. A. Doig, *Theo van Doesburg*, Cambridge University Press, Cambridge, 1986, p. 13.

Van Doesburg contributed from 1912 to 1916, was a typical vehicle for such speculations.[15] Four-dimensionality is a major theme of the series of articles which the Italian ex-futurist Gino Severini contributed to the early numbers of *De Stijl*. Severini introduces the topic in the fourth issue, February 1918, declaring that 'to the ordinary three dimensions [painters] strive to add a fourth dimension which incorporates them, and which is differently expressed, but which constitutes the goal, so to speak, of the art of all epochs'.[16]

In the eighth number he resumes the argument, lending it a spurious scientific legitimacy by citing the eminent French mathematician Henri Poincaré (1854–1912), and concluding that the fourth dimension

is nothing else than *the identification of object and subject, of time and space, of matter and energy*. The parallelism of the 'physical continuum', which for geometry is merely a hypothesis, is realized through the miracle of art. This philosophical and aesthetic conclusion is confirmed by Plato, Bacon, Gracian, and is further supported by mathematics. For according to H. Poincaré the synthesis of ordinary space with time gives rise to a hyperspace of four dimensions.[17]

Such verbal outpourings are relatively easy; the more difficult problem that Van Doesburg and his fellow artists had to face was how the dynamic dimension of time could be expressed in the inherently static medium of painting. At first Van Doesburg tried to overcome the problem by choosing subject-matter that itself implied movement, as in his paintings *Dancers* (1916) and *Rhythm of a Russian dance* (1918). But he increasingly realized that such an attempt could at best produce an illusion of movement, and this realization was a major reason for his growing preoccupation with architecture. For whereas a painting can be regarded as something that can be seen as a whole in a single glance, clearly architecture can be experienced only in time, by moving through space.

A moment's reflection shows that this distinction is fallacious, however. Time enters into one's perception of even the simplest painting: one may start by looking at the composition as a whole, but then the eye begins to move around the painting, considering the details singly or as groups, studying the relations between one part and another, and so on. With sculpture in the round, the time element is still more essential, since only one side can be seen at any one time. In the case of architecture this need is more obvious (to see all aspects of an architectural space, one must turn around and build

15. C. Blotkamp, 'Theo van Doesburg', in Blotkamp et al., *De Beginjaren van De Stijl 1917–1922*, Reflex, Utrecht, 1982, p. 39.
16. G. Severini, 'La peinture d'avant-garde', in *De Stijl*, vol. 1, no. 4, 1918, p. 44.
17. Severini, 'La peinture d'avant-garde', in *De Stijl*, vol. 1, no. 8, 1918, p. 95.

up the total picture from the successive impressions) but not fundamentally different. Furthermore, all these 'four-dimensional' perceptions are inherent in the experience of traditional architecture,
sculpture and painting; no revolutionary new art is required.

Nevertheless, Van Doesburg relentlessly pursued his goal of 'trans-
ferring into architecture the ideas that the De Stijl painters had developed on canvas'. After initial, often frustrating, attempts to collaborate
on colour schemes with various architects – with Wils at Alkmaar
(1917), with Oud on the vacation house *De Vonk* (1918) and housing
at Spangen (1921), with Rietveld at Katwijk (1919), and with Cees
Rinks de Boer at Drachten (1921) – he at last found the ideal collaborator in the young Cor van Eesteren (1897–1988). With him he
created a colour scheme for Van Eesteren's thesis project for a hall for
Amsterdam University (1922) and, the following year, the three house
projects for the Parisian gallery owner Léonce Rosenberg, which will
be discussed in Chapter 4. An important sequel to the Rosenberg
projects was the publication in 1924 of two architectural manifestos:
'Towards a Collective Construction' ('Vers une construction collective') and 'Towards a Plastic Architecture' ('Tot een beeldende
architectuur'). They contain the following absurdities:

> We have examined the relation between space and time and
> found that the plastic manifestation of these two elements by
> means of colour gives rise to a new dimension.[18]

> The space-composition projected in two dimensions, *embedded
> in a plan*, will be replaced by an accurate *constructional calculation*,
> a calculation by which the load-bearing capacity must be reduced
> to the simplest but most resistant points of support. Euclidian
> mathematics will no longer be of any use here, but it will be easily
> solved by means of non-Euclidian calculations in four dimensions.[19]

> *Space and time.* The new architecture reckons not only with space
> but also with time. The unity of time and space gives the architec-
> tural phenomenon a new and completely plastic aspect (*four-
> dimensional temporal and spatial plastic aspects*).[20]

In contrast, Mondrian's few references to the fourth dimension as
a sign of the new *Zeitgeist* have a vagueness that suggests perhaps a
lesser interest or a lack of complete conviction:

> It is truly an encouraging sign that recent painting manifests an
> increasingly conscious striving towards a pure and many-sided

18. T. van Doesburg and C van Eesteren, 'Vers une construction collective', point 4, in *De Stijl*, vol. VI, no. 6/7, 1924, p. 91.
19. Van Doesburg, 'Tot een beeldende architectuur', point 9, in *De Stijl*, vol. VI, no. 6/7, 1924, p. 80.
20. Van Doesburg, 'Tot een beeldende architectuur', point 10, in *De Stijl*, vol. VI, no. 6/7, 1924, p. 81.

representation of things, for this indicates a new, more conscious spirit of the age that *aspires to the universal* with a greater determination. This new aspiration has been correctly attributed to a *greater awareness of four-dimensionality*, and in fact the concept of the four dimensional shows itself in the new art *as a partial or complete destruction of three-dimensional, naturalistic representation and the reconstruction of a new representation in accordance with a less limited vision.*[21]

Three years later, he alludes in an aside to the theory of relativity, in connection with De Stijl's break with traditional one-point perspective:

To see architecture as form-making is a traditionalist view. *This is the perspective visual schema, which belongs to the past.* The neoplastic concept gives this up ... Even before the rise of neoplasticism, the new vision is not projected from a single fixed viewpoint: *it establishes its viewpoint everywhere, and is nowhere fixed* (this corresponds to relativity theory).[22]

Despite the reference to relativity, this statement reveals Mondrian's essentially mystical and quasi-religious approach to the question, as Carel Blotkamp has commented:

It is interesting that Mondrian here brings forward relativity theory as an argument, but in my view it serves as a scientific cloak for a purely esoteric way of thinking. One finds confirmation of this in a letter to Van Doesburg, in which Mondrian says that 'in order to arrive at a pure abstract representation (*to see inwardly*, I mean) time, too, must be erased from the mind'.[23]

In a letter to Oud, Van Doesburg himself had earlier criticized Mondrian's wish for a 'timeless' art and his consequent lack of commitment to the 'third' dimension in painting (in Van Doesburg's view painting should have no illusion of depth, so time constituted not a fourth but a third dimension):

Since in his latest article Mondriaan completely denies the time movement and wants to banish it from painting, for *him* 3-dimensional painting (i.e., space-time painting) must be impossible. He remains limited to the 2-dimensional canvas ... Mondriaan as a *man* is *not* modern because, in my opinion, although he has developed psychically towards the new, spiritually he belongs to the

21. Mondrian, 'Natuurlijke', in *De Stijl*, vol. II, no. 12, 1919, p. 137.
22. P. Mondrian, 'De realiseering van het neo-plasticisme in verre toekomst en in de huidige architectuur', in *De Stijl*, vol. V, no. 5, 1922, p. 68.
23. C. Blotkamp, 'Mondriaan ↔ architectuur', in *Wonen TABK*, nos. 4 & 5, March 1982, p. 41.

old. By this I mean that he sees the spiritual as a conceptual abstraction, in other words something like the theosophists. Of life itself *as reality* he is in fact afraid. He *thinks* life, but he does not live it.[24]

This attack indicates that for Van Doesburg four-dimensionality was the key to the concrete realization of the new spirit in art and in everyday life, without which it would remain merely a theoretical conception. However, the conviction that history is governed by discoverable laws of evolution, and the obsession with four-dimensionality and non-Euclidean geometry, are not confined to De Stijl.

1.5 Giedion's 'authorized history' of the modern movement

The historical theory of the modern movement as a whole is derived from, and continues, the nineteenth century project of converting art history into a science (*Kunstwissenschaft*), a discipline aiming at the same kind of objectivity expected of the natural sciences. In Hegel's concept of a necessary process of historical evolution, and of art as a medium of that evolution, can be found the germ of the idea of a *Kunstwollen*, introduced by Alois Riegl in his *Stilfragen* (1893) and adopted by, among others, Wilhelm Worringer in *Abstraction and Empathy* (1908) and Erwin Panofsky in 'Der Begriff des Kunstwollens' (1920).[25] Riegl saw the *Kunstwollen* – variously translated as 'stylistic intent',[26] as 'will-to-form'[27] or as 'that-which-wills-art',[28] – as a *telos*, a goal to which artistic development is drawn with the inevitability of a natural law. He claims in his book *Die Spätrömische Kunstindustrie* (1901) to have been 'the first to advocate a teleological conception of art.'[29]

Panofsky interprets the *Kunstwollen* slightly differently from Riegl,[30] but still as something outside and above the particular circumstances that surround the birth of a work of art: such things as the individual psychology of the artist or the influence upon him of other works. He compares it to an 'Archimedean point', which enables the historian to 'grasp the object of study with necessity and not merely historically'.[31]

This teleological conception can be discovered, moreover, at the very core of the theory of the modern movement in architecture, in the writings of its major historical interpreter, Sigfried Giedion (1888–1968), secretary of CIAM (Congrès International d'Architecture Moderne) from its foundation in 1928. A pupil of Heinrich Wölfflin, Giedion was a direct heir to the tradition of *Kunstwissenschaft*

24. T. van Doesburg, letter to J J P Oud, 12 September 1921, quoted in Troy, *De Stijl Environment*, p. 70.
25. M.A. Holly, *Panofsky and the Foundations of Art History*, Cornell University Press, Ithaca, N.Y., 1984, pp. 46–96.
26. O. Brendel, *Prolegomena to the Study of Roman Art*, New Haven, 1953, p. 31.
27. E.H. Gombrich, *Art and Illusion*, Phaidon, London, 1959, p. 18.
28. O. Pächt, 'Art historians and art critics –VI, Alois Riegl', in *Burlington Magazine* no. 105, May 1962, p. 190.
29. A. Riegl, *Die Spätrömische Kunstindustrie* (1901), Vienna, 1927, p. 9.
30. Holly, *Panofsky*, p. 79.
31. E. Panofsky, 'Der Begriff des Kunstwollens', in *Aufsätze zu Grundfragen der Kunstwissenschaft*, Berlin, 1964, p. 33.

and the concept of the *Kunstwollen*. In his work one finds repeatedly the idea that it is the historian's task to separate within the flux of phenomena those streams that are significant as expressions of the will of the epoch from those that are not. The most glaring examples of this occur in his best known book, the 'official history', so to speak, of the modern movement: *Space, Time and Architecture* (1941). There he embraces unreservedly the Hegelian notion of history as a process of evolution towards the greater self-awareness and self-realization of the epoch. Giedion portrays history as a 'Being' with a will and a consciousness of itself, even a somewhat mischievous character who may try coyly to conceal its true nature from the investigating historian. It is the task of the historian to see through and strip away these disguises:

> We are looking for the reflection in architecture of the progress our own period has made toward consciousness of itself ... However much a period may try to disguise itself, its real nature will show through in its architecture, whether this uses original forms of expression or attempts to copy bygone epochs. We recognize the character of the age as easily as we identify a friend's handwriting beneath attempted disguises.[32]

Like a graphologist, the historian must separate out the genuine character traits from the artificial or superficial disguises. He must distinguish between 'constituent facts' and 'transitory facts': on one hand 'genuinely new trends ... which, when they are suppressed, inevitably reappear' and on the other those 'more or less short-lived novelties' that 'lack the stuff of permanence and fail to attach themselves to a new tradition'.[33] The historian is not only free, he argues, to make the 'not always obvious distinction' between these two kinds of facts, on his own responsibility and using his own judgement; it is his duty to do so.[34]

Besides the iron-and-glass engineering tradition inherited from the nineteenth century, the new constituent fact of the fully developed modern architecture that arose in the second and third decades of the twentieth century, in the works of Le Corbusier and others, is according to Giedion the destruction of the perspective space that had ruled since the renaissance, and its replacement by a four-dimensional non-Euclidean space first developed in cubist painting. This new artistic concept of space corresponds to, and coincides with, the discovery of relativity by Albert Einstein:

> The three-dimensional space of the Renaissance is the space of Euclidian geometry. But about 1830 a new sort of geometry was

32. S. Giedion, *Space, Time and Architecture*, Harvard University Press, Cambridge, Mass., 1941, p. 19.
33. *Ibid.*, p. 18.
34. *Ibid.*, p. 19.

created, one which differed from Euclid in employing more than three dimensions ... Space in modern physics is conceived of as relative to a moving point of reference, not as the absolute and static entity of the baroque system of Newton. And in modern art, for the first time since the Renaissance, a new conception of space leads to a self-conscious enlargement of our ways of perceiving space ... Cubism breaks with Renaissance perspective. It views objects relatively: that is, from several points of view ... The poet Guillaume Apollinaire was the first to recognize and express this change, around 1911 ... The presentation of objects from several points of view introduces a principle which is intimately bound up with modern life – simultaneity. It is a temporal coincidence that Einstein should have begun his famous work, *Elektrodynamik bewegter Körper*, in 1905 with a careful definition of simultaneity.[35]

The use of the words 'temporal coincidence' is disingenuous. Strictly speaking, it implies that there was no *causal* connection between the writing of Einstein's paper in 1905 and the rise of cubism about two years later. And given that Braque and Picasso are highly unlikely to have read Einstein before producing their first cubist works, this is literally true. But the whole passage is emptied of meaning if it is interpreted as saying that the synchronicity of the scientific and artistic discoveries was merely a coincidence. If Giedion's argument – and with it, the whole argument of *Space, Time and Architecture* – are to signify anything at all, the passage must be interpreted as meaning that while these simultaneous developments were causally independent in the sense that one did not influence the other, they were both driven by a common historical force or *Zeitgeist*.

The idea is still widely held among architects that the discovery of other geometries than the Euclidian – and the fact that one of these geometries appears to conform to the observations that confirmed Einstein's general theory of relativity – somehow invalidates parallel straight lines and rectangles in modern architecture. This idea is sheer mumbo-jumbo. As Bernard Cache writes in a recent essay:

The dismissal of Euclidian geometry by architects sounds rather surprising when one notices how appreciated it is by contemporary scientists, even by those who cannot be suspected of orthodoxy, such as Roger Penrose. In his *The Emperor's New Mind: Concerning Computers, Minds, and the Laws of Physics*, Penrose argues that Euclidian geometry comes first in the list of very few theories which deserve the label 'superb' for their phenomenal

35. *Ibid.*, pp. 356–7.

accuracy. Einstein's theory certainly teaches us that space (-time) is actually 'curved' (i.e. not Euclidian) in the presence of a gravitational field, but generally, one perceives this curvature only in the case of bodies moving at speeds close to that of light. Hence the very limited impact of Einstein's theory on technology. Normally, 'over a meter's range, deviation from Euclidian flatness is tiny indeed, errors in treating the geometry as Euclidian amounting to less than the diameter of an atom of hydrogen!' As those familiar with the difficulties created at a building site by the 1/10 millimeter accuracy of prefabricated components surely know, Euclidian geometry is more than sufficient approximation of architectural space.'[36]

Einstein himself repudiated any parallelism between cubism and relativity. When in 1945, four years after the publication of *Space, Time and Architecture*, he was asked to comment on an essay by Paul Laporte entitled 'Cubism and the Theory of Relativity', which put forward a similar argument to Giedion's, he stated categorically: 'This new "language" of art has nothing in common with the theory of relativity.'[37]

According to Picasso's biographer John Richardson, the poet Apollinaire, and the so-called 'salon cubists' Albert Gleizes and Jean Metzinger, who likewise sought to give cubism a fake 'scientific' legitimacy based on non-Euclidean geometry and four-dimensionality, had all earlier been attached to the Abbaye de Créteil community. This was

A principal breeding-ground of the theories that the Salon cubists revered and Braque and Picasso loathed ... And the ultimate expression of their theories is *Du Cubisme*, the book that Gleizes and Metzinger published in 1912 ... Although the book pays lip service to some of his achievements, Picasso dismissed *Du Cubisme* as nonsense. Likewise Braque: 'Look at the daubs it engendered,' he said.[38]

1.6 Rietveld: architecture as the construction of reality

There is at least one great contributor to De Stijl, however, who was blessedly free of the tendency to metaphysical speculation that pervades the writings of Mondrian and Van Doesburg. Gerrit Rietveld believed that verbal rationalizations could never approach the concrete realities they try to explain; therefore he wrote little,

36. B. Cache, 'A plea for Euclid', in *ANY*, no. 24, 1999, p. 54.
37. P. Laporte, 'Cubism and relativity – with a letter of Albert Einstein', in *Art Journal*, vol. XXV, no. 3, Spring 1966, pp. 246–8; quoted in S. Georgiadis, *Sigfried Giedion: An Intellectual Biography*, Edinburgh University Press, Edinburgh, 1993, p. 123.
38. J. Richardson, *A Life of Picasso*, vol. II, Jonathan Cape, London, p. 215.

and destroyed much of the little that he wrote.[39] He begins one of his few published articles with a disclaimer:

> To make a thing, it is in my opinion absolutely unnecessary to be able first to explain or justify why it has to be just so. On the contrary, the need to find expression in an outward form is diminished if one could have said it just as well in words.[40]

This is not to say that he was any less concerned than Van Doesburg or Mondrian with the problems of spatial continuity or the dissolution of boundaries, but that he thought about these things rather more concretely. As a craftsman, his approach was more matter-of-fact and practical. Instead of asserting dogmatically that 'the new architecture has destroyed the separateness of inside and outside', he recognized that complete openness was an impossibility. An entirely unbounded space could not be perceived. To make a continuous space it is not enough just to do away with walls, or to produce an endless grid of modular coordinates. The space must be given scansion; it must be punctuated in some way if its relative openness is to be perceived. Some degree of delimitation is a necessity, therefore, but it need not consist of enclosing walls:

> The means of bringing an undefined space to a human scale can consist of a line on a road, a floor, a low wall, a ceiling, a combination of vertical and horizontal planes, curved or flat, transparent or solid. It is never a question of shutting off, but always one of defining what is here and what is there, what is above and what is below, what is between and what is around.[41]

More specifically, Rietveld draws attention to the role of opaque wall surfaces in directing and reflecting light:

> A large window has little effect if the light immediately escapes again through a second window ... Only if there is a surface next to or opposite the window, which reflects or conveys the light to the other parts of the interior, does a window make sense as a receiver of light. I have sometimes managed to improve the lighting in a house that was being renovated, or a room that was too dark, by bricking up a window.[42]

Secondly, in his more philosophical speculations, Rietveld does not assume that a new architecture is needed because a process of evolution or historical destiny is suddenly driving humanity towards

39. T.M. Brown, *The Work of G. Rietveld, Architect*, A.W. Bruna & Zoon, Utrecht, 1958, p. xi.

40. G. Rietveld, 'Nut, constructie (schoonheid: kunst)', in *i10*, vol. I, no. 3, 1927, p. 89.

41. G. Rietveld, unreferenced remark quoted in *G. Rietveld Architect*, exhibition catalogue, Stedelijk Museum, Amsterdam, 1971 and Hayward Gallery, London, 1972.

42. G. Rietveld, 'Interiors', lecture, Rotterdam Academy of Fine Arts, March 1948.

an unprecedented state of universal spirituality, but rather that people's psychological needs are fundamentally unchanging, and the aim of the new architecture is simply to serve those needs a little better. The basic purpose of making an architectural space, once the practical needs of shelter and physical comfort have been satisfied, is to help 'make the world real for us'. The following quotations illustrate this:

> If for some purpose we divide off, stake out, delimit a piece of what we customarily call universal, unbounded space, and so shelter it from certain forces and bring it to a human scale, then (if it is any good), a little bit of space has come into being which we are able to experience as reality. Such a little piece of space has then been absorbed into our human system. Was it then impossible to experience the universal space as a reality? Not before there was some kind of boundary: clouds, trees, or something else that gave it measure, and which reflected light and sound. In fact, the concept 'universal space', which we presuppose as always existing, can be manifested only as a continuation of that little piece of realized space which has come into being by virtue of its delimitation.[43]

And:

> Delimitation is not an impoverishment, but on the contrary, the necessary and the most human means to experience reality.[44]

The delimitation of a space is not, therefore, an ending but a beginning. Martin Heidegger says something of the same kind when he writes: 'The boundary is not that whereat something leaves off, but on the contrary, as the Greeks recognized, the boundary is that whereat something begins its real being.'[45]

1.7 The Schröder house

If one excludes interiors, exhibitions, works by architects who happened, like Oud, to be associated with De Stijl at the time but that exhibit few or none of its characteristics, and later works that seem to show such characteristics but which were built long after the movement had come to an end, then the only true work of De Stijl architecture is the house that Rietveld designed with and for his friend Truus Schröder-Schräder (1889–1985) in the Prins Hendriklaan in Utrecht in 1924. There one finds all the characteristic elements

43. G. Rietveld, 'Levenshouding als achtergrond van mijn werk' ('Attitude to life as the background to my work'), in Brown, *Work of G. Rietveld*, p. 163.
44. G. Rietveld, 1963, in *Gerrit Rietveld: Texten*, Impress, Utrecht, 1979, p. 36.
45. M. Heidegger, 'Bauen, wohnen, denken', in *Vorträge und Aufsätze*, Günther Neske Verlag, Pfullingen, 1954, pp. 145–62.

defined by Mondrian in 'Neoplasticism in Painting', by Van Doesburg in 'Towards a Plastic Architecture', or in Rietveld's own rare surviving statements: the straight line, the right angle and the rectangular plane coloured red, blue, yellow, white or grey; walls, roofs and balconies that instead of meeting at corners seem to float or slide past each other, delimiting space without enclosing it; even, it can be argued, a kind of four-dimensionality, thanks to the sliding screens which can be opened or shut at different times to unite or subdivide the space (Figure 1.2)

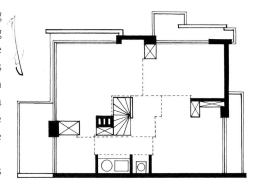

Figure 1.2 Gerrit Rietveld, Schröder house, Utrecht, 1924: upper floor plan

The importance of Truus Schröder's contribution to the design is increasingly recognized: Rietveld supplied the formal vocabulary – the way the house was put together – but without the functional programme which she brought to it, the result would have been very different. For instance, according to her recollections, both the opening up of the main living and sleeping spaces and their subdivision by sliding screens were originally her ideas, or at least originated in response to her suggestions (perhaps Rietveld, if he had outlived her, might have told the story differently):

> I can still hear myself asking, can those walls go, and that's how we ended up with one large space. But I was still looking for the possibility of also dividing up that space. That could be done with sliding partitions. I think that was an idea of Rietveld's, though he found it a shame ... He always regretted it, primarily I think because the space upstairs became considerably more complicated with the placing of the partitions ... In his own house he had one large area.[46]

Reacting against the stiff formality of the life in the rather grand three-storey mansion she and her lawyer husband had lived in from 1911 until his death in 1923, she wanted so far as possible one large space in which she and her three young children could share each other's lives to the full, a space where the children could learn from the conversation of the many artists and intellectuals who came to visit:

> I thought it was very good for the children to live in an atmosphere like that ... To hear those conversations, including those with people who disagreed. In fact, to take part in the exchange of ideas ... I wanted a real exchange of ideas in this house ... I wanted to have people here that you could discuss with. People with a critical attitude, all sorts of people.[47]

46. T. Schröder, interviewed by L Müller and F den Oudsten, in Overy/Müller/Den Oudsten/Mulder, *The Rietveld Schröder House*, Butterworth Architecture, 1988, p. 56.

47. T. Schröder, interview, in *Rietveld Schröder House*, pp. 93–6.

From the start, the Schröder house was intended not just as a response to the particular needs of a given family, but as a social and educational experiment in openness. It was to be a didactic demonstration of the richer and freer life that might result from the breaking down of barriers: the barriers of age and sex that separate the individuals within each family, and the barriers of class and culture that divide the family as a whole from the wider community.

1.8 The De Stijl house as a fragment of a continuous city

The Schröder house was a concrete and specific illustration of De Stijl's more general vision of the house and the city as an architectural and social continuum. In 1926 Mondrian would expound this vision in an article which the following year he published in the first issue of the Dutch avant-garde magazine *i10*, with the title 'Neo-plasticisme: De Woning – De Straat – De Stad' ('Neoplasticism: Dwelling – Street – City'):

'Today as in the past, the dwelling is truly a human 'refuge' … It is entirely natural that the inequality of society should drive each individual to flee the others. The reason is equally to be found in the individual himself: so long as humanity remains a mass of individuals, it will be in no state to create a harmonious environment. In the primitive era collective life was more possible because of the greater equality of the mass of the people … The people then looked to the dwelling only as a shelter from inclement weather, and lived for preference in the open. In the course of civilization this situation changed, and the natural and logical instinct to feel oneself part of a unity was obscured: the possibility of a collective life ceased. And so people occupied themselves more and more with the dwelling, and the 'outside' was reserved for traffic (the street) or for taking the air (the park) … Neoplasticism, however, conceives the dwelling, not as a place in which to take refuge or separate oneself from others, but as *a part of the whole*, a constructive element of the city … The interior of the dwelling must no longer be an accumulation of rooms formed by four walls with nothing but holes for doors and windows, but *a construction of coloured and colourless planes, combined with furniture and equipment, which must be nothing in themselves but constituent elements of the whole*. In just the same way, the human being must be nothing in himself, but only a part of the whole. Then, no longer conscious of his individuality, he will be happy in this earthly paradise that he has himself created.[48]

48.   P. Mondrian, 'Neo-Plasticisme: De Woning – De Straat – De Stad', in *i10*, vol. I, no. 1, 1927, pp. 12–18.

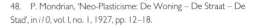

Just as, according to Alberti, the house must be like a little city and the city like a great house, so too, in Mondrian's utopian vision, house, street and city must form a continuity – a continuity composed of fractals, as it were. The neoplasticist city is to be one great open house for the whole community, a continuous space, differentiated here and there, much like the Schröder house, by free-standing screens, but in which neither the separate room nor the private dwelling has any place; conversely the house must be nothing but a fragment or a microcosm of the city.

In Mondrian's view, until society is revolutionized in this way, no true De Stijl architecture will be possible. Meanwhile, the De Stijl artist should stick to painting. In an earlier essay, published in *De Stijl* in 1922, he had envisaged in the 'distant future' a fusion of all the plastic arts into a single work of art, a total habitable environment. But for the present this can only be hinted at in a fragmentary way, through individual works of art:

> Even the neoplastic 'work of art' (as yet more or less individual) still expresses this, its own realization, imperfectly. It cannot represent directly the fullness and freedom of the future life. *The neoplastic conception will go far beyond art in its future realization* ... What was achieved in art must for the present remain restricted to art. Our external environment cannot yet be realized as the pure representation of harmony ... Art is partially disintegrating: but its end *now* would be premature. Its *reconstruction-as-life* is not yet possible, another art is still wanting, but the new cannot be built with old material.[49]

1.9 De Stijl openness *versus* the increasingly private future

The problem is that today not only are we no *nearer* to Mondrian's vision of a society in which the economic, psychological and physical boundaries between individuals melt away, we are moving rapidly *away* from it. Martin Pawley's *The Private Future* (1973)[50] and Richard Sennett's *The Fall of Public Man* (1977)[51] are prophetic analyses of a phenomenon that has become more evident, and become so at an accelerating pace, during the quarter-century since they wrote. The loosening of family bonds, the widening gap between rich and poor and the rapid growth of electronic means of broadcasting and communication are three of the most obvious factors that increasingly motivate each individual to seek a private space within the home and at the same time to engage less directly with the world outside.

49. Mondrian, 'De realiseering', in *De Stijl*, vol. V, no. 3, 1922, pp. 44–7.
50. M. Pawley, *The Private Future: Causes and consequences of community collapse in the West*, Thames & Hudson, London, 1973.
51. R. Sennett, *The Fall of Public Man*, Alfred A Knopf, New York, 1977.

Even in schools, the return to blackboard learning has reversed the late 1960s trend towards open planning and revived the walled-off classroom; but this phase itself is being superseded by the computer screen, which isolates each pupil in a little private world of his or her own. Already in the 1920s, with nothing but a radio to distract them, the Schröder children themselves seem to have found the total openness of the first-floor living space less congenial than their mother hoped:

> A low shelf along the wall in the main living area was intended to be used as a desk where they could do their homework together; in practice, the older children often found the privacy of the small library on the ground floor more appealing.[52]

Can the De Stijl theorists have been entirely on the wrong track? Chapter 4 will question whether the apparent harmony and sociability of primitive communities are possible without a willing surrender of individual liberty to the unquestioned customs of the tribe. Are the members of a tribal group or peasant community – such as that which Mondrian holds up as a model in 'Dwelling – Street – City' – 'free' only in the sense that they are never made aware of the unspoken conventions and limitations that govern their actions and their thoughts? People of the sort that Truus Schröder wanted to attract to her house – 'people who disagreed, people you could discuss with, people with a critical attitude' – are too independent-minded ever to submit to such parochial conformity.

Although powerfully affected by his encounter with De Stijl around 1923–4, Le Corbusier always held to his own ideal of the dwelling as something private and bounded: a 'cell'. Had he a more realistic notion than the De Stijl theorists of what modern life was destined to become – for better or worse?

1.10 Le Corbusier: spatial interpenetration and the new spirit

In the crucial sixth part of early editions of *Space, Time and Architecture*, the concept of 'space-time in art, architecture, and construction' is represented by just three men: one engineer, Robert Maillart, and two architects, Walter Gropius and Le Corbusier (1887–1965). Giedion is careful to stress the latter architect's affinity with the 'non-Euclidian' space newly discovered by the cubist and futurist artists. In this description, in which Le Corbusier appears very close to the principles of Van Doesburg's architectural manifesto, Giedion virtually

52. A.T. Friedman, *Women and the Making of the Modern House*, Harry N Abrams, New York, 1998, p. 77.

repeats the wording of Van Doesburg's eighth point, which demands the destruction of the separateness of inside and outside and the interpenetration of interior and exterior space:

> The spirit of Le Corbusier's houses shows an absolute identity with the spirit that animates modern painting ... Around 1910 Picasso and Braque, as the consequence of a new conception of space, exhibited the interiors and exteriors of objects simultaneously. In architecture Le Corbusier developed, on the same principle, the interpenetration of inner and outer space.[53]

Of Le Corbusier's Villa Savoye (1929–31) Giedion writes:

> It is impossible to comprehend the Savoie house by a view from a single point: quite literally, it is a construction in space-time. The body of the house has been hollowed out in every direction: from above and below, within and without. A cross section at any point shows inner and outer space penetrating each other inextricably.[54]

However, while what Giedion says about the cross-section and the hollowing out of the cube from above and below is certainly true, the striking thing about the exterior of the Villa Savoye is precisely that all these spatial effects are nevertheless contained and held in check by the four-square frame of the walls. And Le Corbusier leaves us in no doubt that this was his intention. Criticizing the centrifugal, fragmented forms of the De Stijl projects exhibited in Paris in 1923–4 as 'arbitrary and tormented', he concludes that once the initial sensation has passed, one will realize the need to return to the discipline of a 'shield of pure form'.[55]

How important it was that this shield should be unbroken is illustrated by the first design for the Villa Savoye, made in 1928. Although somewhat larger, this was broadly similar to the executed design. It included, however, an external staircase giving direct access from the first floor terrace to the ground, and it is remarkable how much this small interruption of the otherwise continuous façade would have compromised its role as an unbroken conceptual boundary between internal and external space. However complex the spatial interpenetrations may be *within* this boundary, the most striking thing about the exterior as built is its complete denial of that 'inextricable penetration of inner and outer space' which Giedion extols.

As regards 'the historic destiny of modern architecture', Le Corbusier undeniably shared the then prevailing belief that humanity was entering a new industrial age, and that this age had an

53. Giedion, *Space, Time and Architecture*, p. 408.
54. *Ibid.*, p. 416.
55. Le Corbusier, 'L'exposition de l'Ecole spéciale d'architecture', in *L'Esprit Nouveau*, no. 23, May 1924.

unstoppable momentum of its own: '... Industry, as formidable as a natural force and overrunning everything like a flood that rolls on to its destined end'.[56]

But it is worth noting that this 'industry' is hardly comparable to Giedion's personified 'History', which is conscious of itself and has its own innate character that it may even try purposely to disguise. Le Corbusier may liken it metaphorically to a force of nature or a river in spate, but it is clear from the context that it consists of nothing more mysterious than the tendency of technologies to develop by a process of learning and experience. Moreover, what for the present holds back technological advance is not some perverse desire of the 'Age' to conceal its true nature, but simply the slowness of the mass of people to recognize and adopt 'the new spirit': 'The right state of mind does not exist.'[57] And the reason for this, too, is quite understandable. Whereas 'tools in the past were always *in man's hands*', today's tools – machines – are literally beyond his grasp. The craftsman of the past owned his own handtools; when he needed them, he simply took them off the shelf. The machine-minder is forced to sell his time to the capitalist machine-owner. Instead of the tool being harnessed to the man, the man is now harnessed to the tool. Not unnaturally, he resists this, and fails to recognize its benefits:

> The human animal stands breathless and panting before the tool that he cannot take hold of; progress appears to him as hateful as it is praiseworthy; all is confusion within his mind; he feels himself to be the slave of a frantic state of things and experiences no sense of liberation or comfort or amelioration ... To pass this crisis we must create the state of mind which can understand what is going on; the human animal must learn to use his tools. When this human animal has put on his new harness and knows the effort that is expected from him, he will see that things have changed: and changed *for the better*.[58]

Where the founders of De Stijl believed that the 'new consciousness of the age' dictated the abolition of all separateness, all categories, all 'harnesses', Le Corbusier sees categories, boundaries and hierarchies as permanent human necessities, essential to any ordered society, to any civilized life, to any developed art. The advance of mechanization is for him not an end in itself, but merely a more efficient means of supplying the elementary and perennial human needs – above all, the one that had been conspicuously forgotten in the headlong rush to industrialization: a decent dwelling for everyone.

56. Le Corbusier, *Towards a New Architecture*, The Architectural Press, London, 1946, p. 211.
57. *Ibid.*, p. 211.
58. *Ibid.*, pp. 211–12.

Thus although the very title of the review that Le Corbusier founded with the painter Amedée Ozenfant in 1920 (*L'Esprit Nouveau* – '*The New Spirit*') *appears* to embody the idea of the *Zeitgeist*, it in fact has little in common with Giedion's 'period progressing toward consciousness of itself', or even with Mondrian's 'human consciousness ... *growing* towards definition'.[59]

Le Corbusier conceives the new spirit, not as a complete break with the past, but rather as a *recovery* of architecture's authentic principles, which he sets out in his 'Three Reminders to Architects'.[60] He writes in *Précisions*: 'Today I am accused of being a revolutionary. I shall confess to you of having had only one master – the past; and only one discipline – the study of the past.'[61]

Like the fresh spring foliage that revitalizes an ancient tree, the new spirit brings new life and a changed aspect to human constants that remain unchanged in their essentials. It cannot be too often stressed that the insertion of the word *New* into the English title of *Vers une architecture* (literally, *Towards an Architecture*) distorts the main argument of the book, which is not to advocate a 'new' architecture but to redirect architecture to its unchanging fundamentals. Architects, in Le Corbusier's view, have lost sight of the four great enduring principles – mass, surface and plan, together with mathematical proportion – and he writes to remind them of these:

> The emotions that architecture arouses spring from physical conditions which are inevitable, irrefutable and to-day forgotten ... A supreme determinism illuminates for us the creations of nature and gives us the security of something poised and reasonably made, of something infinitely modulated, evolved, varied and unified. The primordial laws are simple and few in number.[62]

Still less does the new spirit involve notions of non-Euclidian geometry or simultaneity. A year earlier, in 1919, Ozenfant and Jeanneret (who had not yet adopted the *nom de guerre* Le Corbusier) specifically attacked as 'absurd' the concept of four-dimensionality in painting. In their purist manifesto, *Après le cubisme*, they gave the lie to Giedion's interpretation of Le Corbusier's work as an expression of the space–time continuum:

> When you think about it, the objection raised here towards the fourth dimension only concerns the gratuitous hypotheses of the Cubist theorists; this particular hypothesis has no foundation in palpable reality and, as it is impossible to express it in painting, only adds to the general misunderstanding. In a word, this is why it is

59. Mondrian, 'De nieuwe beelding', in *De Stijl*, vol. I, no. 3, 1918, p. 29.

60. Le Corbusier, *Towards a New Architecture*, pp. 25–62.

61. Le Corbusier, *Précisions* (1930), MIT Press, Cambridge, Mass., 1991, p. 33.

62. Le Corbusier, *Towards a New Architecture*, pp. 28 & 70.

absurd when they claim to be able to express any dimensions other than those we can perceive with our senses. The third dimension of palpable space, known as depth, was banished for a time by some Cubists in favour of a certain 'fourth dimension' which the superficial reading of scientific works had led them to invent.[63]

1.11 Le Corbusier's ordered compartmentation of space and time

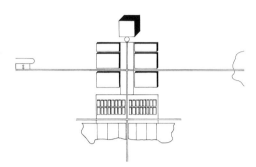

Figure 1.3 Le Corbusier, radiant city, 1929–30: plan

Throughout Le Corbusier's publications one encounters different versions of a recurring image: the human body as an articulated system of specialized compartments – an 'organism'. In *The Radiant City* (1933) it appears as the simplest of diagrams, with the separate parts captioned '*décision*' (the head), '*préhension*' (the hands), '*réservoir*' (the trunk) and '*transport*' (the legs).[64] *The Home of Man* (1948) contains a more elaborate sketch which shows the body in four ways: as skeleton, as outward form, as lungs, stomach and gut, and as circulatory system. The caption runs as follows:

> Nature, the eternal lesson. Architecture, town-planning, determination of functions, classification of functions, hierarchy. Architecture, town-planning = impeccable biology. Final harmony crowning a complex work, an arrangement of perfection. 'The intelligent, correct and magnificent play of forms in light'.[65]

The zoned plans of the 'contemporary city' (1922) and especially the 'radiant city' (1929–30) are direct transcriptions of these diagrams. In the latter, the head is represented by the fourteen towers of the business centre; the neck by the rail and air terminal; the thorax by the residential zone; and, separated from this by a green belt, the abdomen, comprising factories and heavy industry (Figure 1.3).[66]

Together with the body, Le Corbusier found an ideal model of the organic classification of the human habitat in the regulated life of the monastery, in which both space and time are strictly compartmented. The monastic ordering of life suggested a way of solving the great dilemma of industrialized society: the combination of an ever-increasing collectivization of society with a growing isolation of the single individual. Le Corbusier's love affair with the monastery, and with the idea of 'organism', began in 1907 with a visit to the Carthusian monastery of Ema at Galluzzo near Florence, described

63. A. Ozenfant and C.-E. Jeanneret, *Après le cubisme*, Paris, 1918, pp. 16ff.; quoted in S. Georgiadis, *Sigfried Giedion*, Edinburgh University Press, Edinburgh, 1993, p. 132.

64. Le Corbusier, *The Radiant City* (1933), Faber & Faber, London, 1967, p. 82.

65. Le Corbusier and F. de Pierrefeu, *The Home of Man*, The Architectural Press, London, 1948, p. 124.

66. Le Corbusier, *Radiant City*, pp. 141, 168, 170.

by H. Allen Brooks as 'the most profound architectural experience of his life'.[67] Four years later he returned there, and recalled:

> My first impression of the charterhouse was one of harmony, but not until later did the essential, profound lesson of the place sink in on me – that here the equation which it was the task of human wit to solve, the reconciliation of 'individual' on the one hand and 'collectivity' on the other, lay resolved ... The Ema charterhouse is an organism. The term *organism* had been born in my mind.[68]

The monastic plan – more specifically the Carthusian plan, in which each monk lives apart in a self-contained house with its own courtyard garden – combines a high degree of individual privacy (the 'cell') with a structured pattern of collective life: the refectory, the chapter house, the abbey church. The ideal of the private dwelling as 'a vessel of silence and lofty solitude',[69] set within an ordered and comprehensive building – the 'great house' of a complete community – remained the inspiration for all Le Corbusier's housing projects, from the *immeuble-villas* of 1922 to the series of post-war *unités d'habitation*, while its easy application to the monastery of La Tourette (1956) only serves to underline its indebtedness to the traditional monastic plan's balanced, hierarchical ordering of private and communal spaces. As Le Corbusier's collaborator André Wogensky writes of the *unités d'habitation* of the 1940s and '50s:

> The first two motivating ideas of the *Unité d'habitation* are simple and objective: first, to protect individuals and families from all outside intrusion or disturbance. To do this, he set out to design a dwelling in which the family should not see or hear their neighbours, and therefore should neither be seen nor heard by them. Second, he sought to reconcile this protection of privacy with the collective life, to resolve the individual/society dilemma by integrating the dwelling units into a community – what he called the vertical village. Those who claim that the high-rise or tower blocks, the scourge of our present age, are the result of Le Corbusier's ideas, are fools. For these large blocks do not fulfill either of his two conditions.[70]

The key to Le Corbusier's solution to the problem of living harmoniously in an industrialized society is the classification and compartmentation, not only of space but also of time, which in *Towards a New Architecture* he calls 'the three eights':[71] eight hours for work, eight hours for sleep and eight hours for recreation and

67. H.A. Brooks, *Le Corbusier's Formative Years*, University of Chicago Press, Chicago and London, 1997, p. 105.
68. Le Corbusier, in J. Petit, *Le Corbusier lui-même*, Geneva, 1970, p. 44; quoted in R. Walden (ed.), *The Open Hand*, MIT Press, Cambridge, Mass., 1977, pp. 218–19.
69. Le Corbusier, *Radiant City*, p. 67.
70. A. Wogensky, foreword to Walden, *Open Hand*, pp. ix–x.
71. Le Corbusier, *Towards a New Architecture*, p. 255.

meditation. 'Now and always,' he writes in *The Decorative Art of Today* (1925), '… there is a hierarchy. There is a time for work, when one uses oneself up, and also a time for meditation, when one recovers harmony. There should be no confusion between them … Everything has its classification; work and meditation.'[72]

The principal object of meditation in the cell is to be the purist painting. For Le Corbusier, the work of pure art is a 'moment of profound discourse … inseparable from being, a truly indissoluble source of exaltation with the power to bestow pure happiness.'[73]

1.12 The tree and the semi-lattice

In section 1.9 I pointed to the conflict between the De Stijl ideal of spatial openness and today's growing tendency to separation and privacy, and asked whether Le Corbusier's principle of hierarchical compartmentation might not be better fitted to the real social and psychological demands of modern life. But when one looks beyond his seductive sketches of café terraces overlooking landscaped parks, one discovers that the kind of life described in Le Corbusier's writings and provided for by the physical structure of his urban utopias is grimly deterministic, regimented and stratified. He had a long-lasting (though opportunistic) commitment to ideals of leadership and authority, reflected in his involvement with the right wing of the French syndicalist movement and his flirtations with Russian communism and Italian fascism in the 1920s and '30s, and ending with the fruitless and humiliating months spent in Vichy courting Marshal Pétain during the occupation.[74]

The already quoted phrase 'Everything has its classification; work and meditation' continues:

> The classes too have their classification: those who struggle for their crust of bread have the simple ideal of a decent lodging … And those well-enough endowed to have the ability and the duty to think.[75]

Virtually the same words appear in *Towards a New Architecture*, with a still more overtly elitist and authoritarian tone:

> On the one hand the mass of people look for a decent dwelling … On the other hand the man of initiative, of action, of thought, the LEADER, demands a shelter for his meditations in a quiet and sure spot.[76]

72. Le Corbusier, *The Decorative Art of Today*, The Architectural Press, London, 1987, p. 86.
73. *Ibid.*, p. 118.
74. R. Fishman, 'Le Corbusier's plans and politics, 1928–1942', in Walden, *Open Hand*, pp. 244–83; also J.-L. Cohen, *Le Corbusier and the Mystique of the USSR*, Princeton University Press, Princeton, N.J., 1992.
75. Le Corbusier, *Decorative Art of Today*, pp. 86–7.
76. Le Corbusier, *Towards a New Architecture*, p. 24.

And the title page of *The Radiant City*, published in the very year that Hitler came to power in Germany, bears the proud inscription:

This work is dedicated to AUTHORITY. Paris, May, 1933.

Like the monastery, the modern factory gave Le Corbusier an ideal model of ordered classification and hierarchical organization. In *Towards a New Architecture* he exults in the rigid discipline and monotonous regimentation characteristic of industrialized production:

machinery is at work in close collaboration with man; the right man for the right job is coldly selected; labourers, workmen, foremen, engineers, managers, administrators – each in his proper place ... Specialization ties man to his machine; an absolute precision is demanded of every worker ... The father no longer teaches his son the various secrets of his little trade; a strange foreman directs severely and precisely the restrained and circumscribed tasks. The worker makes one tiny detail, always the same one ... perhaps during years of work, perhaps for the rest of his life. He only sees his task reach its finality in the finished work at the moment when it is passed, in its bright and shining purity, into the factory yard to be placed in a delivery-van.[77]

Besides this pride in the finished product, the worker's reward for his eight hours of work will be a mass-produced house, a 'decent dwelling' for his relaxation and enjoyment in his sixteen hours of freedom. This dwelling will replace

the old and rotting buildings that form our snail-shell, our habitation, which crush us in our daily contact with them – putrid and unproductive. Everywhere can be seen machines which serve to produce something and produce it admirably, in a clean sort of way. The machine that we live in is an old coach full of turberculosis.[78]

But even at home the factory worker cannot be trusted to be left entirely to his own devices. He can hardly be expected to relax from his hours of toil by meditating on a purist painting in his 'clean cell'; that is a privilege reserved for the intellectual elite, the managerial class who 'have the ability and the duty to think'. To keep the workers healthily occupied, and to ensure that they have not time for potentially subversive thought, organized sports are provided:

77. *Ibid.*, pp. 254–5.
78. *Ibid.*, pp. 256–7.

Sport at the very door of one's house is needed, so that everyone – men, women, and children – on reaching home, can change their things and come down for play and exercise, to fill their lungs and strengthen their muscles.[79]

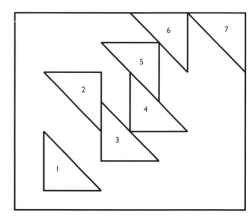

Figure 1.4 Simon Nicholson, abstract composition (redrawn interpretation by the author)

Private gardening is not to be encouraged, however; it is 'selfish and unsporting, which induces sterile fatigue and tendencies contrary to those of sound physical culture'.[80] Instead, close to the housing, there will be 'agriculture of an industrialized and intensive kind, a large yield ... A farmer acts as superintendent and manager'.[81] Even in his hours of recreation, the worker is never unsupervised, never entirely free.

In both the 'contemporary city' and the 'radiant city', each function – housing, education, culture, government, business, industry, and so on – is segregated in a discrete zone, each zone being connected to others by transport routes which, unlike the traditional street, are likewise separated from the functions that they serve. The social and economic drawbacks of such hierarchically organized cities, compared with the apparently chaotic – but in reality more complexly ordered – 'natural' city, were pointed out by many writers in the 1960s and '70s: notably by Jane Jacobs in *The Death and Life of Great American Cities* (1961)[82] and Christopher Alexander in 'A City is not a Tree' (1965).[83] Cities based on an alternative kind of organization, which Alexander defines as a 'semi-lattice', are characterized by 'overlap, ambiguity, multiplicity of aspect'. They are 'not less orderly than the rigid tree, but more so. They represent a thicker, tougher, more subtle and more complex view of structure.'[84]

From this point of view, Le Corbusier's principle of classification and separation of functions is no better than, indeed perhaps worse than, the De Stijl ideal of total openness. Both opt for one simple, all-embracing solution; they are, in fact, the opposite faces of a single, greatly overvalued coin. However, what Alexander calls the 'natural' city – if there ever was such a thing in the sense of one that has grown entirely without conscious human intention – is today neither possible nor desirable. If we want complexity and overlap, we must design it. This argument will be resumed in Chapter 8.

Unable to show an example of a designed semi-lattice city, Alexander takes as his model an abstract painting by Simon Nicholson (Figures 1.4 and 1.5), superficially not unlike certain works of Mondrian (e.g. *Composition with grid 1*, 1918), Van Doesburg or Bart van der Leck. He discovers altogether thirty-six overlapping relationships between the seven similar triangles that make up the painting:

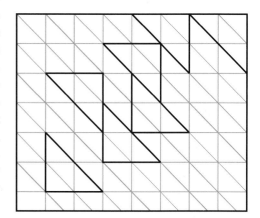

Figure 1.5 The same painting with superimposed regular grid

79. Le Corbusier, *The City of Tomorrow* (1924), The Architectural Press, London, 1971, p. 202.

80. Le Corbusier, 'Response to Moscow', 1930, published in *Planirovka goroda*, Moscow, 1933; quoted in Cohen, *Le Corbusier and the Mystique of the USSR*, p. 146.

81. Le Corbusier, *Towards a New Architecture*, p. 233.

82. J. Jacobs, *The Death and Life of Great American Cities*, Random House, New York, 1961.

83. C. Alexander, 'A city is not a tree', in *Architectural Forum*, April–May 1965.

84. *Ibid.*

The fascination of this painting lies in the fact that although it is constructed of rather few simple triangular elements, these elements unite in many different ways to form the larger units of the painting. If we make a complete inventory of the perceived units in the painting, we find that each triangle enters into four or five completely different kinds of unit, none contained in the others, yet all overlapping in that triangle.[85]

Alexander numbers the triangles and pairs them in various ways as visual units. Thus the pairs 1–2, 3–5 and 4–6 are units because together they form rectangles; 2 and 4 form a parallelogram; 2–3 and 4–5 form Z-shapes; 3–4 and 5–6 point the same way and share the same axis of symmetry; 7 is like the shadow of 6 shifted sideways; and so on:

It seems almost as though the painter had made an explicit attempt to single out overlap as a vital generator of structure ... And when we wish to be precise, the semi-lattice, being part of a large branch of modern mathematics, is a powerful way of exploring the structure of these images. It is the semi-lattice we must look for, not the tree.[86]

The resemblance between Nicholson's painting and some De Stijl works is not, I think, accidental, nor is it just a superficial question of using geometrically simple elements. The doctrinaire theoretical statements of Mondrian and Van Doesburg belie the actual pluralism of their work, to which I now return.

1.13 Purist containment *versus* De Stijl continuity and multivalence

In a purist painting such as Le Corbusier's *Composition with guitar and lamp* (1920) (Figure 1.1) everything is determined by the frame. The composition is conceived as a *complete thing* – a small self-contained world. In this particular case, the shape of the canvas comprises two juxtaposed golden or 1.618 rectangles, i.e. the ratio of total breadth to height is 1.236:1. The composition can be analysed in the following way.

First, the two golden rectangles are again halved, restoring the original shape of the whole. Next, a square is superimposed centrally. The square is then broken down into smaller squares and golden rectangles, and the process continued until the whole canvas is reduced to a symmetrical grid (Figures 1.6–1.11). The significant point,

85. *Ibid.*

86. *Ibid.*

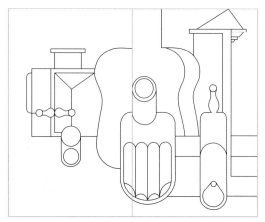

Figure 1.6 C.-E. Jeanneret (Le Corbusier), *Composition à la guitare et à la lanterne*, 1920. Vertical division of the whole canvas into two golden rectangles

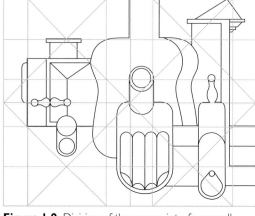

Figure 1.9 Division of the square into four small squares separated by four golden rectangles, with a still smaller square at the centre

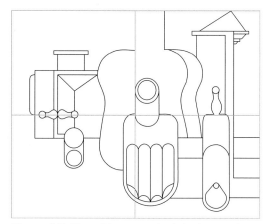

Figure 1.7 The golden rectangles halved to produce four rectangles similar to the whole

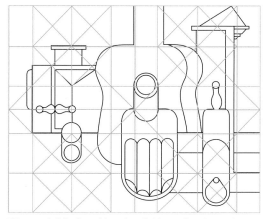

Figure 1.10 Quadripartite division of each small square

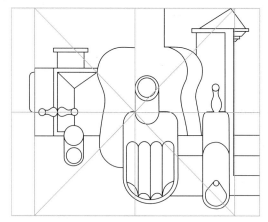

Figure 1.8 Central superposition of a large square

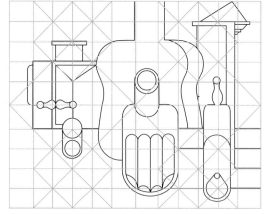

Figure 1.11 Further subdivision giving the final grid composed of 80 squares and 40 double golden rectangles which repeat the shape of the whole painting

in the present context, is that the composition starts out from a pure, contained whole, which is compartmented into smaller, similar shapes, like a piece of furniture with compartments designed to display various objects. The objects themselves – guitar, lamp, flask, wine bottle, glass – are then placed on the separate 'shelves'. The process is exactly comparable to Le Corbusier's recipe for architectural composition in the succeeding years: internal complexity contained within the discipline of a simple frame, or, as he said, 'a pure whole, covering abundance with a mask of simplicity.'[87]

The De Stijl approach was the exact opposite. So far as possible, the frame, conceived as the limit of the composition, was done away with. What appeared on the canvas was regarded as merely a fragment of a boundless continuity. This is most clearly demonstrated by a trio of small paintings (each only 35 cm square) that Van Doesburg began in 1920 and titled *Composition XVIII in three parts* (Figure 1.12).[88] No less than the paintings themselves, the space between and around them, which the artist specified in a drawing (Figure 1.13), forms part of the total composition, which by implication could continue indefinitely beyond them. Van Doesburg must have described this breakthrough to Mondrian, who objects in a surviving letter that the composition still has a centrepoint, even though in Van Doesburg's scheme this lies in the empty space midway between the three canvases. For Mondrian, a De Stijl painting must have no focal or vanishing point:

> Bear in mind that ... *it is not just a question of displacing the centre, but of abolishing it, doing away with it altogether* ... If you merely place the centre point *outside* the canvas, it still remains *a canvas*: your painting then just becomes a part of a larger painting, doesn't it?[89]

According to Carel Blotkamp, 'Mondrian objects that this method reduces paintings to arbitrary fragments of an imaginary greater whole.'[90] What Mondrian finds objectionable is not that the composition continues beyond the canvas, but that the 'whole' of which the canvas is a fragment is still conceived *as* a whole; that is, as a self-contained unity. In fact, Van Doesburg's diagram for the hanging of the three paintings shows a modular proportional scheme of squares governed by very Corbusian-looking 'regulating lines', the whole contained within a single notional frame. Merely to conceal part of this whole is for Mondrian not enough; it must be destroyed entirely.

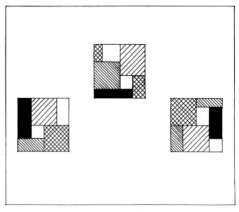

Figure 1.12 Theo van Doesburg, *Composition XVIII in three parts*, 1920

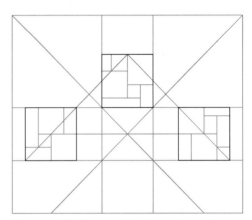

Figure 1.13 Theo van Doesburg, *Composition XVIII in three parts*, 1920, proportional analysis of arrangement on wall

87. Le Corbusier, 'L'exposition de 'Ecole spéciale d'architecture', in *L'Esprit Nouveau*, no. 23, May 1924.
88. Illustrated in *De Stijl*, vol. V, no. 12, 1922, p. 210.
89. P. Mondrian, letter to T. van Doesburg, 12 June 1920.
90. Blotkamp, 'Theo van Doesburg', p. 38.

Following the series of grid and checkerboard compositions of 1918–19, Mondrian strove progressively to destroy the boundary of the painting by making the edge as ambiguous as possible and so implying that the composition continued beyond it. This intention is most clearly seen in a number of very simple lozenge-format compositions consisting of nothing but black – and in one case yellow – lines, made between 1926 and 1933. Sometimes there are four lines, sometimes three, and in the simplest composition, *Composition with two black lines* of 1931, only two (Figure 1.14). Generally only two lines intersect within the canvas, while in the last of the series, *Lozenge composition with four yellow lines* (1933), the lines do not meet within the painting at all.

In the very simple 1931 painting with two lines, the white square of the canvas, set at 45 degrees to the horizontal, is traversed by a vertical and a horizontal black line which intersect close to the middle of the lower left-hand edge of the painting. The horizontal is almost imperceptibly thicker than the vertical. There is a strong implication that the lines continue into an unseen space beyond the frame. Do they form part of an implied rectangular grid? Or are they Mondrian's ultimate (and perhaps unconscious) abstraction of a frequent theme in his earlier landscapes of 1906–8: the perpendicular geometry of the flat Dutch landscape, seen by moonlight? That the theme was of lasting importance to him is indicated by the fact that he returns to it more than ten years later, in the first of a series of imaginary conversations serialized in *De Stijl* between August 1919 and August 1920:

> In this landscape, the horizontal – with regard to ourselves – is represented determinately only by the horizontal of the skyline ... The sky appears as an indeterminate plane, on which, however, the moon appears as a point, therefore *exactly*. The plane is also determined *from this dot to the horizon*: this determination is a *vertical line*. Although the latter does not appear in nature, it is nevertheless there. Were we to draw it, then the opposite of the horizontal would be represented *determinately* ... And it is the *balanced* relation of position – the rectangular composition of lines and planes – that plastically represents *repose*.[91]

In his 1978 essay 'Mondrian: Order and Randomness in Abstract Painting' Meyer Schapiro makes a detailed analysis of the working of the first of these monochrome linear compositions: *Painting I: lozenge composition with four lines and grey* (1926) (Figure 1.15). The whole canvas appears in black-and-white reproduction as a white square set at 45 degrees to the horizontal. (A small part of the whole is not in

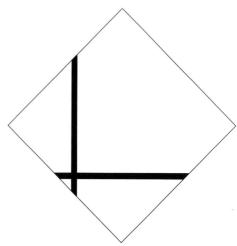

Figure 1.14 Piet Mondrian, *Composition with two black lines*, 1931

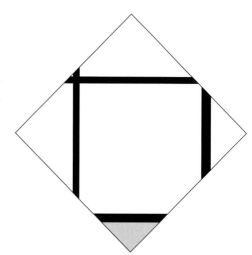

Figure 1.15 Piet Mondrian, *Painting I: lozenge composition with four lines and grey*, 1926

---

91. Mondrian, 'Natuurlijke', in *De Stijl*, vol. II, no. 8, 1919, pp. 86–7.

fact white but pale grey.) Within the whole, at first glance, four black lines of slightly different widths seem to intersect to form a smaller square. The angles of the smaller square nearly coincide with the midpoints of the four sloping edges of the painting, but in fact only one of the four intersections occurs within the frame, so the square appears to extend into an implied space beyond the bounds of the canvas. This space has an apparent depth: the black lines seem to continue *underneath* the edge, and to lie *in front of* the white ground. Furthermore, the fact that the black lines not only meet but intersect slightly at the only visible corner of the square implies that it is not just a solitary square but part of an indefinitely extended grid (Figure 1.16). This effect is reinforced by the 'arbitrary' lozenge shape of the canvas, which prevents the edges from engaging with the orthogonal pattern of lines, as would those of a conventional upright canvas.

But despite this, other intentional ambiguities in this deceptively simple painting invite contrary readings. For instance, the fact that the triangle in the bottom corner of the diamond is not white like the rest, but pale grey, invites the viewer to see it, and thus by implication the remaining white areas, as separate polygonal figures (Figure 1.17). The figure–ground relations are now reversed: the black lines, which before on account of their greater apparent density seemed to stand out in front of a white ground, are now read as part of a continuous *black* ground, visible through narrow gaps between floating white and grey figures. (The figure–ground phenomenon will be discussed more fully in Chapter 7.)

Despite all Mondrian's insistence in his writings on 'determinate relations', he seems intent, in his paintings, on achieving exactly the opposite: to create *indeterminacy* – and therefore complexity and overlap – with the fewest and simplest possible means. Schapiro concludes:

> In this art that seems so self-contained and disavows in theory all reference to a world outside the painting, we tend to complete the apparent forms as if they continued in a hidden surrounding field and were segments of an unbounded grid. It is hard to escape the suggestion that they extend in that virtual space outside.[92]

1.14 The role of the corner junction in architecture

In retrospect, Mondrian saw his whole work as a struggle to destroy the external and internal boundaries of the traditional painting. First, he eliminated the representation of appearances (around 1916), reducing the painting to a rectangular grid of lines and coloured

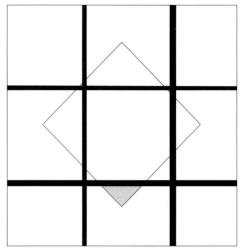

Figure 1.16 Piet Mondrian, *Lozenge composition with four lines and grey*, 1926, indefinite extension of grid

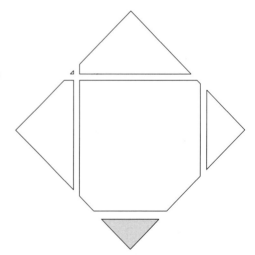

Figure 1.17 Piet Mondrian, *Lozenge composition with four lines and grey*: white and grey areas as figures

92. M. Schapiro, 'Mondrian: order and randomness in abstract painting', in *Mondrian: On the Humanity of Abstract Painting*, George Braziller, New York, 1995, pp. 33–4.

planes; then he strove progressively to undermine the unity of the abstract composition itself, culminating in the final 'Boogie-Woogie' paintings done in New York in 1942–4, where the lines themselves are dissolved into ribbons of tiny blocks of different colours. Asked why he continually struggled to destroy what he had made, he answered: 'I don't want pictures, I want to find things out.'[93] Shortly before his death on 1 February 1944, he saw his whole development as a series of destructions:

> The great struggle for artists is the annihilation of static equilibrium in their paintings through continuous oppositions (contrasts) among the means of expression. It is always natural for human beings to seek static balance. This balance of course is necessary to existence in time. But vitality in the continual succession of time always destroys this balance. Abstract art is a concrete expression of such a vitality ... The intention of Cubism – in any case in the beginning – was to express volume. Three-dimensional space – natural space – thus remained. Cubism therefore remained basically a naturalistic expression and was only *an abstraction* – not true abstract art. This attitude of the cubists to the representation of volume in space was contrary to my conception of abstraction which is based on belief that this very space *has to be destroyed*. As a consequence I came to the destruction of volume by the use of the plane. This I accomplished by means of lines cutting the planes. But still the plane remained too intact. So I came to making only lines and brought the color within the lines. Now the only problem was to destroy these lines also through mutual oppositions. Perhaps I do not express myself clearly in this, but it may give you some idea why I left the Cubist influence. True Boogie-Woogie I conceive as homogeneous in intention with mine in painting: destruction of melody which is the equivalent of destruction of natural appearance; and construction through the continuous opposition of pure means – dynamic rhythm. I think the destructive element is too much neglected in art.[94]

A similar effort to eliminate or render ambiguous the boundaries of the spatial composition – in effect, to destroy space as a defined volume – reappears in De Stijl architecture, particularly that of Rietveld. In the view of Bruno Zevi, the key question is extraordinarily simple: it comes down to how the walls meet – or fail to meet – at the corners. If the walls meet, forming closed corners, the effect is of a discrete space *within* walls. If, on the other hand, the walls appear not to meet, and especially if one wall runs past the end of the other

93. C. Holty, 'Mondrian in New York', in *Arts*, September 1957, p. 21.

94. P. Mondrian, in 'Eleven Europeans in America', in *Bulletin of the Museum of Modern Art*, New York, XII, 4 & 5, 1946.

without touching it, we get a continuous space *between and around* walls. At the conclusion of his book *Poetica dell'architettura neoplastica* (1953), Zevi draws attention to the crucial role of the corner junction in our reading of architecture:

> In the critical interpretation of a building, the analysis of the corners, of how two walls connect or intersect, of how one surface terminates or penetrates another, is highly instructive ... It was natural, as we have seen, for neoplasticism to focus its attention on the corners: setting out to eliminate mass and volume, it had first of all to remove gravity and stability at the point where two walls meet. Well then: from the Greeks up to today, the design of the corner of a building is an immediate and clear reflection of the creative energy and skill of the architect. Consequently anyone who has learnt from De Stijl to judge angles with sensibility and precision will have progressed far along the road to an understanding of architecture.[95]

The aim of the present book is similar. In writing it, I have not sought to take sides in the debate between openness and closure – between De Stijl and Le Corbusier – but to explore their opposite viewpoints in the hope of 'understanding architecture a little better'. Each side claimed to have a single, self-sufficient recipe for the new architecture. Both recipes, by themselves, were incomplete; but the conflict between them, in which each provided as it were the antidote to the other, was often fruitful, and still has lessons for us.

95. B. Zevi, *Poetica dell'architettura neoplastica*, Libreria Editrice Politecnica Tamburini, Milan, 1953, p. 152.

2

De Stijl's Other Name

2.1 The meanings of words

In January 1921 the journal *De Stijl* appeared in a new horizontal format with a radically redesigned typography. On the cover, the title DE STIJL, which originally had stood alone, was now superimposed in black capitals against the larger red initials NB (Figure 2.1).

The letters 'NB' stand for *nieuwe beelding*, a phrase which requires interpretation even in Dutch, and which in English has no obvious equivalent. The usual, almost meaningless translation 'neoplasticism' – which Mondrian himself introduced in both his French and his Dutch writings, still confuses or alienates English-language commentators on De Stijl:

> Neoplasticism, one of the most annoying instances of catachresis[1] in Modern art history, ... can be a stumbling block to understanding Mondrian. *Plastic* usually means the art of molding sculpture from malleable materials such as clay or wax, but Mondrian meant something entirely different.[2]

Confronted by this obstacle, we either ignore it altogether, and stick to the more easily comprehensible but hardly more enlightening title of the journal – *De Stijl* – or we pretend to understand it, much as, in Hans Christian Andersen's story, mature respectable citizens pretend to see the emperor's new clothes. Perhaps, worse still, we make a punning connection between the two meanings of 'plastic', subconsciously linking Mondrian's rejection of nature with an artificial art of brightly coloured smooth rectangular surfaces, a sort of formica art.

But the words *nieuwe beelding* are too important to be either ignored or misunderstood. *De Stijl*, after all, was only the name of the magazine, and tells us little or nothing about the movement or its goals. And for once, with *nieuwe beelding*, in contrast to impressionism, fauvism or cubism, the name of an art movement was chosen by its members, not its enemies, and chosen with care to express its aims.

Beeld and its derivatives *beelden, beeldend* and *beelding* appear constantly in the pages of *De Stijl*: in the title of Mondrian's long

Figure 2.1 Theo van Doesburg, title design for the journal *De Stijl*, 1921

1. 'Incorrect use of words' (*Concise Oxford Dictionary*).
2. C.A. Riley II, *The Saints of Modern Art*, University Press of New England, Hanover and London, 1998, p. 31.

serialized essay 'De nieuwe beelding in de schilderkunst' ('The new *beelding* in painting'); in Oud's article 'Het monumentale stadsbeeld' ('The monumental city-*beeld*'); in Van Doesburg's architectural manifesto 'Tot een beeldende architectuur' ('Towards a *beeldende* architecture'); and in his 1918 essay 'Denken – aanschouwen – beelden' ('Think – observe – *beelden*'), which provides the mainspring of the present chapter. The words stand for an attitude to the role of art which was the driving force behind the De Stijl movement, and without an understanding of their meaning it is impossible to begin to comprehend its goals, achievements and shortcomings.

I have so far avoided translating *beeld* in its various forms because no English word exactly fits all these applications. In order to find the least inadequate translation we may as well start with the Dutch dictionary:

beeld   image; portrait, picture, likeness ...

beeldend   expressive ...

beeldende kunsten   plastic arts ...

beeldendienst   image-worship, idolatry

beeldhouwer   sculptor (*houwen* means 'to hew', so a *beeldhouwer* is literally an 'image-hewer')[3]

There is no problem with *beeld* as such. It means 'image' and its various connotations, and we can safely translate the title of Oud's article as 'The Monumental Image of the City'. But *beelden, beeldend* and *beelding* are more difficult. To translate *beeldende* in 'Tot een beeldende architectuur' as 'expressive' – still less 'imaging' or 'imaginary' – surely cannot be right. In fact *beelden* and *beelding* are abnormal in Dutch, like their equivalents 'to image' and 'imaging' in English. This enabled the De Stijl artists to give the words a particular meaning, distinct from and contrasting with the normal equivalents *afbeelden, afbeelding*, which the dictionary gives as 'represent, portray, depict' and 'representation, portraiture, depiction'.[4] In much the same way, four years before, Ezra Pound had appropriated and given a special meaning to the word 'Imagism'.[5]

The usages *beeldend* and *beelding* first appeared in the writings of the ex-priest, mystical philosopher and art theorist Mathieu Schoenmaekers (1875–1944). Schoenmaekers treats *beelding* as synonymous with yet another Dutch word, *uitbeelding* (literally 'imaging-out'), which the dictionary translates as 'depiction, rendering,

3. K. ten Bruggenkate, *Engels Woordenboek*, Wolters-Noordhoff, Groningen, 1978, p. 74.

4. *Ibid.*, p. 29.

5. E. Pound, 'A few don'ts by an Imagiste', in *Poetry*, March 1913; reprinted in *Literary Essays of Ezra Pound*, Faber & Faber, London, 1954, p. 4.

impersonation', as in the representation of a character on the stage. He reserves *uitbeelding* for the representation of an inner reality beyond mere appearances, as opposed to *afbeelding* (literally *'imaging-off'*), or representation in the usual sense of depiction. His example was followed by Mondrian, who came strongly under Schoenmaeker's influence during the time he lived at Laren (1915–19), and also by Van Doesburg – as can be seen from the tailpiece the latter added to the February 1919 issue of *De Stijl*, opposing the art of De Stijl to 'Baroque', his habitual byword for everything he disliked:

> Pure modern art is *beelding* from innerness outwards ...

> All Baroque arises from *beelding* from the outside, by means of imaging-off *[afbeelding]*.

> Style arises through *beelding* from the *inside outwards*, by means of imaging-out *[uitbeelding]*.[6]

The contrasting meanings given by the De Stijl artists to *afbeelding* and *uitbeelding*, both of which mean 'representation', suggest at last a solution to our problem: does *beelding* too mean 'representation', but in a particular sense? The clue lies in the philosophical sources of De Stijl.

'Representation' can alternatively be rendered by the Dutch word *voorstelling*, which is the same as the German *Vorstellung*; and this of course appears in the title of the principal work of Arthur Schopenhauer (1788–1860): *Die Welt als Wille und Vorstellung* (*The World as Will and Representation*). The book is a crucial source of the De Stijl idea, and Schopenhauer, like the De Stijl artists, uses the word 'representation' in two senses.

In the first sense it corresponds to Kant's limitation of that which can be known to a phenomenal world constructed by the interaction of the mind and the senses. For Immanuel Kant (1724–1804), the 'laws of nature' are dictated by the mind: '*The understanding does not derive its laws (a priori) from, but prescribes them to, nature.*'[7] The opening words of *Die Welt als Wille und Vorstellung* are:

> 'The world is my representation': this is a truth valid with reference to every living and knowing being, although man alone can bring it into reflective, abstract consciousness. If he really does so, philosophical discernment has dawned on him. It then becomes clear and certain to him that he does not know a sun and an earth, but only an eye that sees a sun, a hand that feels an earth.[8]

6. T. van Doesburg, 'Fragmenten III: Beelding van innerlijkheid en uiterlijkheid', in *De Stijl*, vol. II no. 4, February 1919, p. 48.

7. I. Kant, *Prolegomena*, trans. P. Carus, Open Court Publishing, La Salle, Illinois, 1902, p. 82.

8. A Schopenhauer, *The World as Will and Representation*, trans. E.F.J. Payne, Dover Publications, New York, 1969, vol. I, p. 3.

According to Kant, while we may infer the existence of some ultimate reality – a 'thing-in-itself' – underlying the constructed world of
representations, it remains completely beyond our grasp.
Schopenhauer, on the other hand, is prepared to define this underlying ground of existence quite precisely: it is the will.

It is often implied that Schopenhauer describes the will as the
embodiment of evil and the source of all suffering; but this is not
exact. The will, strictly speaking, is for him neutral: 'a blind, irresistible
urge',[9] indifferent to the desires and consequent suffering of
individuals:

> In fact, absence of aim, of all limits, belongs to the essential nature
> of the will in itself, which is an endless striving ... Every individual
> act has a purpose or end; willing as a whole has no end in view.[10]

Evil and suffering arise from the plurality of phenomena: from the
mutual struggle for survival of numberless individuals, and from what
Schopenhauer calls 'the principle of sufficient reason':

> the will as thing-in-itself lies outside the province of the principle of
> sufficient reason in all its forms, and is consequently completely
> groundless, although each of its phenomena is entirely subject to
> that principle. Further, it is free from all *plurality*, although its
> phenomena in time and space are innumerable.[11]

The second, more positive aspect of the world as representation
is identified by Schopenhauer with the platonic Idea and its
objectification in art. Art occupies a central place in Schopenhauer's
system of the world. It is the only means by which human beings
escape from their individual desires and fears and thus transcend the
suffering and pain inherent in individual life. Because art is disinterested, the work of art is able, despite being an object in the world of
phenomena, to represent the will in its eternal aspect, as universality.
'The artist lets us peer into the world through his eyes.'[12] When we
contemplate the world with the artist's disinterested vision,

> Raised up by the power of the mind, we relinquish the ordinary
> way of considering things, and cease to follow under the guidance
> of the forms of the principle of sufficient reason merely their rela-
> tions to one another, whose final goal is always the relation to our
> own will ... We *lose* ourselves entirely in this object ... in other
> words, we forget our individuality, our will, and continue to exist
> only as pure subject, as clear mirror of the object ... If, therefore,

9.   *Ibid.*, p. 275.
10. *Ibid.*, pp. 164–5.
11. *Ibid.*, p. 113.
12. *Ibid.*, p. 195.

the object has to such an extent passed out of all relation to something outside it, and the subject has passed out of all relation to the
will, what is thus known is no longer the individual thing as such,
but the *Idea*, the eternal form, the immediate objectivity of the will
at this grade. Thus at the same time, the person who is involved in
this perception is no longer an individual, for in such perception
the individual has lost himself; he is *pure* will-less, painless, timeless,
subject of knowledge.[13]

This raises a number of questions. If the will is 'eternal becoming,
endless flux',[14] how can its 'adequate objectification' be the Platonic
Idea, which according to Plato 'is always real and has no becoming'?[15]
And how can art, as the direct representation of the will, be beautiful
and even pleasurable, if the will itself is the source of suffering? The
answer to the first question is simply that Schopenhauer's concept of
the Idea differs fundamentally from Plato's. The answer to the second
is that the will, as such, is beyond good and evil, and indifferent to the
suffering of individuals:

> For it is not the individual that nature cares for, but only the
> species ... The individual, on the contrary, has no value for nature,
> and can have none, for infinite time, infinite space, and the infinite
> number of possible individuals therein are the kingdom. Therefore
> nature is always ready to let the individual fall, and the individual is
> accordingly not only exposed to destruction in a thousand ways
> from the most insignificant accidents, but is even destined for this
> and is led towards it by nature herself, from the moment that indi-
> vidual has served the maintenance of the species. In this way,
> nature openly expresses the great truth that only the Ideas, not
> individuals, have reality proper, in other words are a complete
> objectivity of the will.[16]

The Idea is thus knowable through pure, unattached, objective
contemplation or inwardness – through the state in which 'the
perceived individual thing is raised to the Idea of its species, and the
knowing individual to the pure subject of will-less knowing, and now
the two, as such, no longer stand in the stream of time and of all other
relations'.[17] The first example Schopenhauer offers is the work of the
Dutch still-life painters of the seventeenth century:

> those admirable Dutchmen who directed such purely objective
> perception to the most insignificant objects, and set up a lasting
> monument of their objectivity and spiritual peace in paintings of

13. *Ibid.*, pp. 178–9.

14. *Ibid.*, p. 164.

15. Plato, *Timaeus*, trans. F.M. Cornford, *Plato's Cosmology*,
Routledge & Kegan Paul, London, 1937, p. 22.

16. Schopenhauer, *World as Will and Representation*, vol. I, p. 276.

17. *Ibid.*, p. 197.

still life. The aesthetic beholder does not contemplate this without emotion, for it graphically describes to him the calm, tranquil, will-free frame of mind of the artist which was necessary for contemplating such insignificant things so objectively, considering them so attentively, and repeating this perception with such thought.[18]

By rising above individual striving and its bondage to time, space and causality, art allows us, Schopenhauer tells us, to achieve a state of liberation from suffering. Art performs, in Schopenhauer's thought, the role conventionally ascribed to religion. This is a reasonably accurate description of the role that the De Stijl artists gave to art, and of the level of reality that they set out to represent in their paintings. It is worth reflecting that in the years leading up to and immediately following the foundation of *De Stijl* (1914–18), the killing fields of Flanders, just over the frontier from neutral Holland, provided the most horrifying confirmation that anyone could ask for of Schopenhauer's bleak view of the human struggle:

Many millions, united into nations, strive for the common good, each individual for his own sake; but many thousands fall a sacrifice to it. Now senseless delusion, now intriguing politics, incite them to wars with one another; then the sweat and blood of the great multitude must flow, to carry through the ideas of individuals, or to atone for their shortcomings.[19]

It is no wonder that a philosophy in which art presents itself as the sole means by which human beings may escape their bondage to an endless struggle for worthless or unattainable goals should have a particular appeal in those years. In Schopenhauer's aesthetic, art becomes a substitute, and more than a substitute, for a defunct religion. In the fourth number of *De Stijl* van Doesburg writes:

The human being is imprisoned in nature, the illusion arising from the erroneous relativity of the individual. In the past he tried to free himself from this illusion by means of religion. Religion is revered as the interpretation of an emotion which transcends the relativity of the individual. However, religion can only interpret this emotion by means of art in all its forms: music, word, dance and the plastic arts. The new representation *[nieuwe beelding]* has overcome this powerlessness of religion *by itself* to interpret an emotion that rises above the relativity of the individual. Modern art is the direct intermediary between human beings and the absolute. The modern artist destroys the illusion of false

18. *Ibid.*, p. 197.
19. Schopenhauer, *World as Will and Representation*, vol. II, p. 357.

relationships. His aesthetic consciousness reacts solely to that which is above the relative: the universal. By destroying the false illusion of the individual – of nature – he brings to the fore the elementary plastic proportions [*elementair-beeldende verhoudingen*] that govern the world. He reconstructs the world in accordance with a pure aesthetic principle, by means of relations between extremes (dissonances) and correspondences (consonances) of colour and form. In the *aesthetic emotion* which the observer experiences in the presence of a pure plastic work of art, he immediately *recovers* ... the *absolute*.[20]

To translate the title of Mondrian's essay as 'The New Representation in Painting' and Van Doesburg's two pieces as 'Towards a Representational Architecture' and 'Think – Observe – Represent' may sound a bit strange at first; but only because we too readily categorize De Stijl as a movement dedicated to *non-representation* in art, and we think of representation only as the depiction of appearances. Mondrian and Van Doesburg did indeed intend their paintings as representations, however; it is just that what they set out to represent was something previous art had rarely attempted. (The art of Islam is the outstanding exception: see Chapter 5, section 5.5.) The 'new representation', *de nieuwe beelding*, was to be a representation of pure contemplative thought, pure innerness. It was not to be the representation of the world of appearances, but of something resembling Schopenhauer's 'Platonic Idea'. Provided one bears in mind this special meaning which the *Stijl* artists, like Schopenhauer, gave to it, 'representation' is, if not a perfect translation of *beelding*, at least a better one than 'plasticism', 'formation', 'expression' or 'creation', by which it has variously been rendered in English up to now.

We can thus compose a short 'De Stijl–English Dictionary' as follows:

beeld   representation, image

beelden   to represent

beeldend   representational

beelding   representation

Except where 'plastic' or 'plasticism' is necessary to avoid confusion, these translations will be adopted through the rest of this book. In the present chapter and the following one, the original Dutch word is also included, partly in order to show the extraordinary frequency

20. T. van Doesburg, 'Fragmenten I', in *De Stijl*, vol. I, no. 4, February 1918, pp. 47–8.

with which *beeld* (or its derivatives) occurs in De Stijl texts, and thus the importance of finding an adequate English equivalent.

2.2 'Chinese, Greek and German philosophy'

In his important essay 'Think – Observe – Represent' (1918) Van Doesburg distinguishes three levels of thought and three corresponding phases of art:

(1) *Concrete thought* – thought about sensory observation; this is reflected in 'physioplastic' or naturalistic art, from the palaeolithic era to the present.

(2) *Deformative thought* – an intermediate stage, still derived from observation, but in which this is recast by conceptualization; this appears in 'ideoplastic' art, from the neolithic era up to Van Gogh.

(3) Finally there is *pure abstract thought* – thought about thought, in which 'no representation (*voorstelling*) of phenomena is involved', these being replaced by 'exact mathematical figures' and 'number, measure, proportion and abstract line'. This kind of thought is manifested in two modes: rationally, in 'Chinese, Greek and German philosophy', and aesthetically, in 'the new representation [*nieuwe beelding*] of our time'.[21]

The mention of Chinese (or more properly Indian) philosophy seems to refer to the Buddhist doctrine – important also to Schopenhauer – that the goal of life is liberation from the tragic condition of separate selfhood. Throughout his series of articles 'The New Representation [*Nieuwe Beelding*] in Painting' Mondrian stresses that the aim of the new art of De Stijl is '*liberation from the individual* and the *achievement of a clear depiction [uitbeelding] of the universal*'.[22]

The work of art can express the consciousness of the time

either in its relation *to the universal*, or in its relation to *ordinary life, the individual*. In the first case, art is *truly religious*, in the second, *profane* ... So long as the consciousness of the time is dominated by the individual, art remains *bound to (ordinary) life* and is primarily the expression of that life.[23]

Conversely, if in some distant future the universal should become completely dominant, art would become superfluous:

When the universal dominates, life will be so permeated by universality that art, which will be so unreal compared to such a

21. T. van Doesburg, 'Denken – aanschouwen – beelden', in *De Stijl*, vol. II, no. 2, December 1918, pp. 23–4.

22. P. Mondrian, 'De nieuwe beelding in de schilderkunst', in *De Stijl*, vol. I, no. 9, July 1918, p. 102.

23. Mondrian, 'De nieuwe beelding', in *De Stijl*, vol. I, no. 5, March 1918, p. 51.

life, will decay, and a *new life* will take its place, a life which actually realizes the universal.[24]

This condition seems to resemble the Buddhist ideal of complete delivery from individual existence. Mondrian's attention is not directed, however, to this ultimate state, but to the achievement of a harmony between the two extremes; a harmony in which art will play an important part:

> The universal finds its purest, most direct expression *in art* only where there is a balanced relation between the individual and the universal, for then through *representation [beelding]* the individual can receive the universal: in art it is possible for the universal to manifest itself as appearance without becoming bound to the individual, to individual existence.[25]

The distinction between the universal and the individual, reality and appearance, being and becoming, also preoccupied the Greek philosophers, the second group whom Van Doesburg refers to as having revealed pure, intellectual thought. Plato states the distinction most succinctly in the *Timaeus*: 'What is that which is always real and has no becoming, and what is that which is always becoming and is never real?'[26]

The question opposes two possible views of reality. On one hand there is the opinion, which in the *Theaetetus* Plato attributes to the Sophist Protagoras (who in this seems to anticipate Kant), that the only realities are our separate sense-perceptions. In the dialogue Socrates quotes Protagoras:

> He says, you will remember, that 'Man is the measure of all things – alike of the being of things that are and of the not-being of things that are not' ... He puts it in this sort of way, doesn't he? – that any given thing 'is to me such as it appears to me, and is to you such as it appears to you,' you and I being men.[27]

On the other hand, there is Plato's own doctrine, most famously stated in the parable of the cave in the *Republic*,[28] that the real is the intelligible and the eternal, and consists in the universal Forms of which the sensible world is merely the shadow. The passage quoted above from the *Timaeus* continues:

> That which is apprehensible by thought with a rational account is the thing that is always unchangeably real; whereas that which is

24. *Ibid.*, p. 51.
25. *Ibid.*
26. Plato, *Timaeus*, p. 22.
27. Plato, *Theaetetus*, in F.M. Cornford, *Plato's Theory of Knowledge*, Routledge & Kegan Paul, London, 1960, pp. 31–2.
28. Plato, *The Republic of Plato*, trans. and ed. F.M. Cornford, Oxford University Press, Oxford, 1941, pp. 222–6.

the object of belief together with unreasoning sensation is the thing that becomes and passes away, but never has real being.[29]

Lastly, by 'German philosophy' Van Doesburg means above all Schopenhauer and Hegel. We have already noted the affinity between Schopenhauer's concept of the redemptive function of art and the aims of the De Stijl artists. The influence of Hegel was stronger still, and supplied the other fundamental ingredient of De Stijl's artistic doctrine: the idea that the long and inevitable progress of history towards its ultimate goal, the full self-awareness of the universal Mind, was nearing fulfilment. This teaching was acquired both directly (Van Doesburg was reading Hegel at this time[30]) and as interpreted by the Dutch Hegelian philosopher G.J.P.J. Bolland. Van Doesburg's three categories correspond exactly to the three modes which, according to Hegel in *The Philosophy of Fine Art*, 'are due to the notion of the absolute Spirit (Mind) itself':

Spirit, in its truth, is essential substance brought home to itself. It is, therefore, no essence which lies outside and in abstract relation to objectivity, but rather … the re-collected presence of the substance of all objects within finite spirit. It is the finite which grasps its own essential universality, and in doing so, grasps essential Being in the absolute sense. The *first* mode of this comprehension is an immediate one, that is to say, it is a sensuous cognition, a cognition in the form and semblance of the object of sense-perception, in which the Absolute is presented directly to the understanding and feeling. The *second* form is that of the *conceptive* or imaginative consciousness. *Last* of all, we have the *free thought* of absolute Spirit.[31]

That Hegel intends art too to aspire to the condition of 'free thought' appears from the introduction to the same work:

Fine art is not art in the true sense of the term until it is also thus free, and its *highest* function is only then satisfied when it has established itself in a sphere which it shares with religion and philosophy, becoming thereby merely one mode and form through which the *Divine*, the profoundest interests of mankind, and spiritual truths of widest range, are brought home to consciousness and expressed.[32]

Which kind of reality, then, is it possible for art to represent? Van Doesburg's elevation of the *beeldend* art that represents a universal, abstract reality above the sort of art that either mimics appearances

29. Plato, *Timaeus*, p. 22.

30. J. Baljeu, *Theo van Doesburg*, Studio Vista, London, 1974, p. 29.

31. G.W.F. Hegel, *The Philosophy of Fine Art*, 1916 English edition, vol. I, no. 139, quoted by A. Doig, *Theo van Doesburg: Painting into architecture, theory into practice*, Cambridge University Press, Cambridge, 1986, p. 7.

32. *Ibid.*

directly or is derived from them through distortion seems to fit Plato's distinction between the realm of eternal Forms and that of shifting phenomena, and Hegel's between the 'conceptive or imaginative consciousness' and the 'free thought of absolute Spirit'. But does it?

In his Bauhaus book *Principles of Neo-Plastic Art* – published in 1925, but which he claimed to have 'completed in about 1917'[33] – Van Doesburg writes that the aim of art 'is *to give form to the fundamental essence through artistic means and nothing else*'.[34] He demonstrates this by describing the process of transforming a photograph of a cow, through two stages of 'ideoplastic' simplification, into his fully abstract composition *The cow* of 1917. He writes: 'A *transfiguration takes place between the sensory impression and the aesthetic experience. The natural phenomenon is reconstructed in aesthetic accents which re-embody the essence of the object in a new way*.'[35]

Clearly, when he speaks of his abstract re-creation of the cow as 're-embodying the essence of the object in a new way' he envisages a process by which, not the appearance of this or that particular cow at this or that moment, but the universal Form or platonic Idea of the cow, the *cowness* of all cows, can be represented in two dimensions on canvas.

However, in 1917 Van Doesburg's painting was still some way from the representation of 'pure thought, involving no images derived from phenomena'. He was in the process of emerging from an extreme form of 'conceptualization' or 'ideoplasticism' (to use his own terminology): an attempt to reduce phenomena down to their 'primary' or 'platonic' attributes, which he defined as 'aesthetic accents'. But one is hard put to see how his final abstraction from the photograph of the cow can be regarded as 'a representation of pure thought' in the same way as a philosophical proposition or a mathematical construction. As Allan Doig objects:

The analytic process which is prescribed is followed, but the result is not quite what is promised. It does demonstrate the higher abstractions of order in and relationship among what have been defined as the plastic elements, but they demonstrate nothing of the type or ideal of 'cow', so what is the point of starting with a cow, squaring up the blotches and pushing them around until they have a 'pure plastic balance'? Whatever happened to the Neo-plasticism which arose from pure thought rather than the accidental world (in this case, an accidental cow)?[36]

In fairness to Van Doesburg, it must be pointed out that he added a footnote (presumably when the essay was published in 1925) in

33. T. van Doesburg, *Grundbegriffe der neuen gestaltenden Kunst* (1925); trans: *Principles of Neo-Plastic Art*, Lund Humphries, London, 1969, p. 4.

34. *Ibid.*, p. 25.

35. *Ibid.*, p. 18.

36. A. Doig, 'De architectuur van De Stijl en de westerse filosofische traditie' ('The architecture of De Stijl and the western philosophical tradition') in *Wonen TABK*, no. 15–16, 1982, pp. 49–50.

which he says that the method of starting out from a cow or other object is only a means to an end, and can be circumvented:

> My reconstruction of natural objects is adduced only in order to illustrate the creative process. It is not, therefore, the intention to elevate this manner of representation into a dogma or to call for a similar reconstruction for every work of art. In order to avoid misunderstanding it should be expressly stated that the method of reconstruction was only our means to an end. It becomes super-fluous, however, when the artist's aesthetic experience rests only on relationships and ratio. This transfiguration which is demon-strated here by means of forms borrowed from nature takes place in the creative consciousness of the artist. Thus it will also be clear that the creation of relationships by the use of elementary artistic means is not abstract but 'real'. Only during a period of transition was there question of an 'abstract' art in connexion with a representational manner of artistic creation.[37]

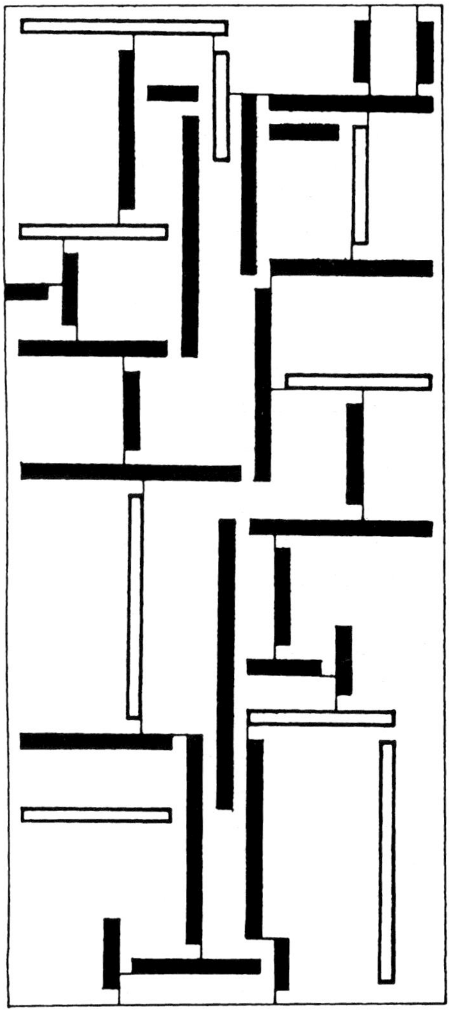

Somewhere between 1918 and 1925 Van Doesburg made the transition from the method of abstraction from a natural object to the construction of 'real' representations no longer derived from phenomena but composed directly by means of pure proportion: 'relationships and ratio'. His painting *Rhythm of a Russian dance* (1918) looks at first sight like a pure geometrical construction, a composition of vertical and horizontal lines which slide past each other in a way which has often been seen as a precursor of the plan of Mies's 'brick country house' project of 1923–4 (Figures 2.2 and 2.3). But studies for the very similar painting *Tarantella* (1918) and *Rag-time* (1919) indicate that all three paintings started out from more or less natural-istic depictions of dancers. Exactly the same process of squaring up and editing out, which Van Doesburg applied to the cow, was still being followed for at least a year or two after he claimed to have completed the essay. The transition from 'ideoplasticism' to the direct 'representation of pure thought' was made by way of architecture.

2.3 The way forward through architecture

Both Hegel and Schopenhauer give architecture the lowest place among the fine arts. According to the latter, when architecture is considered as fine art and leaving aside its strictly utilitarian aspects

Figure 2.2 Theo van Doesburg, Rhythm of a Russian dance, 1918

---

37. Van Doesburg, *Principles of Neo-Plastic Art*, p. 18.

ign it no purpose other than that of bringing to clearer
iveness some of those Ideas that are the lowest grades of
ill's objectivity. Such Ideas are gravity, cohesion, rigidity, hard-
i iss, those universal qualities of stone, those first, simplest, and
dullest visibilities of the will, the fundamental bass-notes of nature;
and along with these, light, which is in many respects their opposite.[38]

However, even at this 'low stage of the will's objectivity' (that is, of
the objectivity of the blind, irresistible urge to existence), architecture
can reveal, through discord, the will's inner nature:

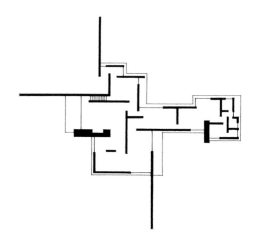

> for, properly speaking, the conflict between gravity and rigidity is
> the sole aesthetic material of architecture; its problem is to make
> this conflict appear with perfect distinctness in many different
> ways. It solves this problem by depriving these indestructible
> forces of the shortest path to their satisfaction, and keeping them
> in suspense through a circuitous path; the conflict is thus
> prolonged, and the inexhaustible efforts of the two forces
> become visible in many different ways.[39]

Figure 2.3 Ludwig Mies van der Rohe, brick country house project, 1923–4: plan

Consequently the highest aesthetic purpose of architecture is
realized in pure structure, the prolongation of the struggle against
gravity, which, left to the original tendency, would reduce the whole
mass of the building to

> a mere heap or lump, bound to the earth as firmly as possible, to
> which gravity, the form in which the will here appears, presses
> incessantly, whereas rigidity, also objectivity of the will, resists ...
> Therefore the beauty of a building is certainly to be found in the
> evident and obvious suitability of every part, not to the outward
> arbitrary purpose of man (to this extent the work belongs to prac-
> tical architecture), but directly to the stability of the whole. The
> position, size, and form of every part must have so necessary a
> relation to this stability that if it were possible to remove some
> part, the whole would inevitably collapse.[40]

Consequently the highest form of architecture is that in which load
and support are most clearly differentiated:

> The purest execution of this theme is column and entablature;
> hence the order of columns has become, so to speak, the thor-
> ough-bass of the whole of architecture. In column and

38. Schopenhauer, *World as Will and Representation*, vol. I, p. 214.
39. *Ibid.*
40. *Ibid.*, pp. 214–15.

entablature, support and load are *completely separated*, and in this way the reciprocal effect of the two and their relation to each other become apparent.[41]

The vault, in which load and support are combined in one form, is a less pure expression of the principle, so it follows that the Gothic cathedral is inferior to the Doric temple. Particularly objectionable, however, are cantilevered balconies, especially if projected from the corners of buildings: 'We do not see what carries them; they appear suspended, and disturb the mind.'[42]

Schopenhauer gives a very clear analysis of the necessary process by which the utilitarian shelter is raised to the level of fine art by the articulation of the wall; first through the piercing of openings, then through the gradual emergence of columns – initially perhaps only painted or applied to the wall surface as pilasters:

> In column and entablature, support and load are *completely separated*, and in this way the reciprocal effect of the two and their relation to each other become apparent. For even every plain and simple wall certainly contains support and load, but there the two are amalgamated. Everything is support and everything load; so there is no aesthetic effect ... In breaking through the wall of a house merely for doors and windows, we attempt at least to indicate the separation by flat projecting pilasters (antae) with capitals, which ... are, if need be, represented by mere painting, in order to express somehow the entablature and an order of columns. Actual pillars ... further realize that pure separation of support and load to which architecture in general aspires ... Only in the row of columns is the separation complete, since the entablature appears here as pure load, and the column as pure support. Accordingly, the relation of the colonnade to the plain wall is comparable to that which would exist between a scale ascending at regular intervals, and a tone ascending little by little without gradations from the same depth to the same height, which would produce a mere howl. For in one as in the other the material is the same, and the immense difference results only from the *pure separation*.[43]

Nothing could be further removed from the kind of architecture envisaged by Van Doesburg, Rietveld or Mondrian than Schopenhauer's ideal of classical trabeated structure. The De Stijl artists aimed at a 'dematerialization' of architecture in which, by exploiting the new possibilities opened up by steel and reinforced concrete – notably the cantilever – the load-bearing structure would

41. Schopenhauer, *World as Will and Representation*, vol. II, p. 411.
42. *Ibid.*, p. 412.
43. *Ibid.*, pp. 411–2.

be minimized or concealed, so that buildings would take on precisely what Schopenhauer objected to: a more or less suspended, floating appearance. Schopenhauer's principle is a kind of 'higher functionalism': not utility, but a functionalism purified of all the particular (and often short-lived) necessities of this or that utilitarian demand. It is a functionalism elevated to the highest possible level of generality or universality, the enclosure of habitable space. He comes close to the later doctrine of Mies van der Rohe, for whom

> Building, where it became great, was almost always indebted to construction, and construction was almost always the conveyor of its spatial form. Romanesque[44] and Gothic demonstrate that in brilliant clarity. Here as there structure expresses the meaning, expresses it down to the last remnant of spiritual value.[45]

Describing his unbuilt project for the Mannheim theatre (1952–3) to Christian Norberg-Schulz, Mies said:

> As you see, we are primarily interested in clear construction ... the entire building is a single large room. We believe that this is the most economical and most practical way of building today. The purposes for which a building is used are constantly changing and we cannot afford to tear down the building each time. That is why we have revised Sullivan's formula 'form follows function' and construct a practical and economical space into which we fit the functions.[46]

Although Mies was in many respects the greatest architectural heir of De Stijl, his mature doctrine of the primacy of structure is completely opposed to the concept of architecture advocated by Van Doesburg and Mondrian. Van Doesburg argued that architecture no less than painting can transcend its material and technical means in order to achieve a totally unified artistic result:

> art is that attribute which absorbs all other attributes, transforming them into its own means. For instance, in good painting the higher aim, the idea, absorbs the technique ... and the material. Well then, is it not possible for architecture to harness all its means of construction ... as representational means in order to realize the artistic moment, one and indivisible?[47]

Mondrian, too, describes the new representational (neoplastic) architecture of the future as one that shall have escaped from

44. Neumeyer's English translation in fact says 'Romantic', presumably a misreading of the German 'Romanik', meaning 'Romanesque'.

45. L. Mies van der Rohe, lecture given in German, Chicago, unknown date, in F. Neumeyer, The Artless Word, MIT Press, Cambridge, Mass., 1991, p. 325.

46. L. Mies van der Rohe, interviewed by C Norberg-Schulz, in Baukunst und Werkform, Nov. 1958, pp. 615–18; republished in Neumeyer, Artless Word, p. 339.

47. T. van Doesburg, 'Slotbemerkingen', in De Stijl, vol. II, no. 10, 1919, p. 119.

precisely that bondage to structure and gravity which Schopenhauer sees as architecture's only intrinsic aesthetic merit, and which Mies upholds as the fundamental principle of good building (*Baukunst*). If and when the new architecture becomes possible, Mondrian maintains, structure and construction will be subordinated to colour, the role of which is destructive, in the sense that it annihilates form:

> Colour is either supported by the architecture, or if necessary it can annihilate it. Colour extends *over the whole architecture*, equipment, furniture, and so forth, so that, in the ensemble, each element annihilates the other. But in this way one also comes in collision with the *traditional conception* of 'structural purity'. There still exists the idea that structure must be 'shown'. The latest technology has already dealt this notion a damaging blow, however. For instance, in reinforced concrete construction, what was defensible in brickwork is no longer valid. If the representational concept *[beeldende begrip]* requires the structure to be visually *[beeldend]* suppressed, then the means must be found to satisfy both structural necessity and the demands of representation *[beelding]*.[48]

The whole De Stijl effort can be seen as a striving to reduce (or to raise) all the visual arts to the condition of music, which Schopenhauer places at the opposite end of the artistic spectrum from architecture. Whereas architecture can represent only 'the lowest grades of the will's objectivity' – matter and gravity – music,

> if regarded as an expression of the world, is in the highest degree a universal language that is related to the universality of concepts much as these are related to the particular things ... For, as we have said, music differs from all the other arts by the fact that it is not a copy of the phenomenon, or, more exactly, of the will's adequate objectivity, but is directly a copy of the will itself, and therefore expresses the metaphysical to everything physical in the world, the thing-in-itself to every phenomenon. Accordingly, we could just as well call the world embodied music as embodied will.[49]

This explains, in my view, why the De Stijl project, despite the surpassing beauty of many of its products, was doomed to remain a noble failure, and especially so in architecture. We shall return to this question in the concluding chapter, where a synthesis between the two opposites, the structuralism of Schopenhauer and the later Mies

48. P. Mondrian, 'De realiseering van het neo-plasticisme in verre toekomst en in de huidige architectuur', in *De Stijl*, vol. V, no. 5, May 1922, p. 69.
49. Schopenhauer, *World as Will and Representation*, vol. I, pp. 262–3.

on one hand and the fluid space of Van Doesburg and Mondrian on the other, will be offered as a possible solution.

For several years, starting in 1921 when he installed himself in Weimar and attempted to take the Bauhaus by storm, Van Doesburg, unlike Mondrian, diverted his best energies from painting into architecture. But at the end of his life, disillusioned by the failure of his architectural masterpiece, the Café Aubette in Strasbourg (1928), to win the public's approval, and his exclusion from the Weissenhofsiedlung the previous year, he came round to Mondrian's negative view. Architecture was impossible, he concluded, in the circumstances of the time, and given the execrable taste of the general public: 'The public wants to live in mire and shall perish in mire. Let the architect create for the public ... The artist creates beyond the public'.[50]

In the last two or three years of his soon to be interrupted life, Van Doesburg turned back from architecture to pure painting.

2.4 The way forward through mathematics

In his last paintings Van Doesburg took a different route, however, from that on which he had set out in 1916–17. Instead of moving towards geometrical abstraction through the progressive simplification of an image drawn from the visual world, he went directly towards pure geometrical construction and mathematical series. His essay 'elementarisme', published after his death in the last issue of *De Stijl*, proclaims that intuitive 'composition' is superseded, and that to allow intuitive judgements to determine the composition of a painting is to rely on personality and the whim of the artist as an individual, which are no less arbitrary and ephemeral than nature itself:

> composition is not the highest thing. it is the transition towards a universal form of representation [*beeldingsvorm*]. only those who do not hesitate to distrust their visual impressions, and are prepared to destroy, are able to produce really great work. perfect work first comes into existence when we surrender our 'personality'. the universal lies beyond our personality. impulse has never produced a work of lasting significance and lasting value. the method leading to universal form is based on calculations of measure, direction and number. the same method underlay the pyramid. up to the stage of composition, personality still has some relevance, but once one has got beyond composition, personality is merely ridiculous and an obstacle. colour preference is like preference for a particular dish – it equates art with the kitchen.[51]

50. T. van Doesburg, letter to A Behne, November 1928; quoted in N.J. Troy, *The De Stijl Environment*, MIT Press, Cambridge, Mass., 1983, p. 176.

51. T. van Doesburg, 'elementarisme', in *De Stijl*, last issue, 1932, p. 15.

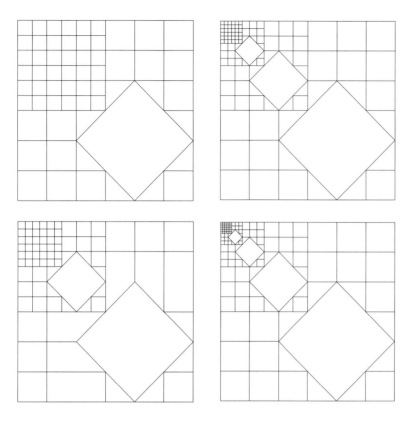

Figures 2.4–2.7
Theo van Doesburg, *Universal form II*, originally 1926: proportional analyses showing four stages of progression based on $\sqrt{2}$. (Redrawn interpretation by the author.)

Plato would have approved. In the *Republic* geometrical figures are presented as the sole example of visible images, existing in the phenomenal world, which nevertheless refer more or less directly to their originals in the world of ideal Forms. Students of geometry or arithmetic, Plato says,

> make use of visible figures and discourse about them, though what they really have in mind is the originals of which these figures are images: they are not reasoning, for instance, about this particular square and diagonal which they have drawn, but about the Square and the Diagonal; and so in all cases. The diagrams they draw and the models they make are actual things, which may have their shadows or images in water; but now they serve their turn as images, while the student is seeking to behold those realities which only thought can apprehend.[52]

In Van Doesburg's late paintings, such as *Universal form II* (1926–9), he finally obeyed the logic of his essay 'Think – Observe – Represent' written ten years before (Figures 2.4–2.7). The visual representation of pure thought was now sought, no longer by means of intuitive

52. Plato, *Republic*, p. 220.

abstract composition, but exclusively by what he then already defined as 'exact mathematical figures' and 'number, measure, proportion and abstract line'.[53]

2.5 The necessity of proportion

The word 'proportion' in the above quotation translates the Dutch word *verhouding*. Like *beelding*, *verhouding* is a word that constantly occurs in De Stijl texts, so it is important to find as accurate a translation as possible. The problem is that, like the German *Verhältnis* and the French *rapport*, *verhouding* means both 'proportion' and 'relation'. In fact, the problem is not with those languages, but with English; for the division in English between 'proportion' and 'relation' is an artificial one, and, because it implies that proportion is something exact and drily mathematical whereas relation has vaguely something to do with human perceptions and feelings (one speaks of the relationship between two lovers, for instance), the division becomes a hindrance to a wider understanding of what proportion really is. 'Relation' in English becomes shadowy and colourless, while proportion (at least in art) is thought of as an abstruse game played by those who enjoy arithmetical or geometrical puzzles.

The concept of proportion/relation is immeasurably enriched when it is understood as a single notion that extends all the way from the relationship between two individuals to the ratio between two numbers. Such an understanding is greatly helped by having a single word for the whole concept. Lacking this in English, we are forced here to make a choice. Existing English translations of De Stijl literature generally opt for 'relation'. Here I propose in most cases to take the opposite course and choose, with some regret that there is no better alternative, 'proportion', and where it is essential to convey both aspects, 'proportional relationship'. The reason for preferring 'proportion' to 'relation' is simply that the more definite word conveys better the essential spirit of De Stijl: its identification of clarity and purity (in Dutch, *schoon* means both 'clean' and 'beautiful') with straight lines, right angles and clear, primary colours. 'Relation', on the other hand, hardly makes any definite impression when you read it. But the reader should always bear in mind that *verhouding*, proportion, is understood by the De Stijl writers in a more comprehensive sense than that in which it is normally understood in our language: that it means both 'proportion' *and* 'relation'.

Van Doesburg gives us a first clue to what *verhouding* might mean when in 'elementarisme' he seems to echo the biblical passage 'thou hast ordered all things in measure, number and weight' by speaking of

53. Van Doesburg, 'Denken – Aanschouwen – Beelden', in *De Stijl*, vol. II, no. 2, December 1918, p. 24.

'measure, direction and number'. He does not say measure and number alone, but direction as well. Of course, direction, too, can be mathematically defined, by angular measurement, but like weight it begins to enlarge somewhat our normal conception of proportion. That concept is broadened still further in Van Doesburg's earlier statement, in 'Towards a Representational Architecture' (1924):

> Against symmetry the new architecture sets the *balanced proportion [verhouding] of unequal parts* – that is, of parts which because of their contrasting functional character differ in posture, measure, ratio *[proportie]* and position.[54]

This translation has presented me with a problem. Van Doesburg, having used *verhouding* in the first part of the sentence, where I have said 'proportion', proceeds to weaken my argument by employing in the second part the less common Dutch word *proportie*. *Proportie* also means 'proportion', but in a narrower, more exclusively quantitative sense than *verhouding*, and without the connotation of relationship. In order not to repeat 'proportion' I am forced to cheat a little by substituting 'ratio'. I believe this subterfuge is justified, however, because translation of *verhouding* as 'proportion' conveys the central importance of proportion for De Stijl, and the fact that proportion is not just, as is often assumed, a matter of shape (the ratio of length to breadth of a coloured rectangle, for example), but also of posture (vertical, horizontal or diagonal), measure (scale) and position (distant or close, left or right, above or below).

The first of Mondrian's series of trialogues, 'Natural Reality and Abstract Reality', begins with a discussion of proportion (*verhouding*) in painting. On a stroll in the moonlit countryside, *Z*, the 'abstract-real' painter (Mondrian's spokesman), argues with *X*, a naturalistic painter, that their art is less fundamentally different than at first appears. *Y*, a layman, keeps the conversation going with occasional common-sense interjections:

> *Z:* You try to draw a line between abstract-real and naturalistic painting, but the distinction cannot be such as to place either beyond the limits of painting ... Let us go back to the source of the work of art: *the emotion of beauty*. Didn't we share essentially the same emotion a moment ago? ...

> *X:* But we see little of that agreement in our art!

> *Z:* Yet that is only apparent. You lay the *stress* on tone, on colour, I stress their outcome: repose; but we *practise the same thing*. For repose *comes about through the representation of propor-*

tional harmony, so indeed I emphasize the *representation of propor-*
tion [verhoudingsbeelding]. Yet the expression of colour and tone is
equally an *expression of proportional relationships*. You represent
proportions just as I do, and I express colour as you do.

Y: Proportion?

Z: We represent through the contrast of colour and line and
this contrast is *proportion*.

X: But in painting don't proportions have to be represented
through nature?

Z: On the contrary: the more the natural is abstracted, the
more proportion comes out. The new painting showed this and
finally arrived at the representation of *pure proportion*.

X: To me nature itself gives expression to proportion, but I'm
not much interested in *pure* proportion. Take this landscape, for
instance: I see the relation *[verhouding]* between the luminous
moon, the air and the land; I also see that the position of the moon
in the landscape is a question of proportion *[verhoudingskwestie]*.
But I don't see why I have to abstract everything for the sake of
these proportions. It is precisely nature that for me brings the
proportion to life!

Z: That is a matter of opinion: for me the representation of
proportion is more alive precisely when it is not shrouded by the
natural but revealed by the flat plane and the straight line ...
Natural appearances generally *veil* the representation of proportion. Therefore if one wants to represent proportion determi-
nately, a more *exact* representation of proportion is necessary.
Proportion as posture is not visible in this landscape in a determinate way for ordinary vision.

Y: What do you mean by *proportion as posture*?

Z: I mean the proportion, not of the measurements of lines and
planes, but of the *posture* of these with respect to each other. The
most complete such proportion is the rectangular: it expresses
the proportion of two extremes.[55]

Once proportion is understood in the wider meaning that Van
Doesburg and Mondrian give to *verhouding*, it ceases to be a marginal
and somewhat questionable game of 'painting by numbers' and is
revealed, as Mondrian here argues, as the essential foundation of all
art, naturalistic as well as abstract. The only difference between the
two is that abstract art, by eliminating naturalistic content, exposes

55. P. Mondrian, 'Natuurlijke en abstracte realiteit', in *De Stijl*, vol. II, no. 8, June 1919, pp. 85–6.

proportion more directly. The sculptor Donald Judd (1928–94) was – like Mies van der Rohe, whom he revered – one of the greatest heirs of the De Stijl movement. In his essay 'Art and Architecture' (1983) he too writes of proportion as something that is not only intellectual but also emotional – being an expression of harmony and repose – and thus as something that has the widest possible significance, not just for art, but for life as a whole:

> Proportion is very important to us, both in our minds and lives and as objectified visually, since it is thought and feeling undivided, since it is unity and harmony, easy or difficult, and often peace and quiet. Proportion is specific and identifiable in art and architecture and creates our space and time. Proportion and in fact all intelligence in art is instantly understood, at least by some. It's a myth that difficult art is difficult … I only want to add that you can't exaggerate the importance of proportion. It could almost be the definition of art and architecture.[56]

Judd goes on to say that, like many people, he was long put off from taking proportion seriously by its association with a quasi-religious belief that particular proportions such as the golden section are inherent in the structure of nature, having been built into nature by God the Creator. This belief certainly sustained the use of proportion in art up to and including the renaissance – although there is little or no evidence for Judd's assumption that the golden section was a typically *renaissance* proportion – and even into the present century. Le Corbusier's *modulor* is the outstanding example. Judd continues:

> Originally I ignored proportion as a subject, although I knew that good art was intuitively well-proportioned, because the subject was associated with the Renaissance and the idea that proportion is a quality of God and Nature, a reality to be deduced or intuited by Man. The Classical Golden Section was a fact of Nature just as the electron is now.[57]

Judd is surely correct in thinking that proportion or regularity – in art, but the same applies to nature – is something that the human mind itself supplies. When we discover order in nature we are regaining from nature what we have already put into nature.[58] Or to repeat Kant's aphorism quoted near the start of this chapter, 'The understanding does not derive its laws (a priori) from, but prescribes them to, nature.' Judd finally became interested in proportion when he realized that a similar conclusion could be applied to art. The idea that

56. D. Judd, 'Art and Architecture' (1983), in *Donald Judd, Complete Writings 1975–1986*, Van Abbemuseum, Eindhoven, 1987, p. 33.
57. *Ibid.*
58. A.S. Eddington, *The Nature of the Physical World*, J.M. Dent, London, 1935, p. 238.

proportion in art is *derived* from some kind of suprahuman ordinance of nature

> wasn't credible to me since proportion is obviously a quality of ourselves. The Golden Section seems unnecessarily fancy, perhaps because of the academic desire for arithmetical justification, but the fact is that we can see the simplest proportions, 1 to 2, 2 to 3, 3 to 4, and guess at more. 1 to 2 is just as particular, is – not 'has' – as much its own quality, as red, or red and black, or black and white, or a material. Also there can be no more than one 1 to 2 rectangle. These can comprise solids and volumes. The proportional rectangles can make a coherent, intelligible space. They can make a credible, intelligent generality. They themselves are specific.[59]

The question of generality and specificity, the universal and the particular, is a whole other argument, however, and one that is of crucial importance for the understanding of De Stijl. It is too large a question to treat in this chapter, and will be the subject of the next.

59. Judd, 'Art and Architecture' (1983), pp. 33–4.

3

The Furniture of the Mind

3.1 Appearance and reality

I have settled down to the task of writing these lectures and have drawn up my chairs to my two tables. Two tables! Yes; there are duplicates of every object about me – two tables, two chairs, two pens.

With these words the English astronomer and philosopher Sir Arthur Eddington (1882–1944) – who in 1919 conducted the first tests that confirmed the predictions of Einstein's general theory of relativity – introduces his Gifford lectures of 1927, published the following year as *The Nature of the Physical World*. One of his two tables, he continues:

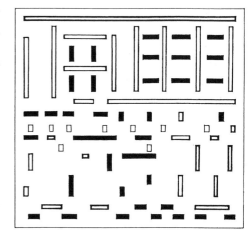

Figure 3.1 Bart van der Leck, *Leaving the Factory (Composition 1917, no. 3)*

> has been familiar to me from earliest years. It is a commonplace object of that environment which I call the world. How shall I describe it? It has extension; it is comparatively permanent; it is coloured; above all it is *substantial* ... Table No. 2 is my scientific table. It is a more recent acquaintance and I do not feel so familiar with it. It does not belong to the world previously mentioned – that world which spontaneously appears around me when I open my eyes ... It is part of a world which in more devious ways has forced itself on my attention. My scientific table is mostly emptiness. Sparsely scattered in that emptiness are numerous electric charges rushing about with great speed; but their combined bulk amounts to no less than a billionth of the bulk of the table itself.[1]

Precisely because of their ordinariness and apparent solidity, tables and other household objects provide philosophers, when they try to communicate with a wider public, with an ideal means of illustrating the problems inherent in our everyday notion of 'reality': a way to undermine our commonsense picture of the world. And to undermine that picture has been the main business of philosophy from its earliest beginnings. Philosophers did not wait for Einstein and Bohr to discover that the 'real' world must be quite unlike the phenomenal one: the 'real' chair, for instance, quite unlike the chair that I appear to be sitting on. How, I wonder, as my chair-shaped

1. A.S. Eddington, *The Nature of the Physical World*, J.M. Dent, London, 1935, pp. 5–6.

piece of empty space sparsely populated by electrical charges continues somehow mysteriously to support me, would the philosophers have managed without tables, chairs and beds?

More generally, the problem of the 'reality' of things comes down, once again, to the question of particulars and universals. The world appears to us in the form of innumerable particular impressions. Since the common-sense view of the world is that it is as it appears, we conclude that the 'real' world comprises a large space containing innumerable particular *things*, such as tables, chairs and people. Broadly, philosophers have asked two kinds of disturbing questions about this. On one hand, if all we know of the world is based on the impressions received by the senses, how do we know that the 'things' we appear to see continue to exist when we no longer perceive them? On the other hand, if there exists a permanent reality underpinning our sense-impressions, what is its nature? Is not *reason* the best guide to the real nature of things, since it is our reason, and not the senses alone, that leads us to infer the existence of this deeper reality? But it is in the nature of reason to deal in universals, not particulars. Therefore, from the Greeks onwards, philosophers who sought an enduring reality behind appearances have described it as composed of some universal substance. The table in front of me may appear to be made of wood, but it is really composed of water, or air, or fire, or numbers, or Ideas, or atoms, or electrical charges.

An example of the tendency to reduce the world to our particular sense-impressions is David Hume, who begins his *Treatise of Human Nature* (1738) with the words:

> All the perceptions of the human mind resolve themselves into two distinct kinds, which I shall call *impressions* and *ideas*. The difference betwixt these consists in the degrees of force and liveliness, with which they strike upon the mind, and make their way into our thought or consciousness. Those perceptions which enter with most force and violence, we may name *impressions*; and, under this name, I comprehend all our sensations, passions, and emotions ... By *ideas*, I mean the faint images of these in thinking and reasoning.[2]

Consequently our particular sensory impressions, together with emotions, are for Hume primary, and our attempts to generalize these impressions, to reduce them to some kind of coherence or rational order, are secondary. The impression is the original, of which the idea is the pale copy. Further on, he states categorically that *'all ideas are copied from impressions'*.[3] When Hume wishes to illustrate

2. D. Hume, *A Treatise of Human Nature*, J M Dent, London, 1911, vol. I, p. 11.
3. *Ibid.*, p. 161.

the application of this principle to one of our most general ideas about the nature of the external world, our concept of space and time, he reflects that

> The table before me is alone sufficient by its view to give me the idea of extension. This idea, then, is borrowed from, and represents some impression which this moment appears to the senses. But my senses convey to me only the impressions of coloured points, disposed in a certain manner. If the eye is sensible of anything further, I desire it may be pointed out to me. But, if it be impossible to show anything further, we may conclude with certainty, that the idea of extension is nothing but a copy of these coloured points, and of the manner of their appearance … Nay, even when the resemblance is carried beyond the objects of one sense, and the impressions of touch are found to be similar to those of sight in the disposition of their parts; this does not hinder the abstract idea from representing both, upon account of their resemblance. All abstract ideas are really nothing but particular ones, considered in a certain light; but being annexed to general terms, they are able to represent a vast variety, and to comprehend objects, which, as they are alike in some particulars, are in others vastly wide of each other.[4]

Hume's standpoint is the exact opposite of that of Plato, who typifies the rationalist view. For Plato, it is the universal, eternal 'Ideas' or 'Forms' that constitute the primary realities of the world, whereas the particular appearances (phenomena) that we experience around us are merely the images or copies of these originals. The first he describes as 'that which is always real and has no becoming', and the second as 'that which is always becoming and is never real'.[5]

Plato too calls to his aid an item of furniture to illustrate the point: in his case it is not a table but a bed. In the tenth book of the *Republic*, justifying his expulsion of the dramatic poets from the commonwealth, he discusses various forms of representation in art. He starts with a question: 'Can you tell me what is meant by representation in general?'[6] He begins by assuming that for every set of things that are called by the same name – such as 'bed' or 'table' – there exists an 'essential nature or Form' made by the Creator, which is the original of all the particular things we see around us in the world of appearances:

> For instance there are any number of beds or of tables, but only two Forms, one of Bed and one of Table … And we are in the

4. *Ibid.,* p. 41.
5. Plato, *Timaeus*, trans. F.M. Cornford, *Plato's Cosmology*, Routledge & Kegan Paul, London, 1937, p. 22.
6. Plato, *The Republic of Plato*, trans. F.M. Cornford, Oxford University Press, Oxford, 1941, p. 317.

habit of saying that the craftsman, when he makes the beds and tables we use ... has before his mind the Form of one or other of these pieces of furniture ... Now the god made only one ideal or essential Bed ... Because, if he made even so many as two, then once more a single ideal Bed would make its appearance, whose character those two would share; and that one, not the two, would be the essential Bed.[7]

All actual beds are derived from this ideal bed. A bed made by a carpenter can be called, therefore, a representation or rather 're-presentation' of the ideal bed. When the carpenter makes it, he has in mind the Form of the object he sets out to make, but since what he makes is necessarily a particular bed, it 'is not the reality, but only something that resembles it ... We must not be surprised ... if even an actual bed is a somewhat shadowy thing as compared with reality.'[8]

For Hume the general idea of 'table', and the still wider, more abstract concept of spatial extension, are nothing but 'copies' or 'representations' of – one might even say, handy *substitutes* for – our innumerable individual sensory impressions. The general concept, which he calls the 'abstract idea', is shadowy and uncertain; it is a representation of, or substitute for, the actual impression. This is the exact opposite of Plato's doctrine that our fleeting sensory impressions are merely copies or pale shadows of the universal Idea. The terms 'image', 'copy', 'abstraction', 'representation' and 'substitution' will crop up throughout this chapter, which thus takes up again some of the arguments put forward in Chapter 2 concerning the De Stijl notion of *beelding* as image and representation.

In his popular introduction to philosophy, *The Problems of Philosophy* (1912), Bertrand Russell picks up, as it were, where Hume leaves off:

It seems to me that I am now sitting in a chair, at a table of a certain shape, on which I see sheets of paper with writing or print ... I believe that, if any other normal person comes into my room, he will see the same chairs and tables and books and papers as I see, and that the table which I see is the same as the table which I feel pressing against my arm.[9]

But Russell's aim is quite different from Hume's, and in some respects closer to Plato's. He regarded Hume's marginalizing of reason, and at the same time 'his rejection of the principle of induction' (that is, of the possibility of inferring general laws from particular

7. *Ibid.*, pp. 317–19.
8. *Ibid.*, p. 319.
9. B. Russell, *The Problems of Philosophy*, Oxford University Press, Oxford, 1998, p. 1.

instances), as representing 'a dead end' and 'the bankruptcy of eigh-
teenth-century reasonableness'. They had led directly to the 'growth
of unreason throughout the nineteenth century and what has passed
of the twentieth'.[10] It was therefore important to find a means of rein-
stating both empiricism and rationality, and of reconciling them with
each other. In his works of the early 1900s, Russell attempts to find in
logic, and in mathematics founded on logic, something equivalent to
Plato's unchangeable world of ideas. He distinguishes two kinds of
entities, *particulars* and *universals*:

> We speak of whatever is given in sensation, or is of the same
> nature as things given in sensation, as a *particular*; by opposition to
> this, a *universal* will be anything which may be shared by many
> particulars ... When we examine common words, we find that,
> broadly speaking, proper names stand for particulars, while other
> substantives, adjectives, prepositions, and verbs stand for univer-
> sals.[11]

Like Plato, Russell contrasts the permanence and definiteness of
universals with the temporary and imprecise nature of particulars.
Particulars can be said to *exist*, in the sense that they are in time (they
exist at a particular moment),

> But universals do not exist in this sense; we shall say that they
> *subsist* or *have being*, where 'being' is opposed to 'existence' as
> being timeless ... The world of being is unchangeable, rigid, exact,
> delightful to the mathematician, the logician, the builder of meta-
> physical systems, and all who love perfection more than life. The
> world of existence is fleeting, vague, without sharp boundaries,
> without any clear plan of arrangement, but it contains all thoughts
> and feelings, all the data of sense, and all physical objects ...
> According to our temperaments, we shall prefer the contempla-
> tion of the one or of the other. The one we do not prefer will
> probably seem to us a pale shadow of the one we prefer, and
> hardly worthy to be regarded as in any sense real. But the truth is
> that ... both are real, and both are important to the metaphysi-
> cian.[12]

By distinguishing universals from particulars, and stressing the reality
of universals, and their *being* outside time whereas particulars exist *in*
time, Russell comes close, not only to Plato, but also (and this is not
merely coincidental) to Mondrian's opposition of the 'timeless'
universal to the 'time-bound' individual:

10. B. Russell, *History of Western Philosophy*, George Allen &
Unwin, London, 1961, pp. 634, 645–6.
11. B. Russell, *The Problems of Philosophy*, Oxford University Press,
Oxford, 1998, p. 53.
12. *Ibid.*, p. 57.

All *style* has a *timeless content* and a *transitory appearance*. We can call the timeless (universal) content the *universal in style*, and the transitory appearance the *characteristic* or the *individual in style* ... The universal in style is eternal, and it is that which makes a style into *style*. It is the representation *[beelding]* of the universal, which, as philosophy also teaches, constitutes the core of the human spirit, although it is veiled by our individuality ... Similarly, although the universal expresses itself *through* nature as the *absolute*, the absolute achieves *representation [beelding]* in nature only by being hidden or veiled in natural form and colour.[13]

Let us return now to Russell's common-sense description of his table. It is the business of philosophy, he holds, to question the assumptions of common sense, and to expose the contradictions that may be hidden behind them:

To make our difficulties plain, let us concentrate attention on the table. To the eye it is oblong, brown, and shiny, to the touch it is smooth and cool and hard; when I tap it, it gives out a wooden sound ... but as soon as we try to be more precise our troubles begin. Although I believe the table is 'really' of the same colour all over ... some parts look white because of the reflected light. I know that, if I move, the parts that reflect the light will be different, so that the apparent distribution of colours on the table will change ... The *shape* of the table is no better. We are all in the habit of judging as to the 'real' shapes of things, and we do this so unreflectingly that we come to think we actually see the real shapes. But, in fact, as we all have to learn if we try to draw, a given thing looks different in shape from every different point of view.[14]

Russell points out ever more discrepancies between appearance and reality that arise when one explores the texture of the table under a microscope, or considers what makes it seem hard to the touch, and so on. These discrepancies have a direct impact on the problem of representational art, to which he now turns.

3.2 Appearance, reality and representation

In everyday life and for most practical purposes, Russell continues, the differences between the table as seen, felt or heard at particular times and from particular viewpoints do not matter, but to the painter they are all-important:

13. P. Mondrian, 'De nieuwe beelding in de schilderkunst', in *De Stijl*, vol. I, no. 2, December 1917, pp. 13–14.
14. Russell, *Problems of Philosophy*, pp. 2–3.

the painter has to unlearn the habit of thinking that things seem to have the colour which common sense says they 'really' have, and to learn the habit of seeing things as they appear. Here we already have the beginning of one of the distinctions that cause most trouble in philosophy – the distinction between 'appearance' and 'reality', between what things seem to be and what they are.[15]

The painter, Russell contends, wants to know what things seem to be, whereas the philosopher, like the practical man, is concerned with what they are – with this distinction: that the philosopher wants to probe more deeply into the question than does the practical man, or even the practical scientist. But is this any longer true?

Already by 1909–11 the cubist and futurist painters were attempting in different ways to penetrate beyond appearances to 'what things are'. And in 1913, the year after *The Problems of Philosophy* was published, Mondrian, having passed beyond cubism, painted his first completely abstract compositions in which the visual source material – trees, cityscapes and so on – entirely disappeared. His aim, too, was to paint the reality behind appearances, but the reality he sought lay still deeper below the surface than that which Picasso or Braque had tried to convey. In general, however, one might say that what distinguishes the art of the twentieth century from that of the four or five hundred years between the renaissance invention of perspective and the discoveries of the impressionists is that it has sought to turn its attention from the 'appearance of things' to some kind of underlying 'reality'. The artist has attempted, in other words, to be in some sort a philosopher. Generally without knowing it, he has retraced the argument of Plato's dialogue.

Still pursuing the problem of the bed, Plato argues along lines similar to Russell's. Besides the carpenter's bed, there is a second way in which the Idea of bed can be represented in the world of appearances. For there also exists a far more versatile kind of craftsman, one who can create, not only every kind of artefact, but also 'all plants and animals, himself included, and earth and sky and gods and the heavenly bodies and all things under the earth in Hades'.[16]

This is the painter. But the work of the painter, in Plato's view, 'is at the third remove from the essential nature of the thing',[17] for what he tries to represent is no longer the essential nature of all beds but the particular bed made by the craftsman. What the painter makes is a copy of a copy. And this copy has the further defect that it shows the carpenter's bed not as it is but only as it appears at a particular moment and from a particular point of view:

15. *Ibid.*, p. 2.
16. Plato, *Republic*, p. 318.
17. *Ibid.*, p. 320.

'I mean: you may look at a bed or any other object from straight in front or slantwise or at any angle. Is there then any difference in the bed itself, or does it merely look different?'

'It only looks different.'

'Well, that is the point. Does painting aim at reproducing any actual object as it is, or the appearance of it as it looks? In other words, is it a representation of the truth or of a semblance?'

'Of a semblance.'

'The art of representation, then, is a long way from reality; and apparently the reason why there is nothing it cannot reproduce is that it grasps only a small part of any object, and that only an image. Your painter, for example, will paint us a shoemaker, a carpenter, or other workman, without understanding any of their crafts.'[18]

The work of the painter, therefore, is inferior to that of the carpenter, not only because it is further removed from the original Form, but also because it is based on a less direct and less profound knowledge of what it means to make a bed; and the same goes for these other craftsmen whom the artist may take as his subject. For

if a man were able actually to do the things he represents as well as to produce images of them, do you believe he would seriously give himself up to making these images and take that as a completely satisfying object in life? I should imagine that, if he had a real understanding of the actions he represents, he would far sooner devote himself to performing them in fact.[19]

Now, if the representation of the things we see around us, such as beds and the makers of beds, is twice removed from the divine Idea, should the painter try instead to represent that Idea directly? Is there a place, that is, in Plato's scheme for Van Doesburg's concept – discussed in Chapter 2 – of the 'new representation' or *nieuwe beelding*, 'in which no representation of phenomena is involved', but instead only of 'pure abstract thought'?[20] Is it possible for the modern painter to bypass the transitory appearance of this or that bed made by a carpenter, and go straight to the ideal Form of all beds conceived by the god? This seems to be what Van Doesburg has in mind when in *Principles of Neo-Plastic Art* he describes his abstract representation of a cow as 'embodying the essence of the object'.[21] If a painting can embody the essence of the object *cow*, it can presumably embody the essence of the object *bed*; but can it?

18. *Ibid.*, pp. 320–1.
19. *Ibid.*, pp. 321–2.
20. T. van Doesburg, 'Denken – aanschouwen – beelden', in *De Stijl*, vol. II, no. 2, December 1918, pp. 23–4.
21. T. van Doesburg, *Principles of Neo-Plastic Art* (1925), Lund Humphries, London, 1969, p. 18.

It is hard to find evidence of support for this idea in Plato. For him, truth must be approached by thinking: it is the task of the mathematician and the philosopher. The artist should stick to his art, and if he cannot be an honest maker of things, the best he can aim at is a sort of half-truth, by trying to be as honest and workmanlike as possible. The best kind of representational art, in Plato's opinion, is the rigidly prescribed, conventional art of Egypt. The Egyptian painter depicts a bed more or less as in a working drawing – that is, in pure elevation. It is as near as he can come, in two dimensions, to the way the carpenter makes it. Egyptian painting therefore has two advantages over the illusionistic art of Plato's Athens: first, it is, arguably, like the work of a carpenter, only once removed from the ideal Form; and secondly it is the product, not of an individual, but of a whole enduring civilization:

> If you examine their art on the spot, you will find that ten thousand years ago ... paintings and reliefs were produced that are no better and no worse than those of today, because the same artistic rules were applied in making them.[22]

From both points of view, Egyptian art had the great merit of *generality*. To this limited extent, at least, it rose above individual sensation and the here-and-now – that is, above plurality and space-time, the factors which reduced everyday experience to that which 'becomes and passes away'. This was, for Plato, as near as art could come to universality and permanence.

3.3 Representation as substitution

Ernst Gombrich's essay *Meditations on a Hobby Horse* (1951) throws light on the meaning of 'representation', on the role in it of function, and on the difference between illusionism or naturalism and the kind of art practised by the ancient Egyptians or by various branches of modernism. It also raises, at least by implication, the question 'Can architecture be said to "represent", in the same sense as painting or sculpture?'

Instead of a bed or a table, Gombrich considers another household object: the hobby horse. He asks: 'Is the hobby horse an "image" of a horse?' To find out, he first consults a dictionary – just as we did in Chapter 2 – and finds 'image' defined as *imitation of object's external form*. The hobby horse is certainly not that. And again like us, he goes on from 'image' to 'representation':

---

22. Plato, *Laws*, trans. T.J. Saunders, Penguin Books, Harmondsworth, 1970, p. 91.

To *represent,* we read, can be used in the sense of *'call up by description or portrayal or imagination, figure, place likeness of before mind or senses, serve or be meant as likeness of ... stand for, be specimen of, fill place of, be substitute for'.* A portrayal of a horse? Evidently not. A substitute for a horse? Yes. That it is.[23]

Picking up the trail suggested by this clue, Gombrich pursues further the idea of representation as substitution. When the first child bestrode a stick and declared 'This is a horse!' it probably bore even less resemblance to an actual horse than its more recent descendants. What made it a horse was that you could ride it; the common factor, the basis of representation, was function, not form:

Or, more precisely, that formal aspect which fulfilled the minimum requirement for the performance of the function – for any 'rideable' object could serve as a horse. If that is true we may be enabled to cross a boundary which is usually regarded as closed and sealed. For in this sense 'substitutes' reach deep into biological layers that are common to man and animal. The cat runs after the ball as if it were a mouse. The baby sucks its thumb as if it were the breast. In a sense the ball 'represents' a mouse to the cat, the thumb a breast to the baby. But here too 'representation' does not depend on formal, that is geometrical, qualities beyond the minimum requirements for function. The ball has nothing in common with the mouse except that it is chasable. The thumb nothing with the breast except that it is suckable.[24]

Gombrich observes that children are apt to reject the 'natural-looking' dolls that adults offer them in favour of some 'monstrously abstract' but 'cuddly' dummy, or even a favourite blanket. In the same way, the primitive effigy may be no more than a standing stone or a piece of wood, but it functions admirably as a god-substitute that can be offered gifts to persuade it to bring rain, or beaten if it fails to do so. This leads him to reflect on 'that great divide' running through the history of art, separating the 'few islands' of naturalistic art (like the illusionistic Greek art attacked by Plato) within the 'vast ocean' of conceptualism, such as the art of children, of primitives and of ancient Egypt and much twentieth century art.

The difference lies in a change of function. Once the object made by the artist ceases to be regarded as a 'real' thing – even if only a substitute – but as the record of a particular momentary visual experience, the nature of 'representation' is fundamentally changed. For the child and the primitive it is far more important that the image

23. E.H. Gombrich, *Meditations on a Hobby Horse,* Phaidon, London, 1963, p. 1.
24. *Ibid.,* p. 4.

possess what they consider to be its relevant attributes, than that it reproduce visual appearances. The Egyptian relief figure must show two hands and two feet in full view, but it matters little that its anatomy is distorted in order to achieve this and to reduce the three-dimensional body to a two-dimensional plane. For much the same reason Picasso might paint a figure with both eyes on the same side of the head, in order to show that there are two. But the figures in Pheidias' Panathenaic frieze, in a post-renaissance painting or in a modern photograph are shown as they would appear momentarily in a projected perspective space, and we unquestioningly supply the hidden limbs or eyes from our imagination.

Paradoxically, *both* kinds of representation depend on omission: the difference lies in *what* they omit. Whereas the conceptual artist leaves out what he regards as inessential features, the illusionistic artist may intentionally obscure the *essential* ones, forcing us to supply them. The expressiveness of a Rembrandt portrait is achieved by leaving in shadow precisely the features in which expression resides: the eyes. The almost shapeless blobs of paint by which Manet brilliantly conveys the illusion of horses racing at Longchamp are no more literal depictions of actual horses than the hobby horse. The image is evoked as much by what we do not see as by what we do:

> No longer is there any need for that completeness of essentials which belongs to the conceptual style, no longer is there the fear of the casual which dominates the archaic conception of art. The picture of a man on a Greek vase no longer needs a hand or a foot in full view. We know that it is meant as a shadow, a mere record of what the artist saw or might see.[25]

Or, as Plato, would have maintained, 'a shadow of a shadow'. Let us, then, try to apply Gombrich's insight to Plato's question: 'Does painting aim at reproducing any actual object as it is, or the appearance of it as it looks? In other words, is it a representation of the truth or of a semblance?' The Egyptian, the child and the primitive 'make' the thing represented much as the carpenter makes the bed; the Greek artist, as Plato complains, merely imitates the semblance. One of the few things shared in common by the many separate and conflicting artistic directions we call collectively the modern movement is the desire to free art from the imitation of a momentary appearance and a particular viewpoint – in other words, from enslavement to a fragment of time and space – and to restore it to its ancient function of 'making': of creating as nature creates. Does this make the paintings of Mondrian and Van Doesburg functional

25. *Ibid.*, p. 9.

objects, like Rietveld's houses and chairs? Or are they intended as 'representations of the truth'?

3.4 The abstraction of function

The answer lies, once more, in the concept of substitution. A house can be described as a 'substitute' for the natural environment, which it replaces in tempered form. Similarly, a chair is a substitute for the natural log or mound of a convenient height and shape that we might otherwise sit on. They are substitutes but also, from a human point of view, mediations and ameliorations. By mediating between ourselves and our natural surroundings, they soften the conflicts inherent in our human relation to nature. Even the hobby horse is an improvement on a real one, if you are the parent of a small child. It can be ridden at any time and anywhere, it is safe, it does not need to be fed or looked after, and your child can cast it aside when bored with it. Likewise, the primitive effigy provides its worshippers with a visible and tangible substitute for unpredictable and uncontrollable natural forces. As Gombrich writes in his earlier book *The Story of Art* (1950), for the primitive there was no fundamental difference between architecture and image-making. Both were primarily functional:

> Those who use these buildings as places of worship or entertainment, or as dwellings, judge them first and foremost by standards of utility ... In the past the attitude to paintings and statues was often similar. They were thought of not as mere works of art but as objects which had a definite function ... Among ... primitives, there is no difference between building and image-making as far as usefulness is concerned. Their huts are there to shelter them from rain, wind and sunshine and the spirits which produce them; images are made to protect them against other powers which are, to them, as real as the forces of nature. Pictures and statues, in other words, are used to work magic.[26]

Can we regard a Mondrian painting of the 1920s or 1930s as a functional object in the same sense? Not, that is to say, as a god, but as a 'presence' that provides us, by the internal cohesion of its composition, with a substitute for the universal harmony that is either lacking in our external world or forever beyond our grasp? Is the pure work of art to be regarded as a 'world within the world', a limited image of the universality we seek and cannot find in the 'real' one?

I think Mondrian and Van Doesburg were mistaken if they supposed that painting could aspire to the condition of pure abstract

26. E.H. Gombrich, *The Story of Art* (1950), Phaidon, London, 1966, pp. 19–20.

thought, on a par with mathematics or philosophy. It is not possible, merely by making abstract, geometrical-looking marks on canvas, to find a short-cut to the universal. The whole project has a certain air of the cargo cult. Like tribesmen who lay out pieces of wood in the forest in the shape of an aircraft in the hope of acquiring the power they associate with the real thing, the De Stijl artists often seemed to suggest that just by using the same figures – straight lines and rectangles – that the geometer uses, they could arrive at an equivalent kind of absolute truth. To be fair to the artists, however, they were not altogether unaware of this problem. Mondrian states it (by his standards) very clearly:

Although the new representation *[Nieuwe beelding]* strongly emphasizes truth, it nevertheless continues to represent *[beelden]* beauty. So it still remains, like all art, relative, even somewhat *arbitrary*. As soon as it might become as absolute as the universal means of representation *[beeldingsmiddel]* allows, it would overstep the bounds of art: it would pass from the field of art into that of truth ... Art *remains* relative, even though the consciousness of the time rises more and more towards the universal, and though intuition – the source of all art – comes from the universal. The *artist*, because he combines inwardness with outwardness, always remains *human*, and therefore unable to rise completely above the subjective.[27]

Mondrian and Van Doesburg were conscious that they were pushing art to the limit, and even beyond the limit, of what art can be. Like primitive tribesmen attempting to make an aeroplane, or an alchemist attempting to transmute base metals into gold, they were pursuing a sort of magic. But the artist remains always a maker of things, not of pure ideas; the best he or she can hope is that these things may sometimes seem to be magical. Peter Smithson has remarked of Gerrit Rietveld that

it is inescapable that the Red-Blue chair and the Schröder house are magical objects, and it is this that drew me to Rietveld in the first place. The work of the members of the De Stijl group is usually wonderful, and some few De Stijl things are magical things. Theo van Doesburg's never are. Mondrian's often, Van der Leck's very often – but child magic not grown-up magic.[28]

The point about magic (child magic or grown-up magic) is that it is founded in the everyday. It takes the ordinary things of everyday life

27. Mondrian, 'De nieuwe beelding', in *De Stijl*, vol. I, no. 9, July 1918, p. 104.
28. P. Smithson, 'Rietveld, builder and furniture designer', in *Bauen und Wohnen*, vol. 19, no. 11, 1965, p. 421.

and transforms them. Fairy tales are full of such transmutations (frog into prince, and so on). The hobby horse is an ordinary walking stick that has been magically transformed into a living, prancing horse. If there is a place for abstract art, it does not lie far from the 'magic' of Van der Leck and Rietveld. The work of both artists was solidly grounded in function: Rietveld's because what he made were useful objects, houses and chairs; Van der Leck's because his paintings are illustrations. Even Van der Leck's near-abstract later paintings were generalized representations of the visual world, rooted in the utilitarian public and social art of the first half of his career. But both artists raised function to a higher, 'magical' level. A Rietveld house or chair, or a Van der Leck painting, is a means of revealing the universal in the particular – to paraphrase Rietveld – a means of enabling human beings to experience reality.[29]

The firm basis for art is therefore function. The only way in which art can transcend the particular function of this or that object, or the depiction of this or that visual impression – can achieve, in short, a degree of universality – is by generalizing, in other words *abstracting*, that function. The bed in Bart van der Leck's study for the mural *Life insurance* (1914) is drawn in pure elevation, much as an Egyptian artist might have represented it.

3.5 Van der Leck and Mondrian: abstract painting *versus* concrete architecture

In the early 1900s, Egyptian art had a strong influence in Holland in the circle of mystically inclined and/or socially committed monumental painters and architects that included Jan Toorop, Antoon Derkinderen, R.N. Roland Holst, J.L.M. Lauweriks (see Chapter 5), K.P.C. de Bazel and H.J.M. Walenkamp. From them the Egyptian influence spread to two younger artists later connected with the Stijl group, who worked together and were close friends from an early age: the architect and furniture designer Piet Klaarhamer (1874–1954) and the painter Bart van der Leck. Van der Leck was among the founders of the De Stijl group; Klaarhamer never joined it, but was closely connected with several of its members, notably Robert van't Hoff and Gerrit Rietveld.

Van der Leck grew up in poverty in the slums of Utrecht. His father, an unemployed house-painter, took no interest in his struggle to become an artist. From his family he did acquire, however, a sympathy with socialism. Apprenticed at the age of fifteen to an Utrecht stained-glass workshop, he remained involved, up to his meeting with Mondrian in 1916 – that is, for a quarter of a century –

29. G. Rietveld, 1963, in *Gerrit Rietveld: Texten*, Impress, Utrecht, 1979, p. 36.

in work that can be broadly described as functional. It was either monumental architectural decoration – murals or stained glass – or more or less directly propagandistic in aim. The propaganda comprised social comment, like the first version of *Leaving the factory* (1910), or advertising, like his poster for the Batavier Line steamship company (1916), or both together. His mural *Life insurance* was both social comment about poverty and sickness and an advertisement for the insurance company 'De Nederlanden van 1845'. The art historian R.W.D. Oxenaar has written that even his colour designs are directed towards the enhancement of life, in the sense of the enrichment of the users' visual experience:

> In this fundamental modesty, both towards architecture and towards the user, is manifested the essence of his vision: simplicity, clarity, facing up to life, down-to-earth, but at the same time radiant, positive, directed to the future and to a new humane monumentality.[30]

The Egyptian influence, which began around 1903, is most evident in Van der Leck's paintings of the years 1912–16, immediately before his brief membership of De Stijl: for instance *Four soldiers* (1912), *The leave-taking* (1913), *Life insurance* and *Cat* (1914). The background is invariably white, suggesting a wall, the figures flat, separate, arranged in a single plane, and either frontal or in profile. Often, as in Egyptian painting, the body is represented frontally but the head and feet in profile.

His paintings of 1916 show a transition from these flat stylized figures towards the pure geometrical abstraction of the following year. In *The storm*, and still more in the *Portrait of the artist's daughter* (composition 1916, no. 1) and the *Mine triptych* (composition 1916, no. 4), natural appearance is simplified, first to straight-edged planes of flat colour, and then to coloured rectangles and parallelograms floating against a black or white ground. He moved that year from The Hague to Laren, where in 1916–17 he came in almost daily contact with Mondrian.

Van der Leck now took the generalization of the image a short step further, reducing the painting to separate vertical, horizontal and diagonal rectangles of primary colour against a white ground. The process can be seen clearly by comparing the sketches and final versions of *Leaving the factory* (composition 1917, nos. 3 and 4) (Figure 3.1), or of *Donkey riders* (composition 1917, nos. 5 and 6). Through most of 1918 he continued to pursue the process of abstraction, in

---

30. R.W.D. Oxenaar, in catalogue, *Bart van der Leck 1876–1958*, Rijksmuseum Kröller-Müller, Otterlo/Stedelijk Museum, Amsterdam, 1976.

such works as *Composition 1918, nos. 1–5*. Even these, however, were derived painstakingly from studies of the visual world.[31]

Donkey riders was the first painting by any artist to be illustrated in *De Stijl*, and the only one included in the first issue, in October 1917, together with Oud's project for seaside housing at Scheveningen. Although its origin in naturalistic subject-matter is still faintly discernible – as Mondrian complained in a letter to Van Doesburg, 'you can still see the donkeys'[32] – Mondrian himself would recall, in the last number of *De Stijl* (1932), how around 1916 his own still 'cubistic and thus more or less pictorial' work came under the influence of Van der Leck's precise technique, flat composition and pure colours.[33] For a short time, at the start of 1917, Van der Leck was 'ahead' of both Mondrian and Van Doesburg in the drive towards pure abstraction. At this point his work was, if one believes that 'progress' is important in art, 'the clearest and most principled painting De Stijl had to offer', as Oxenaar puts it.[34]

Like Mondrian, Van der Leck was deeply suspicious of Van Doesburg's enthusiasm for involving architects alongside painters in De Stijl. His two articles in *De Stijl* – 'The Place of Modern Painting in Architecture' (October 1917) and 'On Painting and Building' (February 1918) – both deal with the problematic relation between architecture and painting, as their titles suggest. In the first, he emphasizes the separate and distinct natures of painting and architecture, and lays claim to an enlarged *lebensraum* for the painter within building – a territory upon which the architect must not presume to encroach:

> Over time, painting has separated itself from architecture, developed independently of it, and by means of experiment and the destruction of the old and the natural, it has come to develop its own essential character, spiritually as well as formally. It still needs the plane surface, and it will always be its ultimate wish to exploit directly the practical surface to which *architecture* necessarily gives rise. More than that, by extending its sphere from the individual to the universal it will claim as its rightful domain the whole colour concept, and that part of the form concept of the building that properly belongs to painting.[35]

No architect, one imagines, would willingly cede so much of his creative territory to the painter. And it is clear from the article that the role of modern painting in architecture is to be essentially destructive. It is not to contribute harmoniously to the functional design, but to subvert the closed, contained and solid character that is

31. C. Hilhorst, 'Bart van der Leck', in C. Blotkamp et al., *De Beginjaren van De Stijl 1917–1922*, Reflex, Utrecht, 1982, pp. 173–81.

32. P. Mondrian, letter to T. van Doesburg, 7 July 1917; quoted in Hilhorst, 'Bart van der Leck', p. 171.

33. P. Mondrian, in *De Stijl*, last number, 1932, p. 48.

34. R.W.D. Oxenaar, 'Van der Leck and De Stijl', in *De Stijl: 1917–1931, Visions of Utopia*, ed. M. Friedman, Phaidon, London, 1982, p. 76.

35. B. van der Leck, 'De plaats van het moderne schilderen in de architectuur', in *De Stijl*, vol. I, no. 1, October 1917, p. 6.

inherent in building, and replace it with openness and light. Whereas architecture constructs, giving rise to massive volumes with closed, finite proportions, modern painting 'destroys corporeality, reducing it to flatness, and comes, through the space concept, to the destruction of the natural materiality associated with the wall-plane, and thereby arrives at *spatial relationship*'.[36]

It must be borne in mind, however, that these texts were written during Van der Leck's brief association with De Stijl and while he was strongly under the influence of Mondrian. Mondrian's article 'The Definite and the Indefinite', published in the December 1918 number of *De Stijl*, develops further the idea expressed in the above quoted passage:

> Through its having progressed to the representation *[beelding]* solely of (aesthetic) proportion *[verhouding]* ... painting is ready to join hands with architecture. Since ancient times, architecture, by its very nature as a mathematical-aesthetic representation of proportion *[verhoudingsbeelding]*, has stood far above its sister arts. Although it has not always given conscious expression to this fundamental characteristic, and although its appearance is also the consequence of necessity and practical demands, architecture went far beyond the *naturalism* of sculpture and painting. Sculpture has as yet only achieved a tautening of its form (Archipenko). Only painting (New Representation *[Nieuwe Beelding]*) brought to the fore the *sole* representation of *proportion*. This is not to say that such painting is a mere *supplement* to architecture; unlike architecture, it is not *constructional* ... Architecture always presupposes enclosure: a building presents itself against space as a *thing* ... Moreover, because of its constructional character and its bondage to material demands, architecture cannot sustain as consistently as painting the contrasts of position, dimension and colour-value which continually counteract each other.[37]

Although this statement was published over a year later than Van der Leck's first article, it probably reflects Mondrian's own view at that time, just as it is entirely consistent with the views on architecture he expressed, for instance, in later essays such as 'The Realization of Neoplasticism in the Distant Future and in Today's Architecture' (1922) and 'Neoplasticism: Dwelling – Street – City' (1927). In the 1922 essay he claims that it will be impossible to realize the new, neoplastic architecture until the far distant future, because architecture must first free itself from its functional and material bonds and become purely abstract. For the present, it might just be possible to

---

36. *Ibid.*, p. 7.
37. P. Mondrian, 'Het bepaalde en het onbepaalde', in *De Stijl*, vol. II, no. 2, December 1918, p. 16.

realize a neoplastic architecture in a single, untypical building, considered as a 'work of art'. However,

> Even as 'artwork' neoplastic architecture is only realizable under certain *conditions*. It demands not only *freedom*, but also *preparation* of a kind unattainable in current building practice. The founders of neoplasticism in painting made great sacrifices in order to bring this 'new' representation *[beelding]* to complete expression; in architecture this is still virtually impossible. Execution in which everything must be *reinvented and worked out from the start* is too expensive or impossible in present circumstances. *Absolute freedom for continual research* is demanded if art is to be achieved.[38]

Van der Leck's views, on the other hand, were about to change, and his attitude to architects to become, as Oxenaar says, more modest. By November 1918 he refused to sign the first De Stijl manifesto, and effectively ended his participation in the movement, although his final break with Van Doesburg came only in May 1920.[39] He had begun as a stained-glass craftsman, and his art had developed in harmony with architecture through monumental wall decoration and advertising graphics. He never gave up his close involvement with architecture and design. Looking back over his life in 1957, a year before his death, he recalled:

> It was in 1917 that *De Stijl* was founded. I very soon distanced myself from it, because I thought I had another starting-point and goal from the others, however similar they might appear. Even then I found the others too one-sided and lacking a solution for a general renewal of painting. Painting has always been for me the representation of visual life. I've never had much use for so-called abstraction ... Built form, or architecture, is the primary ground-form to which painting or colourism must recognize itself to be subordinate.[40]

Having himself grown up in poverty, Van der Leck was far from regarding art as 'free' in a *l'art pour l'art* sense, as Mondrian was inclined to do. He saw painting instead as having a clear social purpose: 'One of the foremost qualities that a painter must have is social insight into the subject matter.'[41]

Whereas Mondrian after 1917 went on to completely abstract composition, not based on any source image derived from the visible world, Van der Leck stepped back from the brink. By 1918 his already worsening relations with Mondrian and especially with Van Doesburg began to be reflected in his art. The *Horseman*, painted at the end of

38. P. Mondrian, 'De realiseering van het neo-plasticisme in verre toekomst en in de huidige architectuur', in *De Stijl*, vol. V, no. 5, May 1922, pp. 66–7.

39. Oxenaar, *Bart van der Leck 1876–1958*.

40. B. van der Leck, interview, 7 June 1957, in Van der Leck memorial exhibition catalogue, Stedelijk Museum, Amsterdam, no. 204, 1959.

41. *Ibid.*

that year, returned defiantly to the just recognizable portrayal of naturalistic subjects, although still far more abstracted than his works before 1916. By 1920 he had broken all ties with the movement.

From 1918 to 1958 Van der Leck continued to work quietly in much the same manner; his subjects drawn from that very same 'ordinary life', from bondage to which, in Schopenhauer's view, art should bring liberation. The paintings themselves are 'liberating' at a certain, purely emotional level: happy, lucid, simple, like brightly coloured wooden toys in the winter light of a sunny nursery. But it is not easy to see where they stand in relation to De Stijl's distinction between two levels of representation. Are they an extreme form of 'deformative' depiction, an *afbeelding* carried to an extreme level of distortion and no more? Or do they attempt, as he himself claimed in the article on painting and architecture which he contributed to the first issue of *De Stijl*, 'to push beyond the depiction [*afbeelding*] of visual reality ... towards cosmic values of space, light, and proportion, in which all earthly modelling or "the particular case" are assimilated and taken for granted'?[42]

The talk of 'cosmic values', almost certainly taken over from Van der Leck's Laren neighbour Schoenmaekers, rings false. Did he seriously believe that his coloured triangles and quadrilaterals floating on a white ground could penetrate through visual appearances towards some cosmic universality? Moreover, its falseness threatens to undermine the real authenticity of the work itself. I prefer to see these paintings as *jeux d'esprit*, things made for the sheer fun of making them: the surroundings of his quiet life in Blaricum, 'portraits of his children, still-lifes, animals, flowers, trees, fruit and people at work'.[43] They are a kind of prolonged playing with the craft which over so many years he had painfully acquired as a young apprentice.

In the forty years from his leaving De Stijl until his death in 1958, Van der Leck continued to be active as a 'functional' designer – of interiors, carpets, furnishing fabrics, ceramics, packaging and typography – for companies like Delftse Slaolie or Metz & Co., or in collaboration with the architects H.P. Berlage and P.J. Elling. Not for nothing was he the son of a house-painter. This functional ground provided the solid foundation for his 'playful' near-abstract compositions. Art and design sustained each other.

3.6 Gerrit Rietveld, furniture maker

Of all the De Stijl artists, the one who seems closest to Van der Leck is Gerrit Rietveld. Both left school early to be apprenticed to a craft – Rietveld, at the age of twelve, in his father's cabinet-making workshop.

42. Van der Leck, 'De plaats', in *De Stijl*, vol. I, no. 1, p. 7.

43. Oxenaar, *Bart van der Leck 1876–1958*.

Much later, he would pursue his education through evening classes in architecture given by Van der Leck's friend Piet Klaarhamer. In both Van der Leck and Rietveld, one finds the same precarious balance between practicality and play, the same almost childlike innocence.

As Mondrian points out in 'The Definite and the Indefinite', one effect (perhaps a side-effect) of De Stijl's reduction of the artistic means to perpendicular lines and rectangles of colour is that it leaves the way open to a fusion of architecture and painting, painting and furniture. But as Mondrian also observes, there are many obstacles in the way, of which the greatest is, in his view, the functional nature of building, and by implication of furniture. Is Rietveld's Red-Blue chair (Figures 3.2–3.7), or the Schröder house, to be regarded as a functional object or as a kind of three-dimensional Mondrian? What is certain is that neither pretends in any way to be a representation of 'cosmic reality', of 'pure abstract thought, or of the platonic Idea of 'chair' or 'house'. If they represent anything beyond their own function (which they perform adequately, but no more) it is ordinary life raised to the level of play. By 'play' I do not mean arbitrariness or frivolity, but on the contrary – just as when I referred above to Van der Leck's later paintings as *jeux d'esprit* – the raising of the merely utilitarian function to a higher plane on which the object is no longer merely expedient, but disinterested: it exists for its own sake, as an enrichment of everyday life. 'Rietveld', says Peter Smithson, 'touched only small things, each was given a life of its own, enriching the town (usually his home town) for its ordinary sake.'[44] Or as Rietveld himself put it:

> If for some purpose we divide off, stake out, delimit a piece of what we customarily call universal, unbounded space, and so shelter it from certain forces and bring it to a human scale, then (if it is any good), a little bit of space has come into being which we are able to experience as reality.[45]

Van Doesburg published illustrations of two furniture pieces by Rietveld, the sideboard and the upright armchair (both of 1919), in *De Stijl* in March 1920, together with a 'poem' in which he compared Rietveld's chair rather bizarrely to a painting by Giorgio de Chirico:

Difference and correspondence.

Difference in intention, in expression, in means.

Correspondence in metaphysical feeling and mathematical indication of spaces.

In both: spaces bounded by spaces.

44. Smithson, 'Rietveld, builder and furniture designer', p. 421.

45. G. Rietveld, 'Levenshouding als achtergrond van mijn werk' ('Attitude to life as the background to my work'), in T.M. Brown, *The Work of G. Rietveld, Architect*, A.W. Bruna & Zoon, Utrecht, 1958, p. 163.

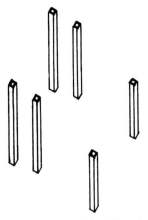

Figure 3.2 Gerrit Rietveld, Red-Blue chair, c.1918 (detail): vertical elements

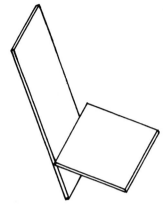

Figure 3.5 Red-Blue chair: diagonal elements (seat and back)

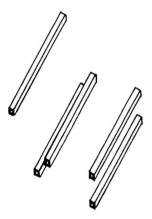

Figure 3.3 Red-Blue chair: transverse elements

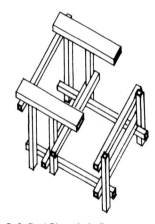

Figure 3.6 Red-Blue chair: linear components assembled

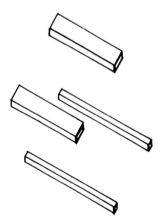

Figure 3.4 Red-Blue chair: longitudinal elements

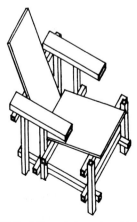

Figure 3.7 Red-Blue chair: seat and back added

Space-penetration.

Space-mysticism.

In Chirico's painting, intentional ... in Rietveld's chair, uninten-
tional, necessary, clear, real: *A SLENDER SPACE-ANIMAL* ...

Rietveld's chair: unpremeditated, but ruthless working of open
spaces with as contrast: *NECESSITY*

SITTING

CHAIR

material delimitation opposed to rich, undisguised and firm representation of open spaces.

CHAIR

dumb eloquence as of a machine.[46]

Unlike Van Doesburg, with his talk of 'metaphysical feelings' and
'space-mysticism', Rietveld always had his feet firmly planted on the
Dutch ground, and was not given to pseudo-mystical effusions. The
first occasion on which his name appeared in *De Stijl* was in July 1919,
when his baby chair was illustrated, accompanied by his own dry,
factual description:

> Proceeding from the known requirements – comfortable, secure
> sitting, adjustable height, washable, not over-strong and heavy,
> one has tried to achieve regularity as clear representation of the
> thing itself, without elaboration. The wood is green, the straps are
> red, the pins that hold the straps in holes in the wooden bars, light
> green. A red leather cushion can be hung from the top rail of the
> backrest. The little gate in front and the table top are removable.[47]

And so on. Rietveld's Red-Blue chair, in its unpainted version,
appeared in the magazine two months later, where the editor
describes it as the answer to the question, 'What place is there for
sculpture in the new interior?':

> Our chairs, our tables, cupboards and other household equip-
> ment will be the (abstract-real) sculptures *[beelden]* in the interior
> of the future. Of the chair's construction Mr Rietveld has written
> us the following: 'With this chair one has tried to make each detail
> as simple as possible, and to leave each element as close as
> possible to the original form natural to the use of the material –
> the form that is best able to enter into harmonious relation with
> the rest.'[48]

46. T. van Doesburg, 'Schilderkunst van Giorgio de Chirico en een
stoel van Rietveld', in *De Stijl*, vol. III, no. 5, 1920, p. 46.

47. G. Rietveld, 'Aanteekening bij kinderstoel', in *De Stijl*, vol. II, no.
9, July 1919, p. 102.

48. 'Aanteekening bij een leunstoel van Rietveld', in *De Stijl*, vol. II,
no. 11, September 1919, p. 133.

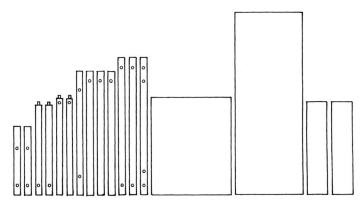

Figure 3.8 Red-Blue chair: the seventeen components before assembly

Even with its original oak painted (at Van Doesburg's suggestion) in abstract black, red, blue and yellow, the chair still retains a certain ordinariness (it is even surprisingly comfortable). And that is its great virtue, as it is of all Rietveld's work. In contradiction to this, however, like all Rietveld's furniture and architecture, it is at the same time rather *extraordinary*. One might resolve the contradiction by saying that it *reveals the extraordinariness of the ordinary, by being more ordinary than 'ordinariness' ordinarily is*. There is always a certain unconventionality, as though the object were saying: 'Yes, I am a chair (or a house); but perhaps I could also be something else!' This unconventionality, this 'extraordinary ordinariness', is connected with the principle of *generality*. A Rietveld design is unique, but every element in it is studied with a view to the greatest possible generality. Thus a chair leg, for example, is reduced to a uniform square section of wood, identical with the horizontal members of the same chair (Figure 3.8), or indeed with the verticals and horizontals of his other pieces of furniture. It could in theory be interchanged with any of these other identical members. He expresses this idea of generality (or transformability) in an essay on the new functionalism *(nieuwe zakelijkheid)* in Dutch architecture:

> The fact that at our better moments we are more comfortable sitting on a table than a chair, or the fact that we don't need a house, table or chair at all, means that the house of the future (the house for the new generation) cannot and must not aim to conform to the notion of 'living' that is now prevalent.[49]

A chair, a house or a painting, if it is to exist at all as an object in the world, is necessarily particular: an individual thing occupying a discrete portion of space, and therefore by its nature removed from the

49. G. Rietveld, 'New functionalism in Dutch architecture', in *De Vrije Bladen*, 1932; English trans. in M. Küper and I. van Zijl, *Gerrit Th. Rietveld 1888–1954*, Centraal Museum, Utrecht, 1992, p. 39.

universal. The nearest it can approach to the universal is by way of the general, that is, the 'almost' or 'relatively' universal. The actually general, one can say, is a *substitute* for the theoretically universal. The more general a work of art is, the closer it comes to a representation of the universal. When Schopenhauer identifies the highest aesthetic manifestation of architecture with structure (see Chapter 2), he is equating it with the general function of all building: the enclosure of space by solid elements.

3.7 Donald Judd: both particular and general

A chair by Rietveld or by Donald Judd reduces the function 'to sit' to its most general terms. Judd, in particular, refused to make different chairs for particular purposes, countering criticism that his chairs were uncomfortable and therefore unfunctional by saying that

> The furniture is comfortable to me. Rather than making a chair to sleep in or a machine to live in, it is better to make a bed. A straight chair is best for eating or writing. The third position is standing.[50]

The case of Donald Judd is particularly relevant to a discussion of De Stijl and 'the furniture of the mind', and for several reasons. He was a sculptor who also made important furniture, and this furniture is often exhibited in art galleries alongside his sculpture. However, he drew a clear distinction between the two categories: 'I'm not arguing ... for a confusion of art and architecture, a fashion now, but for a coherent relationship.'[51] However generalized may be the form of his chairs, tables, beds and buildings, and however much they may resemble abstract sculptures, they are not interchangeable with them:

> Eighteen years ago someone asked me to design a coffee table. I thought that a work of mine which was essentially a rectangular volume with the upper surface recessed could be altered. This debased the work and produced a bad table which I later threw away. The configuration and the scale of art cannot be transposed into furniture and architecture. The intent of art is different from that of the latter, which must be functional. If a chair or a building is not functional, if it appears to be only art, it is ridiculous ... A work of art exists as itself; a chair exists as a chair itself.[52]

50. D. Judd, 'It's hard to find a good lamp', in *Donald Judd Furniture*, Museum Boymans-Van Beuningen, Rotterdam, 1993, p. 21.
51. D. Judd, 'Art and Architecture' (1987), in *Donald Judd: Architektur*, Westfälischer Kunstverein, 1989, p. 196.
52. D. Judd, 'On furniture', in *Donald Judd, Complete Writings 1975–1986'*, Van Abbemuseum, Eindhoven, 1987, p. 107.

For this reason, one suspects that Mondrian's concept of the neoplastic architecture of the future, in which building would cease to be functional and become pure art, was invalid. Where such 'art architecture' has been attempted, it rings false, as in fact do Mondrian's own architectural experiments. His project for a 'Salon for Mme B... in Dresden' and his set design for Michel Seuphor's play *L'Ephemère est éternel* (both 1926) are little more than Mondrian paintings adapted to three dimensions. Such attempts are not to be confused, incidentally, with a 'pure' or 'abstract architecture'. That is something quite different, and perfectly valid, as Mies van der Rohe's Barcelona Pavilion attests. There, it is not a question of 'art architecture', but of architecture reduced to its essentials – to its essential *function*, the delimitation of a habitable space.

All art, according to Judd, must be both particular and general, thus bringing us right back to the discussion of particulars and universals with which this chapter began. He writes:

> Art is simultaneously particular and general. This a real dichotomy. The great thing about proportion, one aspect of art, is that it is both extremes at once. The level of quality of a work can usually be established by the extent of the polarity between its generality and its particularity ... The nature of the general aspects and the particular ones changes from artist to artist and especially from time to time, since the changes are due to broad changes in philosophy ... When the change is progress it reflects the increasing scientific knowledge and the improved values in society. And when the change is not progress, it reflects increasing ignorance and a decline ... In fact, now, art has been declining for fifteen years, following architecture which has already sunk into musical comedy ... A good building, such as the Kimbell Museum, looks the way a Greek temple in a new colony must have looked among the huts ... The temple looks like civilization. The Kimbell is civilization in the wasteland of Fort Worth and Dallas. The Seagram is that in New York.[53]

He defends De Stijl's goal of generalizing – of achieving a coherent language of abstract form across the arts – but at the same time cites a good example of the debasement of painting (in fact a Mondrian painting) into kitsch, by transposing it directly into a useful object:

> I consider the attempted coherence, more breadth than coherence, of De Stijl, the Bauhaus and the Constructivists as live, as normal, and not oppressive ... The three groups did something

53. D. Judd, 'Art and Architecture' (1983), in *Donald Judd: Complete Writings*, p. 34.

tremendous. They didn't impose their work upon the world. On the contrary everyone used and debased their designs. I once went aboard the old Queen Mary or Elizabeth ... One large salon was laid with linoleum that had a design taken from Mondrian. The floor cost more than the four hundred dollars that Sidney Janis paid Mondrian for *Trafalgar Square*.[54]

The balance between the general and the particular must always be maintained. The general cannot be pushed beyond the limit at which it goes over into complete universality without destroying the work altogether, because that balance is lost. The pursuit of absolute universality must end in non-existence, as the Buddhists teach. That is the paradox of De Stijl, and of all abstract art. Every work of art, however abstract, is a tangible material object. As such, it belongs inescapably to the world of particular appearances. If it aims, nevertheless, to represent the world of universal ideas, it can only 'point to' that world; it cannot belong to it. At best, it can be something like the diagram that a student of geometry might use to represent a concept in pure mathematics, as Plato describes in the *Republic*:

> You also know how they make use of visible figures and discourse about them, though what they have in mind is the originals of which these figures are images: they are not reasoning, for instance, about this particular square and diagonal which they have drawn, but about *the* Square and *the* Diagonal; and so in all cases. The diagrams they draw and the models they make are actual things, which may [in their turn] have their shadows or images in water; but now they serve in their turn as images, while the student is seeking to behold those realities which only thought can apprehend.[55]

Like Judd, Mondrian was well aware that although the new representation or neoplasticism aimed at the universal, the precarious balance between the universal and the individual (particular) must be maintained if there was to be art at all. He predicted that

> If ever the universal becomes dominant, it will so permeate life that art – so unreal in comparison with that life – will decay, and *a new life* will take its place, one that truly realizes the universal. The universal finds its purest, most direct representational [*beeldende*] expression *in art* only when there is a balanced relation in the awareness of the age between the individual and the universal, because in *representation [beelding]* the individual can incorporate

54. D. Judd, 'Art and Architecture' (1987), p. 196.
55. Plato, *Republic*, p. 220.

the universal. By means of art the universal is able to manifest itself, without being bound to the individual (to individual existence). Art – although an end in itself – is like religion, a means by which we can know the universal – that is, observe it in its representation [beelding].[56]

To return to our starting point: no matter how 'universal' may be the design of my chair or my table (or my painting), it remains a particular thing, which I know through my sense-impressions. If in my pursuit of universality I try to push the design beyond the limits of the general, it ceases to be a question of making a visible substitute for the abstract idea, but remains that idea, confined to the realm of pure thought. Consequently no work of art can materialize. The universal chair is no chair at all, but only the possibility of sitting; the universal house is no house, merely the piece of personal space that surrounds each of us wherever we are; the universal painting is a blank canvas, or even the absence of a canvas. Malevich's *White on white* (c.1918), Mondrian's *Composition with two black lines* (1931) (Figure 3.9), like the more recent work of Donald Judd, Agnes Martin and others, carry the search for the universal about as far as it can go.

The pursuit of the minimum, of absolute simplicity, is a quest for that elusive holy grail, the universal. In this respect, as Judd recognized, minimalist art is the heir of Mondrian, of Malevich and above all of Mies van der Rohe, who coined the phrase 'less is more'. Mondrian states explicitly that the means by which the new painting can arrive at the representation of the universal is the reduction of the elements of painting to their greatest possible geometric rigour and chromatic definition:

> To make colour definite involves, first, *the reduction of natural colour to primary colour*, second, *reduction of colour to flatness* and third, *the delimitation of colour – so that it appears as a unity of rectangular planes* ... Painting has found this *new* plasticity by *reducing* the representation *[beelding]* of *the corporeality of things to a composition of planes, which give the illusion of lying on a single plane*. These planes, both by their dimension (line) and their values (colour), are able to represent space *[ruimte te beelden]* without expressing it through visual perspective ... If the bounding of form comes about through the *closed line* (contour), then this must be tautened into the *straight line* ... Thus, finally, in the *rectangular* plane, colour is defined a third time, completely.[57]

Like tightrope walkers, Mondrian and Judd explore just how far one can approach absolute simplicity and universality without

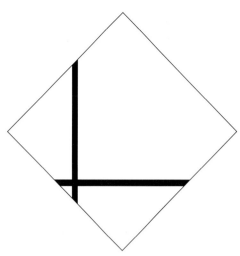

Figure 3.9 Piet Mondrian, *Composition with two black lines*, 1931

56. Mondrian, 'De nieuwe beelding', in *De Stijl*, vol. I, no. 5, March 1918, pp. 51–2.
57. P. Mondrian, 'De nieuwe beelding', in *De Stijl*, vol. I, nos. 3–4, January–February 1918, pp. 29 & 42–3.

exceeding the bounds imposed by the need to make a particular object that exists in the here and now. The fact that this exploration involves risk is what makes such work interesting rather than boring. However apparently simple a work may be, its simplicity can only be relative, not absolute. The making of an ordered thing always involves a certain complexity. For complexity is not the opposite of order, as is often supposed, but an indispensable ingredient of order. Without a certain degree of complexity, no order is possible, and therefore no art.

Moreover, just as complexity is not opposed to order, Judd points out that it is also not a true contrary of simplicity: 'Complicated ... is the opposite of simple, not complex, which both can be.'[58] To complicate is to confuse, mix up; to be complex is to be composite, composed of related parts; and to order is to arrange things so that they do relate as parts of a whole. However, the dictionary defines simple as 'not compound, consisting of one element ... not divided into parts'.[59] Therefore, despite Judd's observation that the simple can also be complex, the search for perfect simplicity, and thereby of absolute universality, is doomed to failure. In Agnes Martin's words:

> We must surrender the idea that this perfection that we see in our mind or before our eyes is obtainable or attainable. It is really far from us. We are no more capable of having it than the infant that tries to eat it. But our happiness lies in our moments of awareness of it. The function of artwork is the stimulation of sensibilities. The renewal of memories of moments of perfection.[60]

Those words describe, better than all the theorizings of Van Doesburg and Mondrian, the actual achievement of De Stijl.

58. Judd, 'On furniture', p. 107.
59. Concise Oxford Dictionary.
60. A. Martin, handwritten lecture notes, in Abstraction – Geometry – Painting, ed. M. Auping, Harry N. Abrams, New York, 1989, p. 166.

4

The Pavilion and the Court[1]

4.1 Encounters

On 15 October 1923, excusing himself for the fact that he had come straight from a building site and had had no time to shave or change out of his muddy clothes,[2] a gaunt, bespectacled man arrived to attend the opening of an architectural exhibition at the Parisian art gallery *L'Effort Moderne*. The exhibition had been organized by the leader of the De Stijl group, Theo van Doesburg. The visitor, as is well known, was Le Corbusier. Both were 'universal men' in the renaissance tradition – painters, writers, designers, and editors of avant-garde reviews – and both fed on controversy and confrontation. Six years before, in the same year that Van Doesburg had founded the magazine and movement *De Stijl*, Le Corbusier had left Switzerland, settled in Paris and joined forces with the painter Amedée Ozenfant, who had recently launched another movement: 'purism'. Together, they had published *Après le cubisme* in 1918, and founded the magazine *L'Esprit Nouveau* in 1920. In 1922 Le Corbusier had built his first houses since leaving Switzerland – a villa at Vaucresson and a studio for Ozenfant – and produced a project for 'a contemporary city for three million inhabitants'. Both houses were basically simple cubes – 'pure prisms' – and the *ville contemporaine* was an ideal city as symmetrical and axial as Versailles.

Van Doesburg had only recently established himself in Paris, having spent most of the previous two years in Germany, where he had been instrumental in helping to bring about a revolution within the Bauhaus, and had come into contact, and conflict, with Mies van der Rohe. Both Le Corbusier and Mies were profoundly affected by their encounters with Van Doesburg and De Stijl, and everything they designed in the succeeding period, 1923–9, is in one way or another infected with the De Stijl idea. This chapter will focus on two buildings, both designed in 1929, which represent the final resolution of their response to and conflict with De Stijl: the Villa Savoye and the Barcelona Pavilion. In another sense, however, one can say that these conflicts have never been resolved, or that the resolution achieved in 1929 was only illusory. The problem which was tackled at Poissy and Barcelona is fundamental to the debate about the validity of the modern movement as a whole.

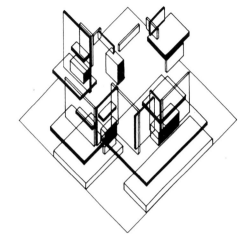

Figure 4.1 Theo van Doesburg, counter-construction based on private house project, 1923

1.   This chapter is an edited and expanded version of the article first published in the *Architectural Review*, December 1981, pp. 359–68.

2.   R. Blijstra, *C. van Eesteren*, Meulenhoff, Amsterdam, 1971, p. 8; the reference is taken from Van Eesteren's journal.

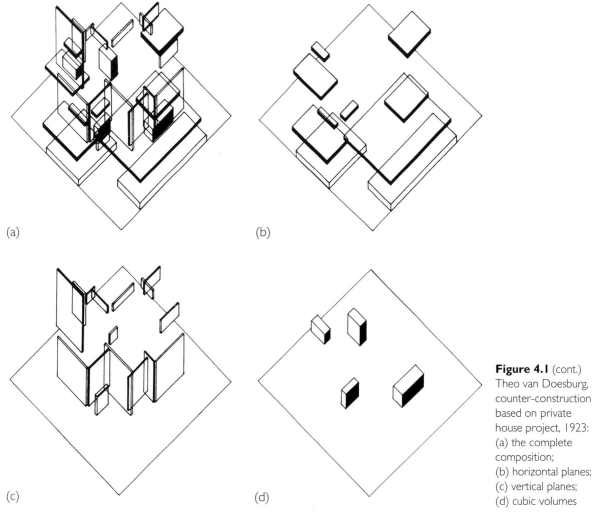

(a)

(b)

(c)

(d)

Figure 4.1 (cont.)
Theo van Doesburg,
counter-construction
based on private
house project, 1923:
(a) the complete
composition;
(b) horizontal planes;
(c) vertical planes;
(d) cubic volumes

4.2 Three house projects

Although the exhibition at *L'Effort Moderne* included work by other
members, ex-members and non-members of the De Stijl group (J.J.P.
Oud, Jan Wils, Willem van Leusden, Vilmos Huszar and Mies van der
Rohe), it was dominated by the drawings and models illustrating
three house projects designed by Van Doesburg himself in collaboration with the architect Cor van Eesteren. The first of these, made in
response to a commission from the gallery owner, Léonce
Rosenberg, and apparently substantially designed by Van Eesteren
before he joined Van Doesburg in Paris,[3] was the most conventional:
externally a rather loose, extended arrangement of interlocking
cubes, internally a series of self-contained rooms on clearly separated

3. J. Baljeu, *Theo van Doesburg*, Studio Vista, London, 1974, p. 58.

floors. The second, a private house with similar accommodation, which seems to have resulted from a closer and more equal cooperation,[4] was a far more compact and tightly organized design, arranged pivotally around a central hall from which the living spaces were spun out centrifugally. Van Doesburg explored the implications of the design in a series of analytical 'counter-constructions' (Figure 4.1a–d) in which the solid volumes were dissolved into floating, interpenetrating coloured planes. According to Van Eesteren the third design, for a studio house, was largely the work of Van Doesburg alone;[5] in it he carried further the three-dimensional interpenetration of spaces and volumes and use of colour, and introduced a frame and panel construction that gave a clear separation of the functions of support and enclosure.

4.3 Tent and pavilion

Although to attribute these designs to the direct influence of Frank Lloyd Wright would be unjustified, they can be linked at a deeper level with Wright's prairie houses of 1900–12. Whereas in the first phase of De Stijl architecture Van't Hoff, Wils and Oud had used borrowings from Wright in designs which were otherwise still relatively conventional, the private house and the studio house seem to go back beyond Wright to the same ground on which his work was rooted: to the primitive shelter isolated in open space. Wright held up the ideal of the nomad's tent in opposition to the cave and the protective walls within which the static, conservative city-dweller sought refuge:

> An idea ... that shelter should be the essential look of any dwelling put the low spreading roof ... with generously projecting eaves over the whole. I began to see building primarily not as a cave but as a broad shelter in the open.[6]

The tent (*papilionem*) or pavilion is the most primitive, pre-urban house-type – the type from which all other types are probably derived. Spatially, it represents unlimited expansion outwards from a concentrated focal point: the hearth, Wright's 'fire burning deep in the solid masonry of the house itself'. The development of house-forms from the centrifugal, multi-directional pavilion type – first the elongated uni-directional *megaron* and later the introspective, centripetal court-house – was a movement from exposure to enclosure, and from the loose clustering of relatively small numbers of individual family units to the city and the state.

4. *Ibid.*, p. 60.
5. *Ibid.*, p. 62.
6. F.L. Wright, *The Natural House*, Horizon Press, New York, 1954; p. 16 in Mentor edition, 1963.

It is significant that the ideal of the primitive hut and the cottage was revived in the mid-eighteenth century, at the moment when, with the breakdown of the syncretic, centralizing system of the baroque, European culture was beginning to polarize into two opposed but complementary ideals: Jean-Jacques Rousseau's cult of the romantic individual, increasingly aware of his isolation and autonomy, and the rational, scientific approach to the objective world represented by the *Encyclopédie* of Jean d'Alembert and Denis Diderot. Marc-Antoine Laugier published his *Essai sur l'architecture* in 1753, two years after the first volumes of the *Encyclopédie*, and with the aim of providing architecture with a systematic theoretical foundation such as already existed for the sciences. Yet in basing his theory on a hypothetical 'natural' state of man and on the building of the first *petite cabane rustique* he also paralleled Rousseau, whose *Discourse on the Origins of Inequality*, with its strikingly similar description of man – 'just as he must have come from the hands of nature ... satisfying his hunger at the first oak, and slaking his thirst at the first brook; finding his bed at the foot of the tree which afforded him a repast; and, with that, all his wants supplied'[7] – appeared in the same year. Fifty years later Claude-Nicolas Ledoux illustrated the publication of his works with an engraving showing a naked man seated under a tree – *L'abri du pauvre*. There is clearly a link between the ideal of the primal hut that lies at the root of neoclassical architecture and Rousseau's concept of the natural man and the free society. Rousseau's definition of the social contract as 'a form of association ... in which each, while uniting himself with all, may still obey himself alone, and remain as free as before'[8] is paraphrased almost exactly in Emil Kaufmann's description of the 'pavilion system' as an architecture in which 'the part is free within the framework of the context'.[9]

4.4 Romanticism and the pavilion system

In his book *Von Ledoux bis Le Corbusier* (1933) Kaufmann writes:

In classic-baroque art all the parts had been intimately connected, almost fused together. Now the parts are united, while each maintaining its own autonomy ... The new principle of independence of the parts constituted the most important step in the process of architectural renewal during the late eighteenth century ... The age sought and found the justification of its ideas in nature itself, from which Rousseau claimed to be able to derive the principles of society, and Ledoux those of art. Ledoux explained the

7. J.J. Rousseau, 'A discourse on the origin of inequality', in *The Social Contract and Discourses*, J M Dent & Sons, London, 1913, p. 163.
8. J.J. Rousseau, 'The social contract', in *Social Contract and Discourses*, p. 12.
9. E. Kaufmann, *Da Ledoux a Le Corbusier*, Gabriele Mazzotta, Milan, 1973, p. 40.

separation of the buildings in his second project for Chaux with the words: 'Return to first principles ... consult Nature; man is everywhere in isolation.'[10]

At the end of the eighteenth century the pavilion model, symbol of the romantic ideals of closeness to nature, personal freedom and romantic love, was transformed into the picturesque suburban villa, and has remained the dream and often the reality of the modern house throughout the world. The continuity of this ideal can be traced through the eighteenth and nineteenth centuries to Wright:

1753   Marc-Antoine Laugier: *Essai sur l'architecture*

1778   Claude-Nicolas Ledoux: project for Chaux

1803   John Nash: Blaise Hamlet, Bristol

1817   Thomas Jefferson: University of Virginia, Charlottesville

1818   John Buonarotti Papworth: *Rural Residences*

1829   Karl Friedrich Schinkel: Charlottenhof, Potsdam

1854   Henry David Thoreau: *Walden*

1869   Frederick Law Olmsted and Calvert Vaux: plan for Riverside, Illinois

1876   Edward W. Godwin, R. Norman Shaw and others: Bedford Park, London

1891   William Morris: *News from Nowhere*

1898   Ebenezer Howard: *Tomorrow*

1902   Frank Lloyd Wright: Ward Willits house, Highland Park, Illinois

The Van Doesburg/Van Eesteren projects are linked to this development not only on account of their nuclear, centrifugal character, but also specifically because of the De Stijl principles of *independence of the parts* and *interpenetration*, which Kaufmann discerned as one of the principal patterns of 'antithesis' in revolutionary architecture:

The pattern of interpenetration can be visualized either by the crossing of masses, or by volume (space) intruding into mass. Interpenetration was almost exclusively a spatial pattern. It played an important part in the nineteenth century, and like the other patterns of antithesis it plays a still greater role in our time.[11]

10. *Ibid.*, p. 93.

11. E. Kaufmann, *Architecture in the Age of Reason*, Dover Publications, New York, 1955, p.189.

De Stijl statements were often designed to repudiate any connection with romanticism or individualism. The 'First Manifesto of De Stijl' begins: 'There exist an old and a new consciousness of the age. The old is directed towards the individual. The new is directed towards the universal.'[12] Like Marinetti, Van Doesburg specifically attacked 'the old culture, the culture of Jean-Jacques Rousseau, the culture of the heart, the cultureless culture of the petit-bourgeois intelligentsia and its long-haired apostles Morris and Ruskin, the concentric culture, the culture of the "I" and "Mine".'[13]

And in the manifesto 'Towards a Collective Construction' (probably written to support the 1923 exhibition, but not published until this was incorporated in a larger show at the *Ecole Spéciale d'Architecture* in 1924[14]) Van Doesburg and Van Eesteren declared:

Our age is the enemy of all subjective speculation in art, science, technique, etc. The new spirit which already governs almost the whole of modern life is against animal spontaneity (lyricism), against the domination of nature, against coiffure and cuisine in art.[15]

Yet, conclusive though these disclaimers appear, the reality was more complicated. De Stijl had its roots in the same ferment of mysticist-communitarian idealism that produced the Amsterdam School, and which was typified by the magazine *Eenheid* (*Unity*) to which Van Doesburg contributed regularly from 1912, by the theosophist beliefs of Mondrian, and by the political idealism that eventually led Van't Hoff (a member of the Dutch Communist Party) to give up architecture in order to work for a better society.[16] Van Doesburg himself was a complex and apparently self-contradictory personality. His alter egos I.K. Bonset and Aldo Camini, far from being extraneous or schizoid manifestations, were integral elements in a total vision which also showed itself in his close association with dada, his friendship with Kurt Schwitters and Hans Arp, and the essentially *destructive* basis of his 'counter-compositions'.

In reality De Stijl, rather than opposing romanticism and individualism, sought to transcend them. The central theme of Mondrian's essay 'The New Representation *[De Nieuwe Beelding]* in Painting' is the achievement of equilibrium between the individual and the universal, between nature and spirit: 'The new culture will be that of the *mature individual*; once matured, the individual will be open to the universal and will tend more and more to unite with it.'[17] And: 'Our age forms the great turning point: humanity will *no longer move from individual to universal, but from the universal to the individual through*

12. 'Manifest I van "De Stijl", 1918', in *De Stijl*, vol. II no. 1, 1918, p. 2.
13. T. van Doesburg, 'Moderne wendigen in de kunstonderwijs', in *De Stijl*, vol. II, no. 9, 1919, p. 103.
14. Y.-A. Bois and N. Troy, 'De Stijl et l'architecture à Paris', in *De Stijl et l'architecture en France*, Pierre Mardaga, Brussels, 1985, p. 50.
15. T. van Doesburg and C. van Eesteren, 'Vers une construction collective', in *De Stijl*, vol. VI, no. 6/7, pp. 89–90; reprinted in H.L.C. Jaffé, *De Stijl*, Thames & Hudson, London, 1970, p. 191.
16. E. Vermeulen, 'Robert van't Hoff', in *De Beginjaren van De Stijl*, Reflex, Utrecht, 1982, pp. 210 and 228.
17. P. Mondrian, 'De nieuwe beelding in de schilderkunst', in *De Stijl*, vol. I, no. 2, p. 17; reprinted in H.L.C. Jaffé, *De Stijl*, Thames & Hudson, 1970, p. 53.

which it can be realized. For the individual becomes *real* only when it is transformed to universality.'[18]

But Van Doesburg saw that this equilibrium could never be static; as soon as it was achieved it had to be destroyed and re-created:

> If the tension between extreme opposites, as we conceive them – for instance the polarity of nature/spirit – is neutralized through a satisfactory plastic equilibrium, then, due to the ineluctible need for evolution, it is still necessary to establish a new point of view to this equilibrium. If this were not so, then the spirit would become crippled within the established equilibrium and would represent a dead end.[19]

As Oud wrote after Van Doesburg's death, 'he was possessed by an idea; the impulse to renewal was the force which drove him'.[20]

4.5 Le Corbusier, classical architect

Le Corbusier, by contrast, stood in 1923 for the static, eternal values of classicism. Although a native of La Chaux-de-Fonds, with its strong anarchist tradition and associations with Rousseau, Bakunin and Kropotkin, by 1910 he had rejected, following the experiences of working for Perret and Behrens and his travels through Italy and Greece, the arts and crafts/art nouveau ideals of his master L'Eplattenier.[21] The ideals that animate his books *Vers une architecture* (1923) and *Urbanisme* (1924) are on the one hand the classical urban tradition, and on the other the machine and its products. The Delage *Grand-Sport* 1921 was confronted with the Parthenon: 'A standard is necessary for order in human effort ... Culture is the flowering of the effort to select. Selection means rejection, pruning, cleansing; the clear and naked emergence of the Essential.'[22]

In a diagram in *Urbanisme*, Le Corbusier opposed the eternal classical values (the primary geometry of the square, the triangle and the sphere) to the 'barbarism' of a gothic cathedral or Robert van't Hoff's craggy design for a newel-post.[23] He declared:

> This modern sentiment is a spirit of geometry, a spirit of construction and synthesis. Exactitude and order are its essential condition ... With what astonishment do we regard the spasmodic and disordered impulses of Romanticism! ... We prefer Bach to Wagner, and the spirit that inspired the Pantheon to that which created the cathedral. We love the *solution*, and we are uneasy at the sight of failures, however grandiose or dramatic. We behold

18.   Mondrian, 'De nieuwe beelding, in *De Stijl*, vol. I, no. 11, p. 128; reprinted in Jaffé, *De Stijl*, p. 185.

19.   T. van Doesburg, 'Van kompositie tot contra-kompositie', in *De Stijl*, vol. VII, no. 73/74, 1926, p. 25; reprinted in Jaffé, *De Stijl*, p. 204.

20.   J.J.P. Oud, in *De Stijl*, final number, 1932, p. 47.

21.   The key period was probably that spent working for Behrens between November 1910 and April 1911; cf. Chapter 7; also H. Allen Brooks, *Le Corbusier's Formative Years*, University of Chicago Press, 1997, pp. 209–53.

22.   Le Corbusier, *Towards a New Architecture*, The Architectural Press, London, 1946, pp. 125, 128.

23.   Published twice in *De Stijl*: in vol. I, no. 6, April 1918, and in the retrospective issue, vol. V, no. 12, December 1922.

with enthusiasm the noble plan of Babylon and we pay homage to the clear mind of Louis XIV; we take his age as a landmark and consider the *Grand Roy* the first Western townplanner since the Romans.[24]

Not surprisingly – especially in view of what Yve-Alain Bois and Nancy Troy call the long and intimate enmity (*'une longue et intime inimitié'*[25]) between himself and Van Doesburg – Le Corbusier's attitude to the De Stijl works in the exhibition at *L'Effort Moderne* was that they were the products of a 'rudely simple' and barbarous aesthetic. The event was barely acknowledged in the pages of *L'Esprit Nouveau*; Le Corbusier finally broke his silence, however, in an article published in 1924 after the works had been transferred to the exhibition at the *Ecole Spéciale*:

After the initial flourish we encounter here, of multiple forms pushing against one another, of craggy and tormented silhouettes, creating at first the effect of a rich architectural sensation, the time will come when it will be realized that light is more generous with a simple prism. Then this complexity, this abusive richness, these exuberant forms, will become disciplined under the shield of pure form. One will know that the whole possesses a greater value than five or ten parts. This tendency towards the pure envelope which covers abundance with a mask of simplicity, can be the only outcome. We can afford to wait.[26]

This was not merely a negative reaction provoked by rivalry, but the affirmation of a principle that was central to Le Corbusier's attitude to architectural space in the early 1920s. The following year he would use an almost identical language in a letter to his client Mme Meyer:

We aim to build you a house as smooth and uniform as a beautifully proportioned chest, unbroken by a multiplicity of features which create an artificial and illusory picturesqueness but respond badly to light and merely add to the surrounding tumult. We are opposed to the prevailing fashion both here and abroad for houses with complex and craggy outlines. We believe that the whole is stronger than the parts.[27]

24. Le Corbusier, *The City of Tomorrow* (1924), The Architectural Press, London, 1971, pp. 44–5.

25. Bois and Troy, 'De Stijl et l'architecture à Paris', p. 55.

26. Le Corbusier, 'L'exposition de l'Ecole spéciale d'architecture', in *L'Esprit Nouveau*, no. 23, May 1924, quoted in B. Reichlin, 'Le Corbusier vs. De Stijl', in *De Stijl et l'architecture en France*, Pierre Mardaga, Brussels, 1985, p. 106.

27. Le Corbusier, letter to Mme Meyer, Paris, October 1925; printed in *Le Corbusier et Pierre Jeanneret 1910–1929*, Girsberger, Zurich, 1956, p. 89.

4.6 Van Doesburg's architectural programme

In 1924 Van Doesburg countered with the manifesto 'Towards a Representational *[Beeldende]* Architecture', which is the most complete summary of the architectural aims of De Stijl. Its fifth and eleventh points are a direct repudiation of Le Corbusier's principle of the 'shield of pure form':

Figure 4.2 Concave (centripetal) and convex (centrifugal) compositions contrasted (after Van Doesburg)

> (5) The new architecture ... does not recognize any predetermined aesthetic formal schema, no mould (such as pastrycooks use), into which it casts the functional spaces ... (11) It does not strive to contain the various functional space-cells within a single closed cube, but throws them outwards ... from the core of the cube.[28]

The Van Doesburg archive in The Hague contains several versions of a diagram which appears to illustrate this principle (Figure 4.2). It contrasts a contained, centripetal composition, like that employed by Le Corbusier (left), with the centrifugal development of space outwards from a central core that characterized the private house and the studio house (right). Together with the idea of spatial continuity, this concept can be linked both to Wright and to futurism. Boccioni stated in the 'Technical Manifesto of Futurist Sculpture' (1912) that

> We must take the object which we wish to create and begin with its central core. In this way we shall uncover new laws and new forms which link it invisibly but mathematically to an EXTERNAL PLASTIC INFINITY and an INTERNAL PLASTIC INFINITY.[29]

Compare this with Van Doesburg's fifth point:

> The subdivision of functional spaces is strictly determined by rectangular planes which ... can be conceived as extended to infinity, thereby creating a system of coordinates, of which the various points correspond to an equal number of points in universal, limitless space.[30]

The contrast between Le Corbusier's and Van Doesburg's conceptions of architectural space is paralleled in purist and De Stijl painting. Both stemmed from cubism, but developed it in opposite directions: whereas Ozenfant and Jeanneret (Le Corbusier) based their paintings on proportional frameworks (*tracées régulateurs*)

28. T. van Doesburg, 'Tot een beeldende architectuur', in *De Stijl*, vol. VI, no. 6/7, pp. 79, 81; reprinted in Jaffé, *De Stijl*, pp. 185 & 186.
29. U. Boccioni, 'Technical manifesto of futurist sculpture', in *Poesia*, Milan, 11 April 1912; reprinted in U. Apollonio, *Futurist Manifestos*, Thames & Hudson, London, 1973, p. 52.
30. Van Doesburg, 'Tot een beeldende architectuur', in *De Stijl*, vol. VI, no. 6/7, p. 79; reprinted in Jaffé, *De Stijl*, p. 185.

which they filled out by inserting realistic objects (*objets-types*) (Figure 4.3), Mondrian developed his analytical cubism away from representation towards total abstraction by paring away the object to lay bare the structure underlying it. In a purist painting the abstract structure functioned as a scaffolding for the realistic subject-matter that it supported; in a painting by Mondrian, Van der Leck or Van Doesburg the structure grew out of the subject-matter itself through the process of abstraction, and subject-matter finally became superfluous. In one the object was contained by the frame, in the other the frame was the remaining skeleton of an object which had been dissolved away.

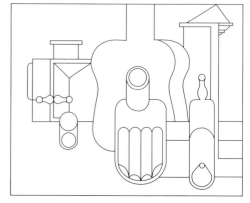

Figure 4.3 C.-E. Jeanneret (Le Corbusier), *Composition à la guitare et à la lanterne*, 1920

4.7 Standardization

De Stijl and purism were also diametrically opposed on the question of standardization, which had dominated architectural discussion since the formation of the Deutscher Werkbund in 1907. Le Corbusier's admiration for the typewriter, the telephone and the mass-production house went back to his experience with Behrens and to the Werkbund Congress of 1911, where Muthesius had said: 'More than any other art, architecture strives for the typical. Only in this can it find fulfilment.'[31]

In Holland, the argument for standardization had been put forward by Berlage at the National Housing Congress held in Amsterdam in 1918:

> The idea of standardization, which simply means order, regulation, the bringing of measure and rule where order is lacking, as such is intrinsic to man ... The repetition of a standard motif is a primary aesthetic principle ... It is ... the rhythmic unfolding of series of dwellings, the continuity of the street façade, which constitutes the spatial element in the architecture of the modern city.[32]

Oud, a close friend of Berlage, put forward identical views in the articles which he contributed to *De Stijl* in 1917–18, in particular 'The Monumental Image of the City'[33] and 'Architecture and Standardization in Mass-construction'.[34] The divergence between his views and those of Van Doesburg would have been enough in itself to make Oud's eventual break with De Stijl inevitable,[35] and even his work of the De Stijl period, with its reliance on symmetry and repetition, is impossible to reconcile with 'Towards a Representational Architecture' – particularly its twelfth point:

31. H. Muthesius, 'Wo stehen wir?', address to Werkbund Congress, 1911, quoted in R Banham, *Theory and Design in the First Machine Age*, The Architectural Press, London, 1960, p. 75.
32. H.P. Berlage, 'Normalisatie in woningbouw', 1918; quoted in Casciato/Panzini/Polano (eds), *Funzione e Senso: Architettura – Casa – Città. Olanda 1870–1940*, Electa, Milan, 1979, pp. 65–6.
33. J.J.P. Oud, 'Het monumentale stadsbeeld', in *De Stijl*, vol. I, no. 1, October 1917, pp. 10–1; reprinted in Jaffé, *De Stijl*, pp. 95–6.
34. J.J.P. Oud, 'Architectuur en normalisatie bij den massabouw', in *De Stijl*, vol. I, no. 7, May 1918, pp. 77–9.
35. In fact, Oud left the De Stijl group in 1922.

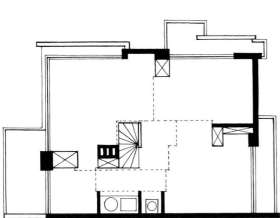

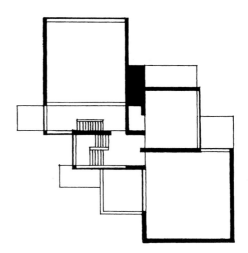

Figure 4.4 Gerrit Rietveld, Schröder house, Utrecht, 1924: upper floor plan

Figure 4.5 Theo van Doesburg and Cor van Eesteren, private house project, 1923: plan

The new architecture has destroyed both monotonous repetition and the rigid similarity of two halves, the mirror image, symmetry. It recognizes neither repetition in time or the street façade, nor standardization. A group of buildings is as much a whole as a free-standing house. The same laws apply to both the building complex and to the city as to the single house. Against symmetry the new architecture sets the *balanced proportion of unequal parts* – that is, of parts which because of their contrasting functional character differ in posture, measure, ratio and position.[36]

4.8 The Schröder house, Utrecht, 1924

Van Doesburg's twelfth point brings us straight back to Rousseau: the idea of the unique, unrepeatable single unit that nevertheless forms part of a harmonious, unified street or city exactly parallels the concept of the individual who remains perfectly free while united with society. It was this ideal of a continuous yet continuously defined and differentiated space that Rietveld attempted to realize in the house that he designed for and in collaboration with Mrs Schröder in Utrecht in 1924 (Figure 4.4). The Schröder house was built in the year of publication of Van Doesburg's manifesto, and it was a conscious attempt to put into practice the centrifugal spatial concept of the house projects exhibited the previous year.

Study of the Van Doesburg/Van Eesteren projects (Figure 4.5) reveals that in fact they have less spatial continuity than Le Corbusier achieved, for instance, in his house for Mme Meyer. Externally, colour

36. Van Doesburg, 'Tot een beeldende architectuur', in *De Stijl*, vol. VI, no. 6/7, p. 81; reprinted in Jaffé, *De Stijl*, p. 187.

is used to create an illusion, which Van Doesburg's analytical axonometrics tend to exaggerate, of planes floating independently in space (Figure 4.1). The reality, however, is very different. The whole plan is contained within a perfect square (Figure 4.6). Within this, the external envelope is broken up into a complex assemblage of over-lapping and intersecting volumes; but these, too, are found to contain an equal number of closed, squarish boxes. Only balconies and cano-pies project as pure planes. Despite – or more accurately, *because of* – the complex 'openness' of the exterior form, each interior space is imprisoned within its own projecting volume.

Le Corbusier realized that an open architectural composition must have a clearly defined frame (even if an implied or partially invis-ible one) if it is not to disintegrate. All architecture depends on at least an implied polarity between interior and exterior space, without which the very possibility of perceiving the space is removed (see Chapter 7). Thus the elimination of the separateness of the interior and exterior, which Van Doesburg demanded in the eighth point of his manifesto, can never be complete. Significantly, he found it neces-sary to draw an imaginary cube around the 'anti-cubic' form in his diagram (Figures 4.2), so that its centrifugality is in fact contained within a hypothetical closed prism. Without this notional contain-ment its openness would be meaningless and ineffectual.

The Schröder house presented Rietveld with the same problem of reconciling an open, floating external expression with the need for a functionally and aesthetically viable interior space. Photographs of the first sketch model and the intermediate development drawings reveal his hard struggle to give an open expression to the essentially box-like plan demanded by the need for interior flexibility. The marvellous fluidity and adaptability which Rietveld achieved within the small dimensions of the house[37] are partly due to the fact that the whole interior space is in fact contained, in contrast to the 1923 projects, within a taut rectangular envelope – in reality, if not in appearance, a Corbusian 'simple prism'. In obedience to De Stijl theory the exterior is dissected visually by the use of coloured planes – white, off-white and grey – cantilevered eaves and balconies, and free-standing columns. Otherwise, nothing projects more than a few inches beyond the surface of the cube. The effect of suspension and openness is attained by a brilliant illusion, a conjuror's sleight of hand.

The open-planned first-floor living space (Figures 4.4) is really of greater interest than the more famous exterior. It provides a total flexibility which perfectly responded to Mrs Schröder's detailed func-tional requirements: as a house to live in, it was for her ideal. The space is differentiated, by means of built-in furniture and sliding

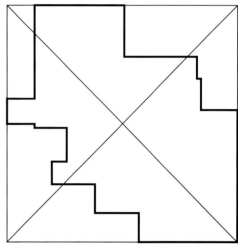

Figure 4.6 Private house plan showing containment within a square

---

37. The overall internal dimensions are 9.5 × 7.0 m.

screens, and by controlled light effects achieved by varied window design, so that it becomes not one uniform space but a collection of intercommunicating *spaces*, each with its own distinctive character and function and subtly implied boundaries. El Lissitzky wrote after visiting the Schröder house that 'cupboards, sofa-beds and tables are arranged like houses in a town in such a way that there are areas for movement and use as if they were streets and squares'.[38]

Rietveld later described the boundary as the starting point of architecture, but his concept of it was the opposite of a total separation. He recognized it as an identifying and linking element, and saw that this always outweighs its purely divisive or protective functions (see Chapter 1, section 1.6). Rietveld was never, even in his *nieuwe zakelijk* period in the 1930s, a functionalist in the narrow utilitarian sense. He realized that the ultimate purpose of architecture is existential: it gives coherence and intelligibility to the world in which we live, through the establishment of a clearly defined and comprehensible system of spatial relations:

> The continuation and growth of our existence depends on direct and actively focussed sensory experience. Sculpture is necessary to us in order that we can experience our sense of form as clarity. We need sculpture that is made without aesthetic or idealistic intentions or symbolic connotations, but merely in order to experience reality more directly ... In the same way, architecture too can bring us to reality. Functional *[zakelijke]* architecture must ... help us to simplify life, to liberate it from superfluities ... Functional architecture must not content itself with slavishly satisfying existing requirements; it must also reveal the conditions of life. It must not be merely the record of space, but the intense experience of it. *Space is the reality which architecture can shape.*[39]

Despite the illusionistic quality of the exterior of the Schröder house, it is a highly effective realization of the De Stijl principle of non-repetition and continuous variation, both in the relationship between its separate elements, and as an individual house in relation to the street and to the town as a whole. For this is not just any house which happens to come at the end of a row – like the end houses in Oud's row of six at the Weissenhofsiedlung. The whole design stems from its special situation as the last house, not only in the row, but on the edge of the town.

Nevertheless, the house ultimately failed to solve the problem posed by Van Doesburg's doctrine of endless variation. If Rietveld had had to design the whole row of houses in the Prins Hendriklaan

38. El Lissitzky, 1926, quoted in T.M. Brown, *The Work of G. Rietveld, Architect*, A W Bruna & Zoon, Utrecht, 1958, p. 58.

39. G. Rietveld, 'Inzicht', in *i10*, vol. II, no. 17–18, 1928, pp. 89–90.

instead of just adding a house to the end of a pre-existing terrace it is hard to see how he could have avoided resorting to either repetition or arbitrary, purely fanciful variation. This was the flaw that Le Corbusier diagnosed in the De Stijl aesthetic: its arbitrariness. Van Eesteren's roughly contemporary design for a row of shops and flats in The Hague, in which Van Doesburg's contribution was restricted to the colour scheme, already reverts, like his town-planning projects of 1925–7 for the Rokin in Amsterdam, Unter den Linden and Paris, to an architecture of mass and repetition. Although the end unit in the row happens to be differentiated by its special function as a café-restaurant, the rest of the block consists of standardized units.

Rietveld himself used repetition in the rows of houses he built at the Wiener Werkbund exhibition and in the Schumannstraat and the Erasmuslaan in Utrecht in 1930–2. And when in the 1950s such heirs of the De Stijl movement as the Opbouw group and Van den Broek and Bakema, as well as Van Eesteren, were faced with the problems of mass housing and the design of whole new quarters like Pendrecht, Alexanderpolder and Slotermeer, they accepted the slab block and the repeated unit, contenting themselves with literally transcribing the formal solutions of De Stijl painting into three dimensions on a vast scale (Figure 4.7). The city was treated like a huge relief sculpture, recalling an abstract composition by Van der Leck (Figure 4.8) or Van Doesburg's *Rhythm of a Russian dance* (Figure 4.9). The pedestrian scale – the scale at which the city is actually experienced by its inhab- itants, that of the individual house and its neighbours – was completely ignored. The effect of this misinterpretation of the De Stijl aesthetic on urban development and redevelopment in Holland and elsewhere since 1945 has been disastrous.

4.9 Mies van der Rohe and De Stijl

The Schröder house had no real successor in Rietveld's work, at least until his 'second De Stijl phase' in the 1950s. By the time the jubilee number of *De Stijl* was published, in 1927, De Stijl as an architectural movement had in one sense come to an end, with Oud's Café De Unie (1925) and Van Doesburg's Café Aubette (1926–8). The foun- dation of the magazines *i10* and *de 8* in that year, and the building of the Weissenhofsiedlung in Stuttgart, marked the beginning of a new, *sachlich* phase of the modern movement, in which – despite Rietveld's solitary voice calling for a broader, mental and sensory, interpretation of function – its objectives would no longer be aesthetic and spiritual but social and technical.

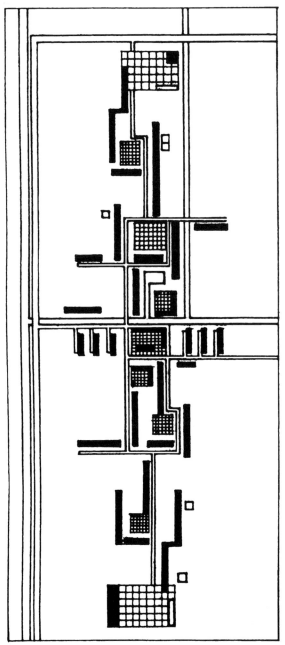

Figure 4.7 Opbouw group with Van den Broek and Bakema, Rotterdam-Alexanderpolder, 1953

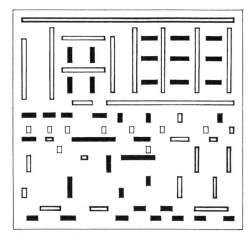

Figure 4.8 Bart van der Leck, *Leaving the factory (Composition 1917, no. 3)*

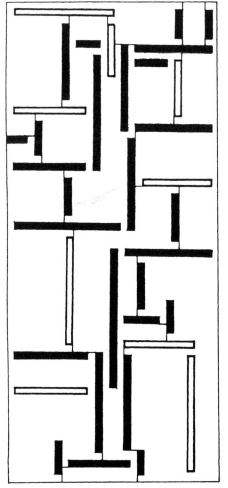

Figure 4.9 Theo van Doesburg, *Rhythm of a Russian dance*, 1918

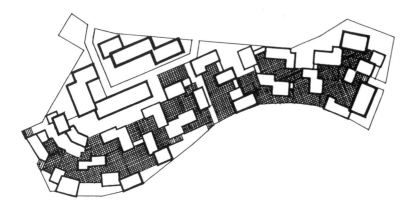

Figure 4.10 Ludwig Mies van der Rohe (or Hugo Häring), early plan for Weissenhofsiedlung, Stuttgart, 1925

Of the two Dutch architects who participated at Weissenhof, Oud had long since broken with De Stijl, while Mart Stam had consistently opposed it in his magazine *ABC*, equating the Van Doesburg/Van Eesteren private house model with Ragnar Østberg's Stockholm Town Hall (1913–23) and Paul Bonatz's Stuttgart Station (1914–22), as examples of 'formalist composition': 'Composition – of cubes, of colours, of materials – is always a makeshift and a weakness. Only functions are important, and should determine form.'[40] And although Van Doesburg acknowledged that 'Thanks to the initiative of the architect Mies van der Rohe ... the collective ideal of a demonstrative exhibition of architecture has been almost completely realized',[41] the closed block-forms and repetitive units of Oud's, Stam's and Mies' own buildings seem to represent the final victory of purism and functionalism over De Stijl. Van Doesburg himself, when he came to build his own house at Meudon two years later, appears to have abandoned the idea of an open, continuous architecture: the house is as prism-like as the *maison Citrohan*, which was one of Le Corbusier's two contributions to Weissenhof.

However, the story is in fact more complex. If one goes back two years to Mies' original, rejected design for Weissenhof,[42] (Figure 4.10) one discovers something that is extraordinarily close to Van Doesburg's conception of the city as 'a balanced relationship of unequal parts' or to Mondrian's vision of '*cities constructed sanely and beautifully by means of a balanced contrast of buildings and empty spaces*'.[43] For the project appears to be conceived, not as an assemblage of separate and self-contained units (which is how it was eventually built) but as an integrated community, a continuous fabric of buildings and terraces interlaced with footways and open squares,

40. M. Stam, in *ABC*, vol. II no. 1, 1926, reproduced in catalogue *Bouwen '20–'40*, Van Abbemuseum, Eindhoven, 1971, p. 59.

41. T. van Doesburg, 'Stuttgart-Weissenhof 1927: Die Wohnung', in *Het Bouwbedrijf*, vol. IV no. 24; reprinted in *Theo van Doesburg: On European Architecture*, Birkhäuser, Basel, 1990, p. 164.

42. P. Blundell-Jones argues in his book *Hugo Häring* (Edition Axel Menges, Stuttgart, 1999, p. 103) that the design, which survives only in photos of a clay model, 'has a distinctly Häringian flavour'; R. Pommer and C.F. Otto, in *Weissenhof 1927 and the Modern Movement in Architecture*, (University of Chicago Press, Chicago, 1991, p. 24), cite correspondence in the MOMA archive confirming that 'Despite Häring's contributions, however, the clay model was attributed from the start to Mies.'

43 P. Mondrian, 'Neo-plasticisme: de woning – de straat – de stad', in *i10*, vol. I, no. 1, 1927, pp. 12–13.

resembling a Mediterranean hill-town: a concrete realization of Mondrian's neoplasticist city, in which

the house will no longer be closed, circumscribed, separate: nor will the street. Despite their different functions, these two elements must form a unity. Hence we must no longer look upon the house as a 'box'. The idea of 'home' (*home, sweet home*) must disappear, as must the conventional idea of 'street'.[44]

The problem, however, is contained in the inviting analogy with a vernacular hill-town. Vernacular architecture is the product of piece-meal growth over a period of time, resulting from additions made by people working spontaneously within an established tradition. To imitate the effects of this organic process in a city quarter designed as a whole is inherently artificial: 'A form born from a process cannot be retrieved without the process sustaining it.'[45] Nevertheless, the design shows Mies to have been one of the most serious, as well as the greatest, contributors to the architecture of De Stijl, and the one who carried forward its development significantly beyond 1927.

Though never a member of the De Stijl group, Mies had close links with it and with Van Doesburg himself through the other contributors to the magazine which he founded and financed: *G*. These were Hans Richter, Werner Graeff, Friedrich Kiesler and El Lissitzky. His attitude to De Stijl in 1923, the foundation year of *G*, was outwardly negative, however. He published in the first number a series of aphorisms which read like a direct repudiation of De Stijl aims: 'We reject all aesthetic speculation, all doctrine, all formalism.'[46] In reaction Van Doesburg reasserted more strongly the importance of painting and sculpture in relation to architecture:

Constructive, purely functional architecture ... leads ultimately towards an anatomical constructive sterility ... Functionalist archi-tecture deals with only the practical side of life or the mechanistic function of life: living and working. However, something exists beyond the demand for the useful, and that is the spiritual. As soon as the architect or the engineer wishes to visualize relation-ship – for example, the relationship between a wall and space – his intentions are no longer solely constructive but plastic as well.[47]

Despite the divergence between these points of view, Mies was invited to participate in the De Stijl exhibition at *L'Effort Moderne*, and Van Doesburg contributed to the first issue of *G*. Furthermore, in the same year Mies produced a design for a brick country house which was

44. Mondrian, 'Neo-plasticisme: de woning – de straat – de stad', p. 18.

45. P. Portoghesi, *Le inibizioni dell'architettura moderna*, Bari, 1975.

46. L. Mies van der Rohe, in *G*, no. 1, 1923; reprinted in P. Johnson, *Mies van der Rohe*, The Museum of Modern Art, New York, 1953, p. 188.

47. T. van Doesburg, 'The significance of colour for interior and exterior architecture', in *Bouwkundig Weekblad*, vol. 44, no. 21, 1923; reprinted in J Baljeu, *Theo van Doesburg*, Studio Vista, London, 1974, p. 139.

not only a pure De Stijl work, but more advanced than anything designed by a member of the De Stijl group at that time. The brick country house (Figure 4.11) is the first product of European modernism that can be compared to Wright's best work of the two previous decades. Unlike the still crude and primitive Van Doesburg/Van Eesteren designs of the same year, or the somewhat strained effects that Rietveld employed in the Schröder house, Mies' design is a total integration of form and expression. What Bruno Zevi says of the Barcelona Pavilion applies with equal if not greater force to this earlier work:

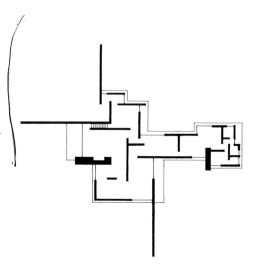

> Mies has no need, like Van Doesburg and Rietveld, to start from a basic 'box', disconnecting its angles, differentiating the walls and cutting them up into varicoloured and more or less projecting rectangles – a fundamentally superficial operation which leaves the spatial rhythm unaltered. For Mies, the box does not exist: Wright has already destroyed it, therefore it is useless to persist in taking it apart. He departs from a continuous space, without interruptions between interior and exterior, never trapped between four walls, and directs its flow by means of planes which, extending beyond the floor and roof slabs, create a continuous dialogue between the open building and the surrounding environment. De Stijl? Without doubt, on account of its orchestration of spatial dissonances. But with a methodological variation of incalculable importance: a redirection of the creative exploration from the envelope to the void. Van Doesburg insisted tenaciously on spatio-temporal values; however, he held that they could be attained by operating at a purely sculptural level: to animate the voids, he busied himself with the planes; he concentrated his attention on the two-dimensional elements in order to avoid a static three-dimensionality. Mies, on the contrary, creates fluid spaces and subordinates the plastic surfaces to them.[48]

Figure 4.11 Ludwig Mies van der Rohe, brick country house project, 1923–4: plan

The project wove together a number of themes from Mies' previous experience:

1. The feeling for masonry construction that he had acquired in his father's stonecutting workshop.

2. The free neoclassicism of Schinkel's Charlottenhof, in which the house is dissolved into an asymmetrical arrangement of scattered pavilions linked by terraces and pergolas; this theme was a major influence on Mies' pre-war work, in particular the project for the Kröller house in The Hague (1912).

48. B. Zevi, *Poetica dell'architettura neoplastica*, Libreria Editrice Politecnica Tamburini, Milan, 1953, p. 130.

3.   Berlage's insistence on the integrity of the sheer wall-plane:
     'Before all else the wall must be shown naked in all its sleek
     beauty.'

4.   Wright's prairie houses.

5.   De Stijl painting, as is evident from a comparison of Van
     Doesburg's *Rhythm of a Russian dance* (Figure 4.9) with Mies'
     plan.[49]

How did Mies reconcile the obvious formal preoccupations
underlying this design with his stated refusal in *G* 'to recognize problems of form, only problems of building'? It is clear from his later statements that Mies' interpretation of the function of the building was
very much less simplistic than his aphorisms in *G* suggest. In 1927 he
wrote that 'Life is what is decisive for us ... in all its plenitude and in its
spiritual and material relations.'[50] And on the policy of the
Weissenhofsiedlung:

> The battle-cry 'rationalization and standardization' deals with frag-
> mentary problems ... Above all there is the problem of space, the
> creation of a new house. This is a problem of the mind which can
> only be solved by creative force and not by calculation and organi-
> zation.[51]

The brick house project exposes the dilemma inherent in the De
Stijl concept of the open composition determined only outwards
from a centre, and not by any enclosing framework or 'mould': the
problem entailed in the very lack of interruption between interior
and exterior space which Zevi sees as Mies' greatest achievement.
The long walls extending from the house, replacing the spreading
eaves and terraces of Wright, are theoretically endless. In the drawing
they conveniently bleed off the edge of the page, suggesting indefinite
extension into space. In practice they would have to end somewhere
– but where? And how? The problem arises out of the essentially
non-permanent and non-urban nature of the pavilion type. Walls
imply permanent settlement, the enclosure of a domain: inside and
outside. In basing his formal solution on the wall, Mies has inevitably
produced an unresolved conflict between two house-types: the
pavilion and the court. Is the house a pavilion, which happens to have
three walls extending from it, or is it the junction of three courts?
For several years, Mies appears to have seen no way out of this
dilemma. His subsequent designs of the 1920s fall into two
contrasting groups. The first group, which includes the

49.   The comparison must not of course be taken too literally. It is
not a question of the direct *translation* of a given painting into
architecture, but rather that a certain type of formal relation, once
discovered, can open up new possibilities in other fields. For an
opposite opinion, see Yve-Alain Bois, 'Mondrian et la théorie de
l'architecture', in *Revue de l'Art*, Paris, 1981, p. 39.

50.   L. Mies van der Rohe, letter on form in architecture, in *Die
Form*, 1927; reprinted in P Johnson, *Mies van der Rohe*, The Museum
of Modern Art, New York, 1953, p. 193.

51.   L. Mies van der Rohe, foreword to catalogue, 'Werkbund
Exhibition Weissenhofsiedlung', 1927; reprinted in P. Johnson, *Mies
van der Rohe*, The Museum of Modern Art, New York, 1953, p. 193.

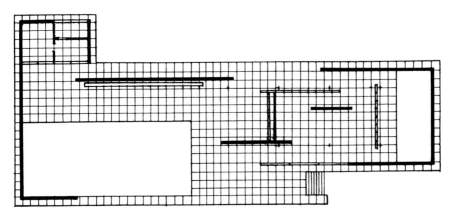

Figure 4.12 Ludwig Mies van der Rohe, Barcelona Pavilion, 1929: plan

Afrikanischestrasse housing (1925), the Weissenhof block and the projects of 1928 for glass office buildings in Berlin and Stuttgart, return to the symmetrical block forms of Mies' neoclassical beginnings, coupled with the straightforward, *sachlich*, use of new materials and technology seen in the concrete office project of 1923. The buildings in the second group are asymmetrical arrangements of closed cubic forms like the concrete house project of 1923; they include the monument to Karl Liebknecht and Rosa Luxemburg (1926), the Wolf house at Guben (1925–7) and (so far as its exterior is concerned) the Tugendhat house at Brno, the design for which was begun in 1928 although it was not built until 1930. None develops the open, planar composition that he had attempted in 1923–4 in the brick country house.

The problem, which neither the De Stijl architects nor Mies himself had been able to solve, was finally overcome by Mies in 1929 with the Barcelona Pavilion (Figure 4.12). The conflict between a continuous centrifugal development of space and the need to create finite spaces and boundaries was resolved by means of a new synthesis. In the same year Le Corbusier, approaching the problem from a diametrically opposite direction, arrived at a similar breakthrough: the Villa Savoye at Poissy.

4.10 Le Corbusier's polychromy: La Roche-Jeanneret and Pessac

The building site from which Le Corbusier hurried away to the opening of the De Stijl exhibition at *L'Effort Moderne* was almost certainly that on which, after protracted and frustrating negotiations

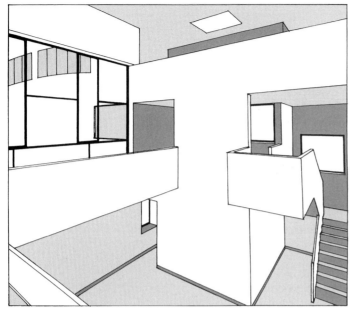

Figure 4.13 Le Corbusier, La Roche-Jeanneret houses, Auteuil, 1923–4: view of entrance hall

with the developers,[52] he was at last about to build the La Roche-Jeanneret houses at Auteuil. Although the design was by then well advanced, and the model would be exhibited at the *Salon d'Automne* the following month, a number of crucial last-minute changes were incorporated in the executed building, which are directly attributable to the impact of the De Stijl projects (Figure 4.13). The changes have been analysed in detail by Bruno Reichlin, who writes:

> the closer the project approached to its definitive form, the more the internal and external openings tended ... to make an angle with opaque areas, either vertical (walls) or horizontal (floors or ceilings), in such a way that the junctions of the delimiting surfaces of the spaces appeared as 'open' at the corners ... This means that an already relatively complete design was transformed by the systematic application of a formal rule ... according to which the envelope is no longer defined by solids pierced here and there by holes for openings.[53]

In the interior, De Stijl influence also appears in the use of colour. In his 1922 article 'The Realization of Neo-Plasticism in the Remote Future and in Today's Architecture', Mondrian had linked the planar character of a future architecture with the necessity of colour:

52. R. Walden, *The Open Hand*, MIT Press, Cambridge, Mass., 1977, pp. 136–41.
53. B. Reichlin, 'Le Corbusier vs. De Stijl', in Bois and Troy, *De Stijl et l'architecture en France*, p. 91.

Because it is essentially planar, neoplastic architecture demands *colour*, without which the plane cannot be for us a living reality. Colour is also necessary to remove the naturalistic appearance of materials: *the pure, flat, determined (i.e. sharply defined, not fluid) primary or basic colour* of neoplasticism, with its complement, *non-colour (white, black or grey)*. Colour is supported by architecture or it dissolves it, according to need. Colour extends *over the whole architecture*: equipment, furniture, etc.[54]

Le Corbusier too saw colour as a means of emphasizing the planar character of architecture. In particular, colour could strengthen relief, by making some surfaces recede and others advance. In his account of the La Roche-Jeanneret houses in the first volume of the *Œuvre Complète*, he writes:

In the interior, the first experiments in polychromy, based on the specific reactions of colours, allow an '*architectural camouflage*': that is to say, the accentuation of certain volumes or, on the contrary, their effacement. The interior of the house must be *white*, but, *in order that this white can be appreciated, one needs a well-regulated polychromy*: the walls in shadow will be blue, those in full light will be red; one can cause an element of the building to disappear by painting it in pure natural umber, and so on.[55]

The Quartiers Modernes Frugès at Bordeaux-Pessac (1925), where colour was used on the exteriors as well as the interiors, show still more clearly the profound impact on Le Corbusier of his encounter with De Stijl. Again, Le Corbusier refers to colour as 'camouflage' – that is to say, colour is to be used (as Mondrian had suggested) to *dissolve* the solid forms of the architecture. The simple prisms of the earlier houses were broken down into arrangements of advancing and receding planes. This dissolution of the solid masses was reinforced by defining each wall-plane with a contrasting colour:

Where the rows of houses form an opaque mass, we have camouflaged each house: the street façades are alternately brown and white. One lateral façade white, the other pale green. The meeting at the corner of pale green or white with dark brown provokes a suppression of volume (weight) and enhances the deployment of surfaces (extension). This polychromy is absolutely new. It is fundamentally rational. It brings to the symphony of architectural elements an extreme physiological power. The effect

54. P. Mondrian, 'De realiseering van het neo-plasticisme in verre toekomst en in de huidige architectuur', in *De Stijl*, vol. V, no. 5, 1922, pp. 68–9.
55. Le Corbusier, in *Le Corbusier et Pierre Jeanneret, 1910–1929*, Girsberger, Zurich, 1956, p. 60.

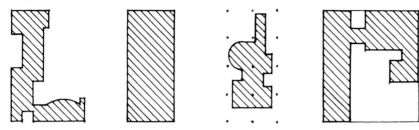

Figure 4.14 Le Corbusier, *The 4 compositions*, 1929

of composing in a coordinated way the physiological sensations of volume, surfaces, contours and colours can be intensely lyrical.[56]

However, in direct opposition to Mondrian and De Stijl, Le Corbusier used colour naturalistically. He not only used 'natural' earth colours, but chose sky blues and greens with the specific intention that certain elements should blend with their natural surroundings:

The site at Pessac is very restricted. The grey cement houses gave an intolerable impression of a condensed, airless mass. Colour can bring us space: we must consider colour as a means of creating space. This is how we established the fixed points. Certain façades were painted *pure burnt sienna*. We have made the lines of houses recede by painting them light ultramarine blue. We have made certain sectors blend with the foliage of the surrounding gardens and forest by colouring the façades pale green.[57]

4.11 Poissy and Barcelona

Le Corbusier's diagram *The 4 compositions* (Figure 4.14), illustrating the evolution of his formal solutions from the loose linear composition of quasi-symmetrical units in the La Roche-Jeanneret houses of 1923, through the simple prisms of Weissenhof or Garches (1927) and the open framework of Carthage II (1929) to the reconciliation of the two themes in the Villa Savoye, reveals his struggle to fuse the discipline of a clear enclosing frame with the plasticity of the free plan.

Mies van der Rohe's Barcelona Pavilion and Le Corbusier's Villa Savoye combine both these elements: the outward-looking plan of the free-standing pavilion and the inward-looking enclosure of the court. Though externally a pure, almost classical pavilion, the villa conceals a 10 m² court carved out of its main living floor. In both buildings, space is marked out by a regular grid of columns and

56. *Ibid.*, p. 85.
57. *Ibid.*, p. 86.

contained by a clear external enclosure. But whereas Mies assembles his free-standing elements in empty space, Corbusier carves his voids out of the solid like a sculptor. Mies' space is held in tension between the centre and the enclosing walls; Corbusier's is compacted and compressed inwards by the square frame of the façades. The villa is the ultimate and perfect expression of the principle which he had stated in his criticism of De Stijl in 1924: 'a pure envelope which covers abundance with a mask of simplicity'.

In terms of the classification of house-form, the Villa Savoye must be seen as *a court contained within a pavilion*. Conversely, the Barcelona Pavilion – although derived from the centrifugal pavilion house of Wright and De Stijl – was no longer a pure pavilion in this sense, but *a pavilion contained within a court*, like the traditional houses of China and Japan. Both Poissy and Barcelona represent a synthesis of these two archetypal house-forms.

The pavilion and the court also correspond to the first two of the three historical space conceptions that Sigfried Giedion defined in later editions of *Space, Time and Architecture*: the first, in which 'space was brought into being by the interplay between volumes', and the second, in which 'the formation of architectural space was synonymous with hollowed-out, interior space'. As such, they mark the culmination of the third space conception, for Giedion the unique and essential achievement of the modern movement, in which

> the space-emanating qualities of freestanding buildings could again be appreciated ... At the same time the supreme preoccupation of the second space conception – the hollowing-out of interior space – is continued ... New elements have been introduced: a hitherto unknown interpenetration of inner and outer space.[58]

4.12 The Barcelona Pavilion as a symbolic form

It is important to realize that the Barcelona Pavilion was not an exhibition stand (the industrial and trade exhibits were housed elsewhere) but a symbolic house/city, like a Greek temple. It represented renascent Weimar culture rather as the Parthenon represented Periclean Athens. In fact, the two historical moments make an interesting comparison. Both Weimar and Athens made extraordinary artistic and scientific achievements *despite* their fatally flawed political, social and economic backgrounds: in Germany, unchecked right-wing violence at home aided by the triumphalism and rapaciousness of the victorious allies; in Athens, a slave economy and a political demagogy that was about to plunge the state into a suicidal war with Sparta. It is

58. S. Giedion, *Space, Time and Architecture*, Harvard University Press, Cambridge, Mass., 5th edition, 1967, pp. lv–lvi.

an irony that in the October of 1929, the year of the Barcelona Pavilion, two disasters struck Germany that would bring to a close five brief years of relative peace and prosperity. The first was the death of Gustav Stresemann, the statesman who almost alone among conservatives had loyally worked for the Republic and steered it through those five 'golden' years; the second, the Wall Street Crash, which marked the beginning of the Great Depression. Thus the Barcelona Pavilion stood, as it were, on the brink of a precipice: in less than four years, Hitler would be chancellor of Germany.

It would be a mistake, moreover, to suppose that a building can be intrinsically a symbol of something other than itself. There is a profound distinction in architecture between *necessities*, which include not only the material functions but also the specific symbolic functions of a particular building, and *essentials*, which are universal properties of all buildings (see Chapter 8, section 8.7). Precisely because it did not have to contain any exhibits or serve any particular material function, the Barcelona Pavilion is an example of 'essential' architecture: a pure spatial construction. As pure architecture, it can be said to represent – that is, *stand for* – architecture in general, so it is not inappropriate to speak of it as 'a symbolic house/city', or even (since the nation can be regarded as a sort of greater city) to stretch that metaphor a little further, to interpret it as a symbol of Germany. But such readings are things that we ourselves choose to bring to the building, they are not specific to it. The same pavilion could equally represent another country if the flagstaff that stood before it carried a different banner.

Thus it is precisely because Mies' pavilion set out to represent no more than 'what it is to make a space', but to represent that completely – the *res privata* as well as the *res publica* – that it could serve so effectively as a symbol of Weimar. From this point of view it is instructive to compare it with Albert Speer's German pavilion at the Paris International Exhibition of 1937. There, architecture was indeed reduced to symbol: the *necessary* was allowed to crush and drive out the *essential*. The result was not only inferior as architecture, but far narrower in its scope as a potential symbol. It excluded everything and everyone that did not fit the Nazi concept of Germany as a uniform (and uniformed) *Volksgemeinschaft*. Paradoxically, Mies' pavilion is in fact more classical than Speer's, despite the latter's use of rudimentary pilasters and entablature. Mies not only avoids the elementary solecism of placing a column in the middle of a symmetrical front; at a more fundamental level, the level of spatial composition, his building is a lucid essay in the subtle interplay of inside and outside.

The pavilion consists essentially of a system of overlapping boundaries, symbols of the subtle interrelationships between private and public domains in actual housing (Figure 4.15). The outermost boundary is defined by a raised plinth, approached by a flight of steps. Within the area of the plinth, free-standing U-shaped walls embrace, without completely enclosing, a contained area, holding the whole composition together like a pair of clamps. Here is Mies' breakthrough: his solution of the problem raised by the endless walls of the brick house. The principle of indeterminacy has been abandoned, and in its place we have a notional frame within which the outflowing space is contained. Space still radiates outwards, but is definite, not infinite. A third type of boundary – shelter – is delineated by a simple rectangle of flat roof, its unbroken outline marking out an imaginary cube of space, reinforcing the effect of containment within a series of frames. Within this cube a smaller interior space is delimited by screen walls of marble and glass; lastly, a final boundary was marked out by the rectangle of carpet which, backed by a wall of onyx, represented the symbolic 'hearth' at the centre of the house. Five elements, thus: plinth, wall-enclosure, roof, interior, and 'hearth'; each time, an 'inside' functions as an 'outside' with respect to an inner space that is still smaller and more enclosed. There is an interesting correspondence between these five elements of Mies' design and the great nineteenth century classicist Gottfried Semper's *Four Elements of Architecture* (1851):

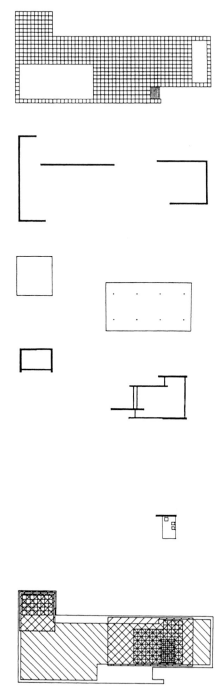

> The first sign of human settlement and rest after the hunt, the battle, and wandering in the desert is today, as when the first men lost paradise, the setting up of the fireplace and the lighting of the reviving, warming, and food-preparing flame ... Throughout all phases of society the hearth formed that sacred focus around which the whole took order and shape ... Around it were grouped the three other elements: the *roof*, the *enclosure*, and the *mound*, the protecting negations or defenders of the hearth's flame against the three hostile elements of nature ... At the same time the different technical skills of man became organized according to these elements: *ceramics* and afterwards metalworks around the *hearth*, *water* and *masonry works* around the *mound*, *carpentry* around the *roof* and its accessories. But what primitive technique evolved around the *enclosure*? None other than the art of the *wall fitter [Wandbereiter]*, that is, the weaver of mats and carpets.[59]

Figure 4.15 Barcelona Pavilion, analysis showing overlapping boundaries

59. G. Semper, *The Four Elements of Architecture and Other Writings*, Cambridge University Press, 1989, pp. 102–3.

4.13 The end of the heroic period of modern architecture

Giedion's 'third space conception' has proved short-lived, although – as I shall argue in Chapters 7 and 8 – not in principle impossible to realize. The two buildings I have discussed represent not only the culmination of the struggle to reconcile the open form and the closed, and to produce a new synthesis: they also marked the close of what one can now see only as a brilliant interlude: the fifteen years from 1914 to 1929, the heroic period during which modern architecture was dominated by revolutionary movements in art – cubism, futurism, expressionism, constructivism and above all De Stijl. As Alison and Peter Smithson observed, after about 1929 'absolute conviction in the movement died':[60]

> Le Corbusier's Pavillon Suisse and his own flat at Nungesser et Coli ... are using the language of the Heroic Period to different ends. There is somehow a loss of force, of revolutionary intent, the beginning of a process of change that finally produced the work of Tecton, in which the language of the Heroic Period is used solely for decorative ends.[61]

The heroic period had been imbued with the idea of revolution, not only in art but in society as a whole. But the political events and non-events of the later 1920s and early 1930s undermined any possibility of belief in such a revolution, and the modern movement consequently began to break up, to be replaced by either post- or late modernism. These two tendencies, which Charles Jencks has categorized as comparatively recent phenomena,[62] were in fact fully established, though unidentified, by about 1935. In those countries where the modern movement had flourished during the heroic period there was now a general reaction against it, often manifested in a return to classicism, and sometimes allied – as with more recent European neo-rationalism – to Marxism. In Russia and Germany this reaction could be regarded as having been imposed from above, but it was no less evident in France and Holland, and in the work of such former members of the radical avant-garde as André Lurçat, J.J.P. Oud, Sybold van Ravesteyn and Hans Schmidt. At the same time, the transplanted modern architecture that began to appear elsewhere – in Britain, Scandinavia, Latin America and the USA – was characterized by a narrowing of aims, an apolitical stance, or at least a rejection of political idealism, that has allowed late modernism to become the willing accomplice of late capitalism in its devastation of the post-war city.

60. A. and P. Smithson, 'The heroic period of modern architecture', in *Architectural Design*, vol. XXV no. 12, December 1965, p. 590.

61. A. and P. Smithson, 'Heroic period', addendum, in *Architectural Design*, vol. XXV no. 12, p. 584.

62. C. Jencks, *The Language of Post-Modern Architecture*, Academy Editions, London, 1984, pp. 6–8.

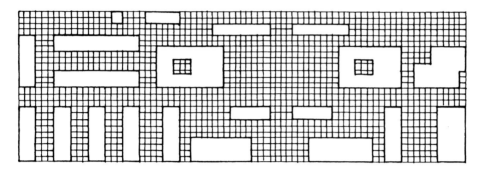

Figure 4.16 Ludwig Mies van der Rohe, IIT Campus, Chicago, 1940: plan

4.14 Mies, Le Corbusier and Van Doesburg after 1929

Although the three main protagonists of this chapter – Mies, Le Corbusier and Van Doesburg – were not unaffected by this change of direction, they do not fit comfortably into either category, post-modernism or late modernism. As each of them moved into the 1930s they came increasingly to regard architecture as above history, rather than expressive of it: they now saw it as concerned, not with a new age or a new vision, but – as to some extent Le Corbusier had always done – with fundamentally unchanging intellectual and exis-tential values. Thus Mies, who in 1923 had spoken of architecture as 'the will of an epoch translated into space: living, changing, new',[63] now, in his address to the Werkbund Congress in 1930, declared:

> The new era is a fact: it exists, irrespective of our 'yes' or 'no'. Yet it is neither better nor worse than any other era. It is pure datum, in itself without value content ... For what is right and significant for any era – including the new era – is this: to give the spirit the opportunity for existence.[64]

At first Mies continued to develop, in his court houses of the early 1930s, the synthesis arrived at in Barcelona; but he appears to have abandoned it when he emigrated to the United States, where he returned to the closed, neoclassical forms from which he had begun. In the IIT Campus (1940) De Stijl openness survives only in the layout of the blocks (Figure 4.16) and in the way the structural grid, as Bruno Zevi says, 'comes to the surface of the prism, generating prodigious but frozen corner solutions; in the Farnsworth House the steel uprights are ejected from the glazed volume, inverting the system explored in Germany'.[65]

63. L. Mies van der Rohe, aphorism on architecture, in *G* no. 1, 1923; reprinted in Johnson, *Mies van der Rohe*, p. 188.
64. L. Mies van der Rohe, 'The New Era', speech to the Werkbund meeting in Vienna, 1930; reprinted in Johnson, *Mies van der Rohe*, p. 195.
65. B. Zevi, *Poetica dell'architettura neoplastica*, 2nd edition, Giulio Einaudi, Turin, 1974, p. 187.

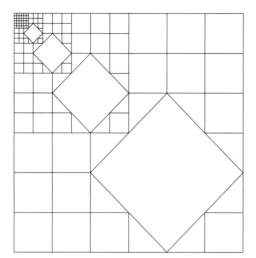

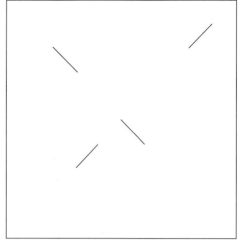

Figure 4.17 Theo van Doesburg, *Universal form II*, 1926/30 (redrawn interpretation by the author)

Figure 4.18 Ad Dekkers, *Drawing*, 1970

The case of Le Corbusier is somewhat different, because he was always less concerned than other leaders of the heroic period with the idea of a 'new' architecture. *Vers une architecture* and *Urbanisme* were arguments, not so much for a *new* architecture or *tomorrow's* city as for the eternal values of architecture: the lessons of Greece, Rome and the Paris of Colbert and Louis XIV. The first works that grew out of these books were rather static, essentially classical compositions, and the new, dynamic element that begins to appear in Le Corbusier's work from about 1924, beginning at Auteuil and Pessac and culminating in the synthesis of Poissy, was at least partly due to his encounter with De Stijl. This anti-classical tendency is carried further in the later buildings, while the one specifically 'modern' element in his work of the 1920s – the machine aesthetic – is dropped. The Errazuris and de Mandrot villas (1930), the *maison de weekend* and the holiday house at Mathes (1935), and the *Murondins* project (1940), with their use of rustic materials and traditional, even archaic building techniques, already point to Ronchamp, La Tourette and the Maisons Jaoul.

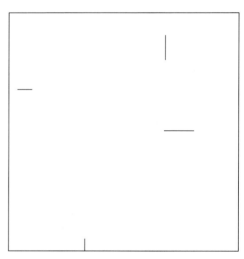

Figure 4.19 Ad Dekkers, *Incised wood panel XXVII*, 1973

In the closing years of his life, 1929–31, Van Doesburg's work too underwent a profound change, though in a quite different direction from Le Corbusier's. Moving away from intuitive composition, he took a new interest in the mathematical basis of art and in classical and universal values. This change led to the foundation in 1930 of a new magazine, *Art Concret*, and was reflected in a fundamental change in his work. His late compositions, such as the *Universal form II* of 1926–9 (Figure 4.17), anticipate the mathematically generated works of such artists as Richard Lohse, Sol LeWitt or Ad Dekkers (Figures 4.18–4.19) in the post-war decades. And his own house at Meudon seems to owe more to purism than to De Stijl. In the manifesto 'From Intuition Towards Certitude', he wrote in 1930:

> What today gives a cultural value to paintings is mathematical or rather arithmetical control. Mathematics has represented not only the basis of all science but also the foundations of art during the great epochs. As soon as the artist uses elementary forms as a means of expression, his work is not merely 'modern', but universal. After having passed through the various phases of plastic creation (the phases of arrangement, composition and construction), I have arrived at the creation of *universal forms* through constructing upon an arithmetical basis with the pure elements of painting.[66]

Van Doesburg's writings of this period reveal a growing resolve to withdraw from the messy 'brown' world of architectural activity into a hermetic 'white' world of pure intellectual, mathematical creation. The work of art is seen as a means of contemplation:

> WHITE. This is the spiritual colour of our times ...; our era is one of perfection, purity and certitude ... We have superseded both the 'brown' of decadence and classicism and the 'blue' of divisionism, the cult of blue sky, the gods with green beards and the spectrum. White, pure white ... Let them amuse themselves, down there in the depths; we want more, we want to mount the heights of truth where the air is pure and can be withstood only by metallic lungs.[67]

And in one of his last, as it were valedictory, pieces of writing, published after his death in the final, memorial number of *De Stijl* (1932), he recommends:

> white, always much white and black, for colour gets its full significance solely from the opposition of white and black. a single colour is already enough to create a work of art, provided this colour, by its measure, direction and position, can suggest to us all other colours ... your studio must be like a glass-bell or a hollow crystal. you yourself must be white. the palette must be of glass, your brush square and hard, always dust-free and as immaculate as a surgical instrument. there is certainly more to learn from medical laboratories than from painters' studios, which are like cages

66. T. van Doesburg, 'From intuition towards certitude', 1930, in *Réalités Nouvelles*, no. 1, 1947, p. 3; reprinted in Baljeu, *Theo van Doesburg*, p. 185.

67. T. van Doesburg, 'Towards white painting', in *Art Concret*, April 1930, pp. 11–12; reprinted in Baljeu, *Theo van Doesburg*, p. 183.

stinking of sick monkeys. your studio must have the cold atmosphere of mountains at an altitude of 3000 metres, with eternal
snows at the summit. the cold kills the microbes.[68]

4.15 It is necessary, not to adapt, but to create

This change of heart was inescapable, because the concept of De Stijl
architecture demanded a total revolution in the basic nature of
human relationships. Without such a radical change in society it could
never develop beyond the one-off fragment – a handful of interiors,
the Schröder house, and the Barcelona Pavilion. Its reliance on 'the
balanced relationship of unequal parts' in place of repetition and
symmetry depended, like the 'changefulness' of arts and crafts architecture, on the kind of man-made Eden envisaged by Mondrian, in
which

> The 'artist' will be absorbed into the *complete human being*. The
> 'non-artist' will be the same, equally imbued with beauty. One
> person may be predisposed to aesthetic, a second to scientific, a
> third to some other activity; but each 'profession' will be an equal
> part of the whole. Architecture, sculpture, painting and decorative
> art will then merge into a single art, i.e. *architecture-as-our-environ-
> ment*.[69]

But such a spontaneously varied environment can be created only
where every man is a builder, or at least where the architect has not
yet appeared on the scene as an intermediary, and often a barrier,
between builder and client. Here again there is an analogy between
De Stijl and anarchism. Such a spontaneous architecture can be
created only by a primitive or folk society – that is to say one that is, in
Amos Rapoport's words,

> tradition-bound, where the few changes that occur happen
> within a frame of a given common heritage and hierarchy of values
> reflected in the building-types ... In most traditional cultures,
> novelty is not only not sought after, but is regarded as
> undesirable.[70]

This conservatism, or rather willing surrender of the individual to
the group, is the necessary precondition for freedom from superimposed order. The need for conscious design, like the need for
government, is then supplanted by taboo. When the architect tries to
imitate the natural and harmonious variation of folk building the

68. T. van Doesburg, 'elementarisme', in *De Stijl*, last issue, 1932, p.
16; reprinted in Jaffé, *De Stijl*, p. 187.
69. Mondrian, 'De realiseering', in *De Stijl*, vol. V, no. 3, March
1922, p. 43; reprinted in Jaffé, *De Stijl*, pp. 164–5.
70. A. Rapoport, *House Form and Culture*, Prentice-Hall,
Englewood Cliffs, N.J., 1969, pp. 5, 7.

result is inherently artificial: an arbitrary arrangement of arbitrarily varied parts. It is for this reason that the attempt to create a De Stijl architecture produced only two masterpieces – at Utrecht in 1924 and at Barcelona five years later – and even these achievements were limited in context and to some extent illusory. Without a surrendering of individuality to a collective ethos it is likewise impossible to bring about the continuity of inside and outside, of private and public, that Van Doesburg demanded in the eighth point of his architectural manifesto:

> The new architecture has *broken through the wall*, thus destroying *the separateness of inside and outside. The walls are no longer load-bearing;* that role is filled by points of support. This gives rise to a new, open plan, totally different from the classical one, in that interior and exterior spaces interpenetrate.[71]

Such a continuity of inside and outside space was achieved in the Schröder house by *trompe l'œil*, and in the Barcelona Pavilion only because it was a symbolic house and not a real one. Bakema and others who later tried to apply De Stijl principles to the city never came to grips with the interiors of their housing blocks, but treated buildings as solid elements; the city was no longer architecture but oversized, inhuman abstract sculpture. In his essay 'Neoplasticism: Dwelling – Street – City' (1927) Mondrian gave a very precise description of the change needed in society if 'architecture-as-our-environment' was to become a reality:

> Today, there is no equality, and consequently no harmony, between the dwelling and the street. This is partly due to climate, but also to a lack of equality between different individuals. It is entirely natural that the inequality of society should drive each individual to flee the others ... In the primitive era collective life was more possible because of the greater equality of the mass of the people ... In the course of civilization this situation changed, and the natural and logical instinct to feel oneself part of a unity was obscured: the possibility of collective life ceased ... In order to create the city of the future, one must first create the new dwelling. Neoplasticism, however, conceives the dwelling, not as a place in which to take refuge or separate oneself from others, but as *a part of the whole*, a constructive element of the city. And this is the great difficulty today: whereas it is already possible to renew the dwelling, the city cannot be changed at present. We need courage and strength to endure a period of disharmony. Precisely

71. Van Doesburg, 'Tot een beeldende architectuur', in *De Stijl*, vol. VI, no. 6/7, p. 80; reprinted in Jaffé, *De Stijl*, p. 186.

because of the fear of disharmony, and because one is habituated to the past, no progress is made. It is necessary, *not to adapt, but to 'create'* ... The interior of the dwelling must no longer be an accumulation of rooms formed by four walls with nothing but holes for doors and windows, but *a construction of coloured and colourless planes, combined with furniture and equipment, which must be nothing in themselves but constituent elements of the whole.* In just the same way, the human being must be nothing in himself, but only a part of the whole. Then, no longer conscious of his individuality, he will be happy in this earthly paradise that he has himself created.[72]

---

72. Mondrian, 'Neo-plasticisme: de woning – de straat – de stad', pp. 12–16.

5

Lauweriks, Van Doesburg and Le Corbusier

5.1 A gardener and a house in Germany

In his book *Le Modulor*, Le Corbusier describes the start of his 'voyage of discovery' in search of the secret of proportion:

> At twenty-three, our man drew on his sketching-board the façade of a house he was going to build. A perturbing question arose in his mind: 'What is the rule that orders, that connects all things? I am faced with a problem that is geometrical in nature …' Great disquiet, much searching, many questions. Then he remembered how once, on a voyage of discovery, as he was looking over a modern villa at Bremen, the gardener there had said to him: 'This stuff, you see, that's complicated, all these twiddly bits, curves and angles, calculations, it's all very learned.' The villa had belonged to someone called Thorn Brick (?), a Dutchman (about 1900).[1]

The story is mystifying. Le Corbusier (or Charles-Edouard Jeanneret as he was then; he renamed himself 'Le Corbusier' in 1920) was born on 6 October 1887. If the date '1900' means anything at all it must refer to the year in which the Bremen villa was built, not to Jeanneret's chat with the gardener; at that time he was only twelve. Apart from a one-week flying visit to Munich and Nuremberg in March 1908, he did not travel in Germany until 1910, that is to say the year in which he turned twenty-three. The façade he was sketching at that age can only have been that of his parents' house at La Chaux-de-Fonds, the Villa Jeanneret-Perret, the design of which was begun as soon as he returned home from Germany, in November 1911[2] – only a few months, therefore, after seeing the villa in 'Bremen'. The phrase 'he remembered how once' – which implies that enough time passed between seeing the mysterious 'villa in Bremen' and the sketching of the façade for the memory of the first event to have become hazy – is therefore entirely misleading.

But who designed this villa, and who was its owner? The name 'Thorn Brick' is suspiciously close to that of the Dutch artist and designer Johan Thorn Prikker (1868–1932), who indeed had a house built for him in Germany at this time – but in 1910, not 1900.

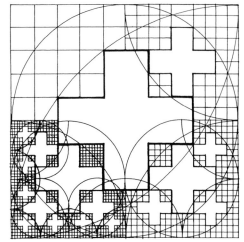

Figure 5.1 Type of square modular grid based on inscribed and intersecting circles used by J.L.M. Lauweriks

---

1. Le Corbusier, *The Modulor*, Faber & Faber, London, 1961, p. 26.
2. H.A. Brooks, *Le Corbusier's Formative Years*, University of Chicago Press, Chicago and London, 1997, pp. 307 and 310.

This house was designed by another Dutchman, the architect J.L. Mathieu Lauweriks (1864–1932).[3] Lauweriks was one of a group of Dutch architects, including K.P.C. de Bazel (1869–1923) and J.H. de Groot (1865–1932), who all based their work on geometrical patterns and systems of proportion. The Thorn Prikker house was not built, however, in Bremen – where Henry Russell Hitchcock fruitlessly searched for it in 1964[4] – but at Hagen in the Ruhr. Peter Behrens was likewise active in Hagen in 1910, so Jeanneret could have had reason to visit the town during the five months he spent working in his office. In any case he certainly went there in 1911, on which occasion he met the client of both Behrens and Lauweriks: the millionaire philanthropist, art patron and collector Karl Ernst Osthaus (1874–1921).

In 1900 Osthaus had commissioned Henry van de Velde to transform the interiors of the recently completed museum he had had built, in a neo-renaissance style, by the Berlin architect Carl Gérard. Apparently Van de Velde transformed not only the building but also its purpose; he is thought to have persuaded Osthaus to change it from a museum of natural history and science into a gallery of modern art, renaming it the Folkwang Museum.[5] This led to the creation on the Hohenhagen – the hilltop estate Osthaus acquired at Eppenhausen, overlooking Hagen – of an artistic garden suburb, rivalling the roughly contemporary Mathildenhöhe at Darmstadt, designed by Joseph Olbrich for Grand Duke Ernst Ludwig of Hesse between 1899 and 1908. The first step was the building of Osthaus' residence on the Hohenhagen, the Hohenhof, to Van de Velde's design (1906–7).

Osthaus met Peter Behrens during the time the architect was a member of the Mathildenhöhe artists' colony. Behrens built his own house there in 1901, but left Darmstadt in 1903 to take up an appointment as director of the School of Arts and Crafts in Düsseldorf. He at first tried to persuade H.P. Berlage to run the architectural course at Düsseldorf; Berlage felt unable to do so, however, and instead recommended Lauweriks, who was appointed in 1904.

The emergence in Behrens' work of 1904–8 of an austere classicism characterized by a strict geometry of squares and circles – for example, the lecture hall at the Folkwang Museum, Hagen (1905), the art exhibitions at Oldenburg and Dresden (1905 and 1906) and the crematorium at Delstern (1906) – has been attributed to Lauweriks' influence.[6] At Düsseldorf, during these years, Lauweriks was teaching a design method based on very much the same kind of geometry. Among the mutually connected motifs used were:

3. N.H.M. Tummers, *J L Mathieu Lauweriks: zijn werk en zijn invloed*, G. van Saane, Hilversum, 1968, p. 29.
4. *Ibid.*, p. 35.
5. A. Windsor, *Peter Behrens: Architect and Designer 1868–1940*, The Architectural Press, London, 1981, p. 58.
6. *Ibid.*, pp. 55–6.

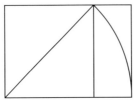

Figure 5.2 Rectangle based on diagonal of square, i.e. $\sqrt{2}$

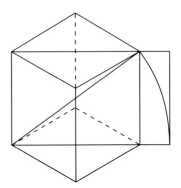

Figure 5.3 Rectangle based on diameter of cube, i.e. $\sqrt{3}$

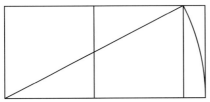

Figure 5.4 Rectangle based on diagonal of double square, i.e. $\sqrt{5}$

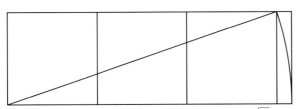

Figure 5.5 Rectangle based on diagonal of triple square, i.e. $\sqrt{10}$

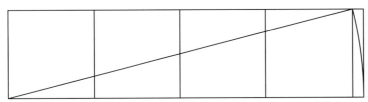

Figure 5.6 Rectangle based on diagonal of quadruple square, i.e. $\sqrt{17}$

1. Square or cubic modular grids generated by inscribed, circumscribed and intersecting circles (Figure 5.1).

2. Square root rectangles defined by diagonals of squares or multiples of squares or cubes, particularly the square roots of two, three, five, ten and seventeen (Figures 5.2–5.6).

3. Zigzags, meanders and spirals suggestive of fractal geometry (Figure 5.7). These appear in Lauweriks' design for the 1909 exhibition of Christian art in Düsseldorf, the houses at Hagen, and many later works. The fractal principle allowed the motif to be repeated at all possible scales, governing the forms of buildings, decorative details and furniture, and urban and landscape layouts. It is interesting to speculate that the Koch curve, one of

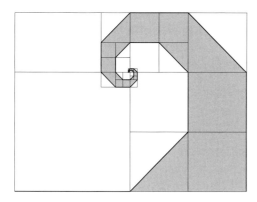

Figure 5.7 Meander design used by Lauweriks   **Figure 5.8** Koch curve

the earliest fractals, was discovered by the Swedish mathematician Helge von Koch in 1904 (Figure 5.8). Can Lauweriks possibly have been aware of this?

Osthaus shared out the design of the Hohenhagen estate between Van de Velde, Behrens and Lauweriks. Van de Velde was to have built a new museum, which was never realized. The first two houses built were designed by Behrens: these were the Schroeder and Cuno houses (1908–9 and 1909–10), to which he later added the Goedecke house (1911–12). N.H.M. Tummers has speculated that Jeanneret visited Hagen in mid-1910 in connection with the technical problems that plagued the Cuno house,[7] but as we shall see, his first visit probably occurred no earlier than April 1911.

On that visit Jeanneret could hardly have failed to notice, or had mentioned to him, the houses that, in 1910, Lauweriks had started to build on the adjoining site. The first of these was for the artist Johan Thorn Prikker. Thorn Prikker was a close friend of Henry van de Velde; as early as 1900 he contributed a monumental wall-painting to the latter's Leuring house at Scheveningen. In 1904 he followed Van de Velde to Germany, where he remained for the rest of his life, teaching first at Krefeld and later in Munich, Düsseldorf and Cologne. He was a member of the Hohenhagen art colony from 1910 to 1919, executing under Osthaus' patronage numerous commissions for mural paintings, stained-glass windows and other works.

The Thorn Prikker house is wound around itself in a tight U, like a taut spring or – to use an organic analogy closer to Lauweriks' own thoughts – a young shoot just emerging from the bud (Figure 5.9). The same tight rectangular spiral reappears in the plasterwork of the dining room ceiling of the house (Figure 5.10). From the U-form of the plan there unfolds a continuous meandering path embodied in

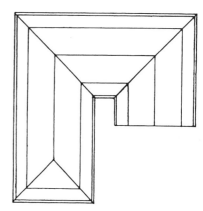

Figure 5.9 J.L.M. Lauweriks, Thorn Prikker house, Hohenhagen, 1910: roof plan

Figure 5.10 J.L.M. Lauweriks, Thorn Prikker house: plan of dining room ceiling

7. Tummers, *Mathieu Lauweriks*, p. 35.

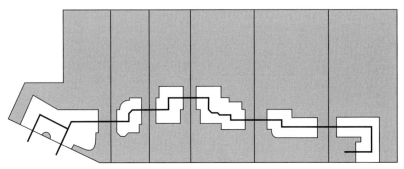

Figure 5.11 J.L.M. Lauwerks, Stirnband, Hohenhagen, 1910–14

the wandering ridge line that binds together all the nine houses Lauweriks built along the *Stirnband* ('head band') – a narrow road that encircled the brow of the hill (Figure 5.11). His first drawing for the site (1910) contrasts strongly with Behrens' axial plan of 1907. It ambitiously incorporates the whole Hohenhagen layout, including the Van de Velde and Behrens portions, in a single meandering line. The same concentric rectilinear patterns, meanders and spirals are echoed in the façades as well as in the garden layouts of the houses. There was ample reason for Le Corbusier's 'gardener' to speak of 'all these twiddly bits, curves, angles'. Tummers points out that the layout of Domino-houses which Le Corbusier designed three or four years later, in 1914–15,[8] 'is extraordinarily closely related to Lauweriks' planning arrangement for Hohenhagen'.[9]

But was it really the gardener that Jeanneret spoke to? As N.H.M. Tummers was the first to point out,[10] when Lauweriks first came to Hagen he was housed in the gardener's cottage of the Hohenhof. Is it more likely that Jeanneret talked to a real gardener, that he genuinely mistook Lauweriks for a gardener because he occupied the gardener's house, or that he deliberately chose to 'misremember' the event, disguising Lauweriks' more sophisticated description in deliberately peasant-like simplicity in order to stress the originality of his own contribution? Surely the latter. Tummers points out that the building permit for the Thorn Prikker house was not obtained until June 1910, so the building cannot have been far advanced before about December of that year; and a house under construction is unlikely to need a gardener. If Jeanneret is assumed to have made his Hagen visit during the five months of his employment with Behrens, Tummers argues,

How, then, can a gardener have shown him the house, if it was not yet built, or at least not yet completed, at the time Jeanneret left Behrens – five months after April, i.e. August/September 1910? ...

8. *Le Corbusier et Pierre Jeanneret, oeuvre complète de 1910–1929,* Girsberger, Zurich, 1956, p. 25.
9. Tummers, *Mathieu Lauweriks,* p. 36.
10. *Ibid.,* pp. 21 and 35.

It is my firm opinion that the explanation about the gardener is ... an indication that Jeanneret met Lauweriks when the latter was living a stone's throw from the Cuno house – in the gardener's dwelling of the Hohenhof! Lauweriks must have shown him the drawings, from which it could be plainly seen how the house was conceived on the basis of a system.[11]

Although more recent research by H. Allen Brooks undermines Tummers' chronology, it confirms the main thrust of his argument. The months which Tummers assumes that Jeanneret spent working for Behrens were indeed passed mainly in Germany, but not in Behrens' employment, which he entered only on 1 November 1910 (having briefly returned home to La Chaux-de-Fonds at the end of July) and did not leave until 1 April 1911.[12] On the other hand, thanks to Brooks' research, the fact of Jeanneret's visit to Hagen is no longer a matter of speculation. There is no evidence that he was sent there by Behrens during his five month *stage*, but he undoubtedly visited the town soon after leaving him, while touring Germany to gather material for his 'Etude sur le mouvement d'art décoratif en Allemagne' (1912). On 9 May he not only came to Hagen but had a meeting with Osthaus, after which he continued to correspond with him.[13] According to Brooks, 'Osthaus was warmly receptive to Jeanneret's visit and subsequently a limited correspondence, though always initiated by Jeanneret, ensued.'[14]

Now, if the encounter with Lauweriks' method is no longer in question, what further inferences can be drawn from Le Corbusier's evasive allusion to it? If he took such trouble to conceal it, why did he bother to mention it at all? If it was so trivial an experience as he makes it appear, what need was there to refer to it, forty years later, in his book on the *modulor*?

The phenomenon is a more general one in Le Corbusier's writings. It seems that in spite of – or perhaps *because* of – its enormous influence on him, he chose to play down, or put a negative slant on, all aspects of the year he spent in Germany. What Brooks says about the period with Behrens can be applied to the German experience as a whole: 'His debt was so great, indeed so profound, that Le Corbusier thought it best that it should be left unknown.'[15]

Yet he could not, one suspects, leave it at that. Because the experience was so significant for him, he was at the same time torn by a contrary desire to reveal it. Like a lover's guilty secret, the stronger the need to keep silent, the more burning was the desire to tell and the greater the subconscious tendency to leave tell-tale clues. The role of Lauweriks' proportion system as a source of the *modulor* was

11. *Ibid.*, pp. 35–6.

12. Brooks, *Le Corbusier's Formative Years*, pp. 208, 226–7, 235–46.

13. H. Hesse-Frielinghaus, *Briefwechsel Le Corbusier – Karl Ernst Osthaus*, Karl Ernst Osthaus Museum, Hagen, 1977, and Windsor, *Peter Behrens*, p. 115.

14. Brooks, *Le Corbusier's Formative Years*, p. 249.

15. *Ibid.*, p. 247.

too important for it to be left out of the story altogether. Le Corbusier responded in the only way his *amour-propre* allowed: he compromised by recounting it in an encoded form.

5.2 Viollet-le-Duc, Cuypers and Berlage

In 1864, the year in which Lauweriks was born, the leader of the gothic revival in France, Eugène-Emanuel Viollet-le-Duc (1814–79), travelled to Roermond in Limburg at the request of his Dutch follower, Pierre J.H. Cuypers (1827–1921), to support him in the controversy surrounding his restoration of the thirteenth century Munsterkerk. The controversy had gone on a long time. Fifteen years before, a campaign to save the church from mutilation was the first act with which the newly qualified Cuypers had announced his entry on the architectural scene of his home town.[16]

On the wider stage of nineteenth century Dutch architecture as a whole, Cuypers would eventually go on to become the unchallenged star. Just as Peter Behrens' office was the training ground for the fledgling leaders of the modern movement – Walter Gropius (who joined Behrens' office on Osthaus' recommendation),[17] Ludwig Mies van der Rohe and Le Corbusier – Cuypers' atelier, and the Quellinus and Rijksmuseum Schools of Arts and Crafts, which he founded in 1880 and 1881, provided in the 1880s and 1890s the nursery for a group of Dutch designers and architects who would emerge as the leaders of the Dutch *Nieuwe Kunst* (Art Nouveau): designers like Theodore Nieuwenhuis, G.A. Dijsselhof and C.A. Lion Cachet, and the architects K.P.C. de Bazel, H.J.M. Walenkamp, and Lauweriks himself.

Cuypers' best-known buildings, the Rijksmuseum (1877–85) and the Central Station (1881–9) in Amsterdam, both exhibit the same forward-looking attitude to gothic architecture which Viollet-le-Duc himself showed in his work – notably in the designs for structures of iron and masonry that illustrate the twelfth lecture of the *Entretiens sur l'architecture* (1863–72).[18] Both Viollet and Cuypers admired Gothic architecture above all as *rational construction*. Even the theory of proportions was seen as the consequence of structural rationality. 'Architectural proportion,' writes Viollet, 'is established primarily by the laws of statics, and the laws of statics are derived from geometry.' John Summerson contrasts this with the more nostalgic approach of Pugin and other English gothicists in his essay 'Viollet-le-Duc and the Rational Point of View':

All of them were as deeply imbued with a love of Gothic architecture as was Viollet-le-Duc; but not one of them was man enough

16. Tummers, *Mathieu Lauweriks*, pp. 3–4.
17. Ibid., p.38.
18. E.-E. Viollet-le-Duc, *Discourses on Architecture*, George Allen & Unwin, London, 1959, vol. II, pp. 51–100.

to think his way through the romantic attraction of style to a philosophical point of view applicable to all buildings at all times. The Englishmen built their Gothic churches, their Gothic schools, their Gothic houses, and within narrow limits they performed creditably. But the Frenchman, though he did build one or two Gothic buildings of an 'occasional' character, left a structure of thought upon which many of our own ideas of modern architecture are based.[19]

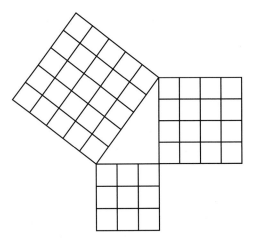

Figure 5.12 'Pythagorean' right-angled triangle

What is true of Viollet-le-Duc is equally true of his disciple, Cuypers.

Lauweriks grew up in the Cuypers household; his father, Jean Hubert Lauweriks, was a Belgian artist whom in 1854 the architect invited to come from Antwerp to take charge of the sculpture studio engaged on the Munsterkerk restoration. The year after his birth, when Cuypers moved north to Amsterdam, the Lauweriks family went with him. It may have been Viollet who persuaded Cuypers to make the move; he wrote to him shortly after the Roermond visit: 'la verve d'une grande ville est nécessaire à un artiste'.[20] In Amsterdam, the Lauweriks lived in a wing of Cuypers' house, breathing its intense atmosphere of Catholic piety and devotion to art. At the age of sixteen, Lauweriks precociously entered the Quellinus School: not as a student, but already as a teacher. He would remain throughout his life more important as an influence on other architects, as teacher, writer and theorist, than as a designer in his own right. His whole architectural output was produced in a period of six years, between 1909 and 1915, when he was in his late forties. None of it was built in Holland.

Viollet-le-Duc narrowly missed being present, therefore, at Lauweriks' birth, and his teachings formed part of the background in which Lauweriks grew up. It is relevant to look at those teachings, and specifically Viollet's theory of proportion, to see to what extent they may have contributed to Lauweriks' system. In his *Entretiens sur l'architecture* Viollet discusses a number of triangles on which he believed the proportions of ancient and medieval buildings were based. These are as follows.

1.   The 'pythagorean' right-angled triangle with sides in the proportion 3:4:5. This proportion allows all three sides to be mutually commensurable while obeying the Theorem of Pythagoras, which states that the square on the hypotenuse of a right-angled triangle equals the sum of the squares on the two perpendicular sides; that is, the square of five equals the sum of the squares of three and four, i.e. $25 = 9 + 16$ (Figure 5.12).

19.   J. Summerson, 'Viollet-le-Duc and the rational point of view', in *Heavenly Mansions*, Cresset Press, London, 1949, p. 141.

20.   Tummers, *Mathieu Lauweriks*, p. 4.

2. The equilateral triangle, with angles of 60 degrees (Figure 5.13).

3. The isosceles triangle formed by the diagonal cross-section of a pyramid, the elevation of which forms an equilateral triangle. This triangle comprises two right-angled triangles, each with a base equal to $\sqrt{2}$, a height of $\sqrt{3}$ and a hypotenuse of $\sqrt{5}$, giving a ratio of height to base-width for the whole triangle of $\sqrt{3}:2\sqrt{2}$ or approximately 1:1.633 (Figure 5.14).

4. The visually very similar 'Egyptian' isosceles triangle, with a base of eight and a height of five units, i.e. a ratio of height to base-width of 1:1.6. The two sloping sides are incommensurable with the height and base, being equal to $\sqrt{41}$, or just over 6.4 units (Figure 5.15). Viollet-le-Duc speculates that 'Perhaps the architects of the ancient world made use of this figure; it is certain ... that the masters of the Middle Ages made it the generator of some of the great buildings.'[21] He discovers in it the basis of the proportions of the basilica of Constantine, Notre Dame in Paris and the cathedral of Amiens. The triangle is in fact superfluous to this construction, however; applied to a façade or a plan it merely serves to generate an 8:5 rectangle, i.e. a perfectly commensurable figure that can be simply composed with squares.

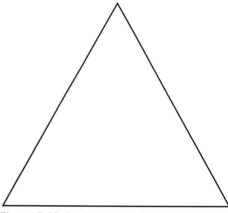

Figure 5.13 Equilateral triangle

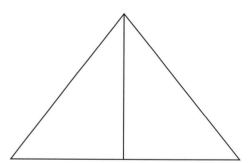

Figure 5.14 Isosceles triangle formed by cross-section of pyramid

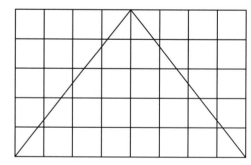

Figure 5.15 'Egyptian' triangle

The Egyptian triangle is the one on which H.P. Berlage (1856–1934) based the façades of his final, 1898, design for the Amsterdam produce exchange (*Koopmansbeurs*). To understand the historical significance of this building one must bear in mind Berlage's unique position as the acknowledged 'father' of modern Dutch architecture, the one man whom all the diverse – and often mutually hostile – avant-garde groupings, including De Stijl, recognized as forerunner and leader. The project had gone through several vicissitudes. An international competition was held in 1884–5. The two designs entered by Berlage and his partner, the engineer T. Sanders, were in a flamboyant Netherlands renaissance style, quite different from the austere building we know today. At the first stage they were placed among the five finalists, but failed to win. However, the winner, the French architect L.M. Cordonnier, was accused of plagiarism, and none of the submitted designs was carried out. Twenty years later Cordonnier would have his revenge. In 1905–6 he won the competition for the Peace Palace in The Hague, in which Berlage's entry was unpremiated.

A new initiative began in 1895. This time there was no competition; Berlage, now an independent architect, was appointed as technical adviser from the start, thanks to his friendship with the city

21. Viollet-le-Duc, *Discourses*, vol. I, p. 400.

councillor and alderman for public works M.W.F. Treub, like Berlage a radical. His first two designs were produced in 1896–7. The proportioning grid makes its first appearance only with the third version, which was put out to contract in 1898. The executed building, which Berlage published as the 'final' design, is a radically simplified reworking of this third scheme. In the lecture that he gave to explain the intentions underlying the project, Berlage expressly acknowledged his debt to Viollet-le-Duc and to the young school of Dutch architects, and explained the use of the Egyptian triangle:

> The investigations of Viollet-le-Duc, and more recently of De Bazel, Lauweriks, and De Groot, are utilized in the design of the façade; the building is constructed according to a 4 by 5 schema and is made up of an arrangement of four-pointed prisms, whose base is a square and whose height stands in a ratio to the side of a rectangle of 5:8 ... The articulation of the façades, the interior architecture, in short, the entire building is constructed according to these proportions.[22]

In a later series of lectures, given in 1908 at the Kunstgewerbe-museum, Zurich, under the title 'Foundations and Development', Berlage returned to the theme:

> Research has proven that the Egyptian triangle, the section of the pyramid with the ratio of 8 long to 5 high, is – according to a whole 'school of archaeology' – nothing less than 'the key to all proportion, the secret of all true architecture' ... Ultimately, any form of triangle can be used, but only if it is implemented in a uniform way. But the simple geometrical and even arithmetical ratios achieve the most beautiful results, in that the trained eye senses and therefore understands this ... As a final example I show you the Stock Exchange building in Amsterdam, which is entirely proportioned after the Egyptian triangle. It consists of a system of built-up pyramids with the ratio 8:5, and can, therefore, be compared with a group of natural crystals.[23]

The base of the pyramid that Berlage refers to acts as the planning module for the whole building. It measures 3.8 metres, so the height of the pyramid is $3.8 \times 5/8 = 2.375$ metres. This is not the floor-to-floor height but acts as a vertical module governing the elements of the façade, such as windows, spandrels, the height and even the slope of the roofs. Starting from a datum about 1.5 metres above pavement level, the general height of the long southern (Damrak) façade

22. H.P. Berlage, 'Exchange Lecture', 1 April 1898, in I. Boyd White and W. de Wit (eds), *Hendrik Petrus Berlage: Thoughts on Style 1886–1909*, The Getty Center, Santa Monica, California, 1996, p. 30
23. H.P. Berlage, 'Foundations and Development' (1908), in Boyd White and de Wit, *Hendrik Petrus Berlage*, pp. 195 & 218.

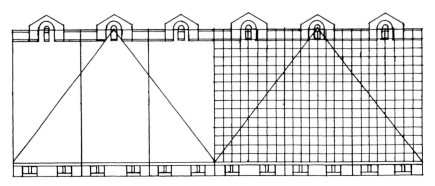

Figure 5.16 H.P. Berlage, produce exchange, Amsterdam, 1898–1901: diagrammatic part elevation showing use of 'Egyptian' triangle

is six modules and that of the clock tower on the corner seventeen modules. Generally, major elements of the same façade are so proportioned that the number of horizontal and vertical modules is in a simple ratio. For instance the first long section of this façade is twelve modules long and six high, so it is contained within two juxtaposed Egyptian triangles (Figure 5.16). Conversely, smaller elements which may appear at first to be arbitrarily dimensioned are in fact disciplined by subdivisions of the same triangular grid. Pieter Singelenberg, in his book on Berlage, describes the following experiment:

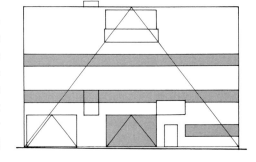

> the division of Berlage's drawing of the Southern façade was transferred to a sheet of transparent paper. This was displaced by a half, a third, and a quarter unit. horizontally as well as vertically. This showed that practically all the elements of the façade have their origin in this 5:8 proportion.[24]

It is tempting to make a direct transition from Berlage's exchange to Le Corbusier's Villa Stein at Garches (1927), where the Egyptian triangle seems to reappear even more clearly as the governing figure of the façade (Figure 5.17). But there is no sound reason, apart from this coincidence, to link the two buildings. If there was a connection, it is more likely to have been an indirect one, by way of a common source in Viollet-le-Duc, whose *Dictionnaire raisonné* Le Corbusier (then still C.-E. Jeanneret) purchased with his first month's pay while working for Auguste Perret in Paris in 1908. He did not, however, buy the *Entretiens*, which might have led him straight to the Egyptian triangle.[25] Anyway, the material facts are these: the overall length of the façade of the Villa Stein is 20.7 metres and its height 13.0 metres,

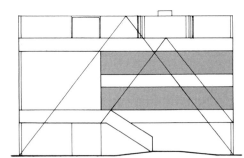

Figure 5.17 Le Corbusier, Villa Stein, Garches, 1927: front and rear elevations with *tracées régulateurs* based on Egyptian triangle

24. P. Singelenberg, *H P Berlage: Idea and Style, the quest for modern architecture*, Haentjens Dekker & Gumbert, Utrecht, 1972, p. 102.

25. Brooks, *Le Corbusier's Formative Years*, p. 159.

a ratio of 1.5923:1 or practically 8:5. The identical figure reappears in the third floor loggia and other features of the façade.

Against this, it must be said that Le Corbusier's published elevations are overlaid with *tracées régulateurs* based on the golden rectangle, and this is more likely to be the proportion he really had in mind (Figure 5.18). The resemblance to the Egyptian triangle is therefore probably only coincidental. It is curious, nevertheless, that since the ratio of the golden section is 1:1.618 it requires a wider margin of error, when applied to the villa, than the analysis based on the Egyptian triangle.

5.3 Düsseldorf and the Werkbund

Lauweriks and K.P.C. de Bazel left Cuypers' office in 1895 to set up an independent 'atelier for architecture, arts and crafts and decorative arts'. In 1897 they established the 'Vahana' course in drawing, art history and aesthetics, and the following year founded the periodical *Bouw- en Sierkunst (Architecture and Decorative Art)*. Between 1900 and his move to Düsseldorf in 1904 Lauweriks taught at the School of Arts and Crafts in Haarlem.

The Düsseldorf appointment came about through Berlage, who as mentioned above was initially approached by Behrens to take up the post. The school was a focus of the wider movement for design reform in Germany, reflected in the establishment of a network of institutions, most notably the Deutsche Werkbund, which became important sources of the post-war modern movement. The moving spirit behind the foundation of the Werkbund in 1907, Hermann Muthesius, had also been the driving force behind the appointment four years earlier of Behrens as the director of the Düsseldorf School.

Lauweriks was thus in a key position to influence all these developments by his example and teaching. One of his students, Adolf Meyer (1881–1929), entered Behrens' office where he worked on the AEG factories. He went on to become the partner of Walter Gropius, with whom he worked on the Fagus factory, Alfeld (1911–13). Meyer played a leading role behind the scenes in the development of the Bauhaus. In 1920 he, Gropius and Fred Forbat met Theo van Doesburg in Berlin, where he had been invited by the art critic Adolf Behne, and subsequently it was with the more sympathetic Meyer rather than Gropius that Van Doesburg negotiated his move to Weimar which precipitated the stormy but fruitful interaction between the Bauhaus and De Stijl in the years 1921–2.[26]

Although Meyer himself was not directly involved in the design of the Bauhaus buildings at Dessau (1926), the swastika form of the plan

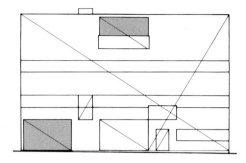

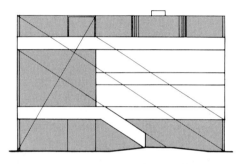

Figure 5.18 Villa Stein, Garches: front and rear elevations with *tracées régulateurs* based on golden section

26. E. van Straaten, *Theo van Doesburg 1883–1931*, Staats-uitgeverij, The Hague, 1983, pp. 98–9

has a striking resemblance to Lauweriks' generation of building-forms by means of rectangular meanders (Figure 5.19). N.H.M. Tummers argues strongly that like other works of the Gropius-Meyer partnership, this shows strong affinities, albeit indirect ones, with Lauweriks' teaching, rather than (as Giedion assumes in *Space, Time and Architecture*) with cubist painting:

> The Lauweriks form is clearly recognizable in various projects that Gropius made together with Meyer; above all in the ground plan of the philosophical academy at Erlangen, and consequently also (though admittedly without Meyer's participation) in that of the Bauhaus itself.[27]

The painting Giedion cites in connection with the Bauhaus building is Picasso's *L'Arlesienne*:

> Two major endeavors of modern architecture are fulfilled here, not as unconscious outgrowths of advances in engineering but as the conscious realization of an artist's intent; there is the hovering, vertical grouping of planes which satisfies our feeling for a relational space, and there is the extensive transparency that permits interior and exterior to be seen simultaneously, *en face* and *en profile*, like Picasso's 'L'Arlesienne' of 1911–12: variety of levels of reference, or of points of reference, and simultaneity – the conception of space–time, in short. In this building Gropius goes far beyond anything that might be regarded as achievement in construction alone.[28]

While Giedion's and Tummers' attributions of the sources of the Bauhaus are both of course speculative, one is bound to ask the question: which story is more believable? In 1912, when Picasso completed *L'Arlesienne*, Gropius joined Behrens' office soon after it opened. This happened in 1907 or 1908, as a result of a chance meeting with Karl Ernst Osthaus while travelling in Spain. As he recalls in a letter written shortly before his death: 'I was nearly a year in Spain during 1907–8, and there I met Osthaus for the first time ... Osthaus brought me to my Master, Peter Behrens.'[29]

The introduction to the Behrens' office was only one of several occasions on which Osthaus befriended Gropius and came to his aid at crucial points in his career.[30] He brought him to lecture at the Folkwang Museum in Hagen (of which Lauweriks, incidentally, was a member of the advisory board[31]) and sponsored his election to the Werkbund.[32]

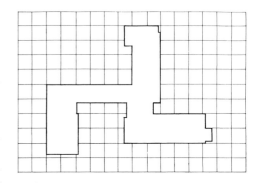

Figure 5.19 Walter Gropius, Bauhaus, Dessau, 1926: diagrammatic plan

27. N.H.M. Tummers, *J L Mathieu Lauweriks: zijn werk en zijn invloed*, G. van Saane, Hilversum, 1968, p. 39.

28. S. Giedion, *Space, Time and Architecture*, Harvard University Press, Cambridge, Mass., 1941, p. 401.

29. W. Gropius, letter to H. Hesse-Frielinghaus, quoted in H. Hesse-Frielinghaus, *Peter Behrens und Karl Ernst Osthaus*, Hagen, 1966, p. 504, n. 6, and in Windsor, *Peter Behrens*, p. 79.

30. R. Isaacs, *Gropius*, Little Brown & Company, Boston, MA, 1983, pp.21, 54, 63.

31. N.H.M. Tummers, *J L Mathieu Lauweriks: zijn werk en zijn invloed*, G. van Saane, Hilversum, 1968, p. 22.

32. E.S. Hochman, *Bauhaus: Crucible of Modernism*, Fromm International, New York, NY, 1997, p.12.

Gropius' connection with Osthaus, and through Osthaus indirectly with Lauweriks, was thus a very strong one. It was further strengthened by his association with Lauweriks' pupil Adolf Meyer, first as colleagues in Behrens' office (which Meyer was one of the first to join), and later as partners, after they had left Behrens' employment together in 1910. In comparison with such solid connections, the supposed link between the Bauhaus building and cubism has an air of fantasy.

In his Zurich lectures of 1908 Berlage showed a student work by Meyer as an example of the geometrical design method taught at Düsseldorf by Lauweriks.[33] Another brilliant ex-Lauweriks student, whose collaboration with Gropius was cut off by his death in 1918, was Fritz Kaldenbach.[34]

Even before Lauweriks entered it, the Behrens-Werkbund circle was no stranger to proportion systems. The revival of interest in these, and particularly in the golden section, began in Germany with the publication of Adolf Zeising's *Neue Lehre* in 1854,[35] and Gustav Fechner's *Vorschule der Aesthetik* in 1876.[36] In 1883 the architect August Thiersch published a theory of proportion based on the repetition of similar figures, in which he stated:

> We have found, in observing the most successful products of art in all important periods, that in each of them a fundamental shape is repeated, and that the parts form, by their composition and disposition, similar figures. Harmony results from the repetition of the fundamental form of the plan throughout its subdivisions.[37]

Thiersch's theory was taken up by the Swiss art historian Heinrich Wölfflin in an article published six years later, containing analyses of a number of Greek temples and renaissance churches and palaces.[38] In 1906–7, while Lauweriks was teaching at the School of Arts and Crafts in Düsseldorf, August Thiersch's son Paul was working in Peter Behrens' Düsseldorf office.[39] Thiersch's theory is very probably the source of Le Corbusier's use of *tracées régulateurs* or 'regulating lines'. He could have been exposed to it either while working in Behrens' office in 1910–11 or during his stay in Munich in April 1910. Having admired en route the churches in Stuttgart and Ulm by the Munich architect Theodor Fischer (1862–1938), on his arrival in Munich Jeanneret 'presented himself at Professor Fischer's office with portfolio in hand'.[40] Fischer was a founding member and the first president of the Deutsche Werkbund, and moreover an enthusiastic subscriber to Thiersch's proportion theory.[41] H. Allen Brooks goes on to relate that although

33. Berlage, 'Foundations and Development', p. 216.

34. Windsor, *Peter Behrens*, p. 55

35. A. Zeising, *Neue Lehre von den Proportionen des menschlichen Körpers*, Leipzig, 1854.

36. G.T. Fechner, *Vorschule der Aesthetik*, Georg Holms, Hildesheim, 1978.

37. A. Thiersch, article on proportion in *Handbuch der Architektur*, Darmstadt, 1883, vol. IV, p. 39.

38. H. Wölfflin, 'Zur Lehre den Proportionen' (1889), reprinted in *Kleine Schriften*, Basel, 1946.

39. J. Paul, 'German neo-classicism and the modern movement', in *The Architectural Review*, London, vol. CLII, no. 907, September 1972, pp. 176–7.

40. Brooks, *Le Corbusier's Formative Years*, p. 213.

41. Ibid., p. 214.

Concerning employment, Fischer was apologetic ... he cordially invited the young Swiss to visit his home the following afternoon (Sunday) where Jeanneret had such a splendid time that he lacked superlatives to describe it ... And Fischer even proffered the use of his tennis court whenever Jeanneret might wish to play![42]

Whether this offer was taken up is not recorded, but such friendly relations between the two men suggest at least the possibility that the subject of proportion systems might have come up in their conversation.

5.4 Cosmic mathematics

In his ground-breaking study of Lauweriks' work at Hagen (1967), N.H.M. Tummers describes it as an important confluence of a number of streams: Jugendstil and art nouveau, the Bauhaus and De Stijl. He points to the striking foreshadowing in Lauweriks' architecture, and in the revolutionary typography of the magazine *Der Ring* which Lauweriks founded in 1908 (Figure 5.20), of the work of – among others – J.J.P. Oud (Figures 5.21–5.22), Piet Mondrian, Walter Gropius and Le Corbusier. These visual parallels are backed up by historical connections: Berlage provides a link with Oud; Adolf Meyer, Fritz Kaldenbach and Osthaus himself all connect Lauweriks with Gropius; and Jeanneret undoubtedly visited Osthaus at Hagen in 1911.

The link with the De Stijl painters – Mondrian, Van der Leck and Van Doesburg – is less substantial. It depends on a presumed affinity (apparently unsupported by documentary evidence of direct influence) between Lauweriks' thought and that of Mathieu Schoenmaekers (1875–1944), ex-priest, mystical philosopher and author of *The New World-Image* (1915) and *Principles of Plastic Mathematics* (1916).[43] Mondrian and Van der Leck were neighbours of Schoenmaekers and fell briefly under his spell while all three were living at Laren in 1915–17. By 1917, however, Mondrian was already warning Van Doesburg that while Schoenmaekers might be a possible contributor to *De Stijl* he found him an 'awful fellow' and doubted the genuineness of his intentions.[44] The invitation to contribute was in fact withdrawn.[45] Another somewhat tenuous connection is through theosophy: Lauweriks became a member of the Theosophical Society in 1894, Schoenmaekers in 1905 and Mondrian in 1909.

The De Stijl artist whose work and thought show the most obvious affinity with that of Lauweriks is not Mondrian, however, but

42. Ibid., p. 213.

43. Tummers, *Mathieu Lauweriks*, pp. 11 & 19.

44. P. Mondrian, letter to T. van Doesburg, 21 May 1917; E. Hoek, 'Piet Mondrian', in C. Blotkamp et al., *De Beginjaren van De Stijl 1917–1922*, Reflex, Utrecht, 1982, p. 59.

45. C. Blotkamp, 'Theo van Doesburg', in *De Beginjaren*, p. 40.

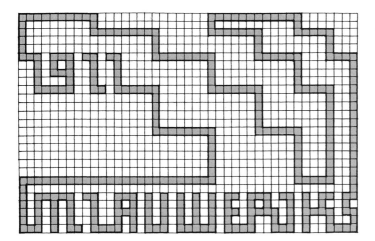

Figure 5.20 J.L.M. Lauweriks, name-card for 1911: proportional analysis showing use of square grid

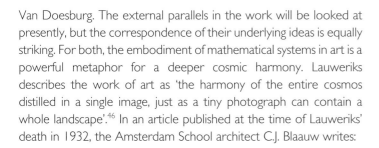

Figure 5.21 J.J.P. Oud, monogram

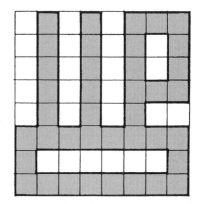

Figure 5.22 J.J.P. Oud, monogram: proportional analysis showing use of square grid

Van Doesburg. The external parallels in the work will be looked at presently, but the correspondence of their underlying ideas is equally striking. For both, the embodiment of mathematical systems in art is a powerful metaphor for a deeper cosmic harmony. Lauweriks describes the work of art as 'the harmony of the entire cosmos distilled in a single image, just as a tiny photograph can contain a whole landscape'.[46] In an article published at the time of Lauweriks' death in 1932, the Amsterdam School architect C.J. Blaauw writes:

> His system was not a search for artistic form through a meaning-less play with line. For him the system was the divine thread with which things were embroidered by a higher force. The artist's life-task was to seize hold of this divine thread and so weave it by creative effort that the work of art would thrill with the beautiful harmony which stamped it as a thing of a higher order.[47]

For Van Doesburg too, art – more specifically, the 'new image' or 'new representation' (*nieuwe beelding*) promoted by De Stijl – will replace religion as a means of direct connection with the divine. In a letter to the Belgian architect Huib Hoste he writes: 'The newly created image *itself* can now, through our step into the future, achieve what previously the Church was able to do through the medium of art, namely create a direct relationship with God.'[48] He says much the same in an article published in *De Stijl* in February 1918 (quoted more fully in Chapter 2, section 2.1):

46.   J.L.M. Lauweriks, 'Het nut en doel der kunst', in *Theosophia*, no. 15, 1906–7.

47.   C.J. Blaauw, 'J.L.M. Lauweriks', in *Bouwkundig Weekblad*, no. 53, 1932, pp. 141–2.

48.   T. van Doesburg, letter to H. Hoste, quoted by A. Doig in *Theo van Doesburg*, Cambridge University Press, Cambridge, 1986, p. 59.

Modern art is the direct intermediary between human beings and the absolute. The modern artist destroys the illusion of false relationships. His aesthetic consciousness reacts solely to that which is above the relative: the universal. By destroying the false illusion of the individual – of nature – he brings to the fore the elementary plastic proportions that govern the world.[49]

Finally, in *Principles of Neo-Plastic Art* (1919), Van Doesburg writes:

Although we cannot grasp the perfect harmony, the absolute equilibrium of the universe, each and everything in the universe (every motif) is nevertheless subordinated to the laws of this harmony, this equilibrium. It is the artist's business to discover and give form to this concealed harmony, this universal equilibrium of things, to demonstrate its conformity to its own laws, etc. The (truly exact) work of art is a metaphor of the universe obtained with artistic means.[50]

The artistic means by which this 'metaphor of the universe' – or this 'direct relationship with God' – was to be obtained were mathematical. 'The development of plastic art is determined by the urge to perception,' writes Van Doesburg in his 1918 essay 'Denken – Aanschouwen – Beelden' ('Think – Observe – Represent'): 'The new representation (*nieuwe beelding*) manifests the urge to perception through the experience of *plastic proportion (beeldende verhouding)*.'[51] In so doing, the new representation will raise art to the level of pure abstract thought, hitherto manifested only in mathematics and philosophy. Art, no longer busying itself with the representation of sensory perceptions of natural phenomena, will now be concerned only with pure conceptual relationships revealed by exact mathematical figures, and by 'number, measure, proportion and abstract line'.[52] Near the end of his life he wrote:

perfect work first comes into existence when we surrender our "personality". the universal lies beyond our personality ... the method leading to universal form is based on calculations of measure, direction and number. the same method underlay the pyramid.[53]

And:

That which today bestows a cultural value on painting is mathematical or, rather, arithmetical control. Mathematics has represented not only the basis of science but also the foundations of art

49. T. van Doesburg, 'Fragmenten I', in *De Stijl*, vol. I, no. 4, February 1918, pp. 47–8.

50. T. van Doesburg, *Principles of Neo-Plastic Art*, trans. J. Seligman, Lund Humphries, London, 1969, p. 33.

51. T. van Doesburg, 'Denken – aanschouwen – beelden', in *De Stijl*, vol. II, no. 2, Dec. 1918, p. 23.

52. Ibid., p. 24.

53. T. van Doesburg, 'elementarisme', p. 15.

during the great epochs. As soon as the artist uses elementary forms as a means of expression, his work is not merely 'modern', but universal.[54]

In the writings of Le Corbusier one meets again with the same insistence on the underlying unity of the cosmos. Mathematical order is for him the foundation of nature's harmony. We are innately sensitive to this harmony, which implies some kind of grand cosmic design; and the same mathematical order is the prerequisite not only for all science, but also for any art of universal significance and lasting value. In *Towards a New Architecture* he writes:

We say that a face is handsome when the precision of the modelling and the disposition of the features reveal proportions which we *feel to be harmonious* because they arouse, deep within us and beyond our senses, a resonance ... An indefinable trace of the Absolute which lies in the depths of our being ... This is indeed the axis on which man is organized in perfect accord with nature and probably with the universe ...; this axis leads us to assume a unity of conduct in the universe and to admit a single will behind it. The laws of physics are thus a corollary to this axis, and if we recognize (and love) science and its works, it is because both one and the other force us to admit that they are prescribed by this primal will. If the results of mathematical calculation appear satisfying and harmonious to us, it is because they proceed from the axis ... If we are brought up short by the Parthenon, it is because a chord inside us is struck when we see it; the axis is touched.[55]

Much the same argument appears, thirty years later, in *The Modulor*: 'nature is ruled by mathematics, and the masterpieces of art are in consonance with nature; they express the laws of nature and themselves proceed from those laws. Consequently, they too are governed by mathematics'.[56]

What led to this remarkable convergence between the thought of Lauweriks, Van Doesburg and Le Corbusier? Was Schoenmaekers the link between the first two? And did Le Corbusier's meeting with Osthaus and perhaps Lauweriks at Hagen in 1911 give him the idea which led forty years later to the *modulor*? And was it to his mind so crucial to the genesis of his system that he felt unable to omit all reference to it in his book?

Van Doesburg met Schoenmaekers on his first visit to Mondrian at Laren in 1916, but seems not to have read *The New World-Image* until

54. T. van Doesburg, 'From intuition towards certitude' (1930); in *Réalités nouvelles*, no. 1, 1947, p. 3; and in J. Baljeu, *Theo van Doesburg*, Studio Vista, London, 1974, p. 185.

55. Le Corbusier, *Towards a New Architecture* (1923), The Architectural Press, London, 1946, pp. 187–96.

56. Le Corbusier, *The Modulor*, Faber & Faber, London, 1961, pp. 29–30.

1918, when he rejects its religious overtones, but approves the reference to space–time:

> I find many of the ideas vague, dreamy, fantastic. For instance, his notion of artistic symbolism seems to me far-fetched. One of the best things for me is his exposition of the concept of time and space. There he expresses certain thoughts which coincide with my own recent thinking, in relation to the fourth dimension: motion.[57]

What Van Doesburg saw as valuable in Schoenmaekers' thought was not anything that might have connected him with Lauweriks, therefore, but the concept of four-dimensionality. This was much under discussion in the popular scientific literature of the time; Einstein had published his general theory of relativity in 1916. The list of books advertised as obtainable by subscribers to *De Stijl* includes Henri Bergson's *Matter and Memory*, Henri Poincaré's *New Mechanics*, and works on four-dimensionality by J.B. Ubink and H.K. de Vries, as well as Schoenmaekers' *The New World-Image* and *Plastic Mathematics*.

If Schoenmaekers is the principal link between Lauweriks and Van Doesburg, he is thus a weak one. Moreover, Van Doesburg's few references to Lauweriks tend to be uncomplimentary. In 1916 Lauweriks returned from Germany to Amsterdam, and in 1918 he joined the editorial staff of the newly founded magazine *Wendingen*, a potential rival of *De Stijl*. Van Doesburg wrote:

> The periodical *Windwijzer* ['weathercock'] … appears under the pseudonym *Wendingen* ['swings' or 'changes'], which describes its contents perfectly (its motto 'you never can tell' or 'where the wind blows, there go I'). It is the Dutch continuation of the periodical *Der Ring*, founded in Düsseldorf in 1908 and edited by the architect Lauweriks (a periodical which smelled strongly of Vienna and the Werkstätte).[58]

One can agree with Allan Doig's conclusion:

> A number of different strands of development can be traced: one through Schoenmaekers and Berlage, to the pioneering work of J L M Lauweriks concerning the rule of system, logic, and mathematics in the cosmos and hence in art as the sign of the Universe; another strand is evident … in the mathematically based designs of J H de Groot, whose ideas were known to Van Doesburg.[59]

57. T. van Doesburg, letter to A. Kok, 22 June 1918, quoted in Blotkamp, 'Theo van Doesburg', p. 40.
58. T. van Doesburg, 'Rondblik', in *De Stijl*, vol. IV, no. 6, June 1921, p. 87.
59. Doig, *Theo van Doesburg*, p. 133.

In other words, Schoenmaekers was only one, and perhaps not the most important, of the many interwoven threads that make up the fabric of artistic and architectural thinking in Holland in the first two decades of this century. Although some or all of these threads may connect Van Doesburg indirectly with Lauweriks, it is not the strength of any individual thread that matters, but the weave and density of the fabric as a whole. Circumstantial connections between individuals (who met whom and when) are less significant in this context than the broad intellectual and artistic climate that these individuals helped to form, and by which they were in turn formed. Doig continues:

> The reason for mentioning these strands of development is not to establish direct lines of inheritance, but to indicate the breadth of the discussion within which Van Doesburg shaped his conception of the mechanical aesthetic and its humanistic, but universal, basis. Within this larger discussion, statements which otherwise seem mystical almost to the point of being cranky reveal their fundamental seriousness.[60]

5.5 Grids

The problem remains, how these grandiose cosmological ideas worked themselves out in practice; in other words, how well the remarkable parallels, which one finds between Lauweriks', Van Doesburg's and Le Corbusier's theories of art, were realized in their work – and specifically in architecture.

This can be most clearly evaluated in the design of elements that are free of the constraints of convenient planning and weathertight construction: in the composition of purely decorative two-dimensional features such as grilles, tessellations and window-framings. All three artists produced asymmetrical patterns based on modular grids, not unlike crossword puzzles. Van Doesburg describes the process as follows:

> The decorative method is always based on a motif ... This motif (or pattern) is repeated, one to the left, once to the right, reversed, or strung out horizontally or rising vertically ... and it will not be difficult for the musically trained ear to discover the same decorative development of the musical 'pattern' in the work of no less a personage than Bach.'[61]

60. Ibid., p. 133.
61. T. van Doesburg, 'Het glas-lood in de oude en nieuwe architectuur', in *Het Bouwbedrijf*, vol. VII, no. 10, 9 May 1930, p. 202; quoted in Doig, *Theo van Doesburg*, p. 90.

Van Doesburg's many designs for stained-glass windows (Figure 5.23) – notably for Oud's Villa Allegonda at Katwijk (1917) – and the tile patterns that he used to decorate the floors of J.J.P. Oud's vacation house, De Vonk, at Noordwijkerhout (1918) (Figure 5.24), are composed of repetitions of relatively simple asymmetrical patterns. The repetition is cleverly disguised by means of various kinds of symmetries: translations, reflections and rotations.[62] As Tummers points out, very similar patterns appear in Lauweriks' work at Hagen and at the Stein house at Göttingen (1912): as fences and gates (Figure 5.25), window-gratings, and again as stained-glass windows (Figure 5.26).[63]

Le Corbusier devotes ten pages of *The Modulor* to a series of Stijl-like compositions which he describes as 'panel exercises' (Figure 5.27):

> You take a square, say, and divert yourself by dividing it up in accordance with the measures of the 'Modulor'. This game can be played indefinitely ... The 'Panel Exercise' has the satisfying effect of showing that in the very heart of this impeccable geometry – which some might think *implacable* – the personality has complete freedom of action. Hanning's 'panel exercise' had a certain special character of its own, that invented by de Looze ... a different one, and that of Préféral a different one again. These documents might serve as tests in a kind of graphology of the plastic emotion of the individual, the psycho-physiological reactions of each player in the game.'[64]

Le Corbusier illustrates no fewer than 325 of these patterns. Although described as 'games', they were clearly intended as more than an amusing pastime or a psychological test. In *The Modulor* he shows in some detail a glazed panel designed on the same principle.[65] He used similar glazing designs in his subsequent architecture, for instance in the window designs of the Maisons Jaoul at Neuilly (1954–6), the monastery of La Tourette (1957–60) and the Centre Le Corbusier in Zurich (1963–7). And if this is not sufficient proof of the seriousness with which Le Corbusier regarded the method, the pattern exercises come at the conclusion of the most high-flown and 'philosophical' section of *The Modulor*: the chapter entitled 'Mathematics'. The chapter begins by restating the connection between mathematical order in art and the fundamental mathematical harmony of nature:

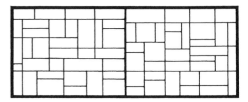

Figure 5.23 Theo van Doesburg, Stained glass composition IX, 1918

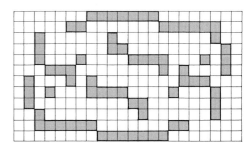

Figure 5.24 Theo van Doesburg, part floor-tile design for vacation house 'De Vonk',

Figure 5.25 J.L.M. Lauweriks, garden gate, Harmann house, Hohenhagen, 1911

62. Doig, *Theo van Doesburg*, pp. 64–81.
63. Tummers, *Mathieu Lauweriks*, pp. 45–61.
64. Le Corbusier, *Modulor*, pp. 92 and 96.
65. Ibid., pp. 163–4.

Mathematics is the majestic structure conceived by man to grant him comprehension of the universe. It holds both the absolute and the infinite, the understandable and the forever elusive. It has walls before which one may pace up and down without result; sometimes there is a door: one opens it – enters – one is in another realm, the realm of the gods, the room which holds the key to the great systems. These doors are the doors of the miracles. Having gone through one, man is no longer the operative force, but rather it is his contact with the universe. In front of him unfolds and spreads out the fabulous fabric of numbers without end.[66]

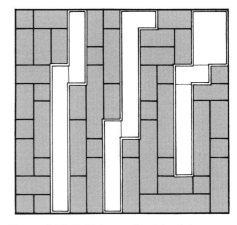

Figure 5.26 J.L.M. Lauweriks, stained-glass window, Stein house, Göttingen, 1912

It is not too far-fetched to conclude, therefore, that Le Corbusier regarded these patterns as a kind of 'spatial music', and thus potentially as 'doors to the room that holds the key to the great systems'. In fact, he draws a direct parallel with music, quoting from Leibniz and Rameau:

> Music is a secret mathematical exercise, and he who engages in it is unaware that he is manipulating numbers. [67]
>
> (Leibniz)

> Music is not a part of mathematics; on the contrary, it is the sciences which are a part of music, for they are founded on proportion, and the resonance of the body of sound engenders all proportion. [68]
>
> (Rameau)

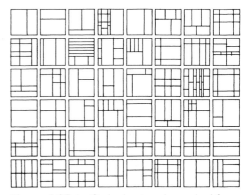

Figure 5.27 Le Corbusier, 'panel exercises' from The Modulor, 1950

In just the same way, Lauweriks conceived his modular zigzags and spirals as images from which might be distilled 'the harmony of the entire cosmos', and Van Doesburg intended his floor tilings and stained-glass compositions as fragments of a universal harmony, 'metaphors of the universe'. The problem with this is one that all the visual arts must confront when they aspire to the condition of music: that is, when they become purely abstract, and therefore essentially decorative. The danger is that, far from rising thereby to the pure heights of universal truth, they sink into triviality. Instead of breathing what Van Doesburg calls 'the cold atmosphere of the mountains at an altitude of 3000 metres ... [where] the cold kills the microbes',[69] they risk suffocating for lack of representational content or purpose.

The outstanding example of such abstraction is Islamic pattern, an art which resulted from the proscription on religious grounds of the representation of visible phenomena. It is against this standard that the pattern-compositions of Lauweriks, Van Doesburg and Le

66. Ibid., p. 71.
67. Ibid., p. 75.
68. Ibid.
69. Van Doesburg, 'elementarisme', p. 15.

Corbusier must be judged. Two aspects of Islamic pattern may explain why it succeeds in achieving universality and avoiding triviality.

First, the patterns themselves are not arbitrary. Each pattern pursues the strict logic of a chosen mathematical ratio – for instance the square root of two or three, or the golden section – manifested in primary geometrical figures such as squares, hexagons or pentagons. Although both Van Doesburg and Le Corbusier employ some of these same ratios and figures, they do so in ways that are comparatively loose, haphazard and mathematically crude.

Secondly, the same geometries which the Islamic artists use in small-scale pattern making, in the form of tilings, carpets or perforated screens, recur at the larger scale in the plans of palaces and mosques. In other words, the order of the whole is reflected in its subdivisions, in much the same way as the branching of a tree is reflected in the veining of its leaves. By this means, the relation between the parts and the whole within the work becomes a powerful metaphor for the relation between the work itself and the world at large. Van Doesburg seems to have had this sort of metaphorical relation in mind when he wrote in his 1924 architectural manifesto:

> The subdivision of functional spaces is strictly determined by rectangular planes which ... can be conceived as extended to infinity, thereby creating a system of coordinates, of which the different points correspond to an equal number of points in universal, limitless space.[70]

The restricted conditions of Van Doesburg's two architectural realizations did not give him sufficient opportunity, perhaps, to demonstrate this great vision. The Café Aubette in Strasbourg of 1927 was a conversion of a historic building (designed by J.F. Blondel in 1764), so walls could not be moved; and the overall form of Van Doesburg's own house at Meudon (1927–30) was governed by the limitations of its narrow site. In painting he had greater freedom, but it is only in the last years of his life that he began to approach a mathematically consistent method of composition. In January 1930 Van Doesburg told his friend the poet Anthony Kok that although unfortunately his need to keep writing to earn money left him too little time to paint, he had recently made a sketch for his next painting, 'on the spatio-temporal ground-form of which I can make *1000 paintings*, since the "universal" is inexhaustible! The new painting will have the following planar relationships: 8:16:32:56, with which the colour must be in accordance.'[71]

70. Van Doesburg, 'Tot een beeldende architectuur', in *De Stijl*, vol. VI, no. 6/7, 1924, p. 79.

71. T. van Doesburg, letter to A. Kok, 23 Jan. 1930; quoted in E. van Straaten, *Theo van Doesburg 1883–1931*, Staatsuitgeverij, The Hague, 1983, p. 169.

The fact that the fourth number in the series is 56 seems odd. If the sketch in question is the one on which he based the most obviously mathematical of all his works – the *Universal form II* (1926–9) (Figure 5.28) – then it consists of a series of diagonally placed squares, each exactly twice the width of the next, so the fourth term should be 64. But since 56 happens to be the sum of the three previous numbers (8 + 16 + 32 = 56) Van Doesburg is perhaps referring to a different, more complex, additive series: one in which each term is the sum of its three preceding terms, i.e. $D = A + B + C$. Dividing his series throughout by eight in order to reduce it to its simplest numerical terms, and extending it downwards and upwards, it becomes the interesting sequence 0, 0, 1, 1, 2, 4, 7, 13, 24, 44, 81 ..., which converges towards a constant ratio of approximately 1:1.84. It is not easy to find an example of such a complex series among Van Doesburg's late paintings, however. Can the number 56 be simply a mistake? If it is, such slipshod arithmetic casts doubt on the seriousness of his claim that 'mathematical or, rather, arithmetical control'[72] must be the basis of any art of universal value. His quest for a mathematical route to universal significance seems then to have been little more than a romantic dream.

In the case of Le Corbusier one is struck by the fact that he apparently made no attempt to apply the *modulor* to the overall proportions of such buildings as the *Unité d'Habitation* at Marseilles (1947–52) or La Tourette (1956–7). In *The Modulor* he gives the overall dimensions of the *Unité* as '140 metres long, 24 metres wide and 56 metres high'.[73] He does not mention, however, that these dimensions are not far from the closest *modulor* measures: 139.01, 25.07 and 53.1 m respectively. Presumably he regarded the *modulor* measures as intrinsically anthropometric, and therefore significant only when not too far removed from the actual dimensions of the human body. Consequently he restricted them to relatively small elements of the building, such as the internal dimensions of the individual apartments and the superstructures on the roof: elements that can be grasped or reached with the hand or measured out with a few paces.

5.6 The entire cosmos in a single image

Lauweriks was the only one of the three artists who consistently applied the system of proportions to the whole as well as to the parts. The same meandering line that appears in the design of details like metal railings and window grilles recurs in the layout of the gardens at Hagen and as the line that unites the roof ridges of all the houses (Figure 5.11) and which in his ideal plan he extends beyond

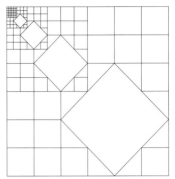

Figure 5.28 Theo van Doesburg, *Universal form II*, 1926 (redrawn interpretation by the author)

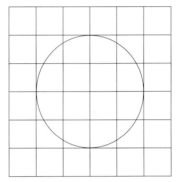

Figure 5.29 Christian Bayer, church project, 1909: modular grid, first stage – circle inscribed on

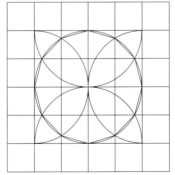

Figure 5.30 Christian Bayer, church project, 1909: modular grid, second stage – dodecagon defined by intersecting half-circles

72. T. van Doesburg, 'From intuition towards certitude' (1930) in *Réalités nouvelles*, no. 9, 1847, p.3, and in Baljeu, *Theo van Doesburg*, p.185.
73. Le Corbusier, *Modulor*, p. 132.

the group he actually built, to embrace the whole suburb. The repetition of the same motif at a succession of scales is a logical consequence of Lauweriks' fractal-like system, in which small patterns combine to form larger ones, and these in turn to form still larger ones. In his own work – exemplified by the 1915 project for a war-memorial park – he usually disguises the underlying modular grid under an elaborate system of complex curves strongly suggestive of 'Julia sets'. Julia sets were, coincidentally, being developed at almost the same time, during the first world war, by the French mathematicians Gaston Julia and Pierre Fatour.[74]

In contrast to these curves – aptly described by Le Corbusier's fictitious 'gardener in Bremen' as 'all those twiddly bits' – the church design by Lauweriks' student Christian Bayer, published in *Der Ring* in 1909,[75] provides a straightforward didactic demonstration of his compositional method. The design is based on a six-by-six grid of squares, framing a circle with a radius equal to the width of two squares (Figure 5.29). The circle circumscribes a twelve-sided figure – a regular dodecagon – defined by arcs of the same radius as the circle (Figure 5.30). The resulting figure, which can be resolved into over-lapping patterns of equilateral triangles, hexagons and squares, combines the root two and root three proportions. It is the key diagram for many Islamic patterns (Figures 5.31–5.32). That Lauweriks' method should recall Islamic designs is not surprising, given that oriental art and architecture in general were a major inspiration for him and for K.P.C. de Bazel, and for the teaching of the Vahana course which they founded together in 1897.

The basic motif (Figure 5.33) is reiterated at six different scales in the plans and elevations of the church and in the urban layout of the surrounding district. The basic circle-in-square motif, which determines the wall thickness, is multiplied thirty-six times to give the width of the church and fifty-four times to give its length and height (Figure 5.34). It comprises one of the thirty-six squares that compose the next larger unit, six times the dimension of the first: this defines the side-chapels and structural bays. The third unit, nine times the dimension of the basic motif, defines the narthex, and the fourth, twice as large as the third, defines the nave and the diameter of the tall lantern that surmounts the central dome. The fifth figure, twice the dimension of the fourth, determines the great central space of the church, the overall width of the building and the height of the twin towers that frame the central cupola. Finally, this dimension is again multiplied six times to produce the overall width and length of the urban space that surrounds the church (Figure 5.35).

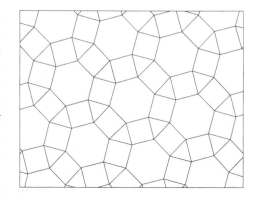

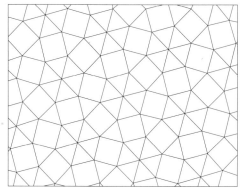

Figure 5.31–32 Typical Islamic tessellations based on dodecagons, squares and equilateral

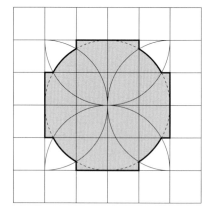

Figure 5.33 Christian Bayer, church project: basic motif

74. J. Gleick, *Chaos*, Sphere Books, London, 1988, p. 221.
75. Tummers, *Mathieu Lauweriks*, pp. 14–18.

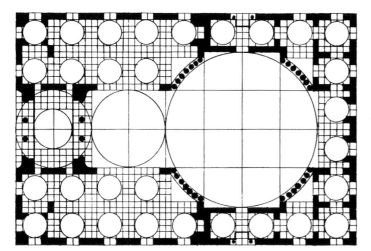

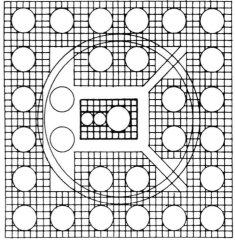

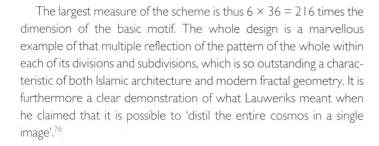

Figure 5.34 Christian Bayer, church project: plan

Figure 5.35 Christian Bayer, church project: site plan

The largest measure of the scheme is thus $6 \times 36 = 216$ times the dimension of the basic motif. The whole design is a marvellous example of that multiple reflection of the pattern of the whole within each of its divisions and subdivisions, which is so outstanding a characteristic of both Islamic architecture and modern fractal geometry. It is furthermore a clear demonstration of what Lauweriks meant when he claimed that it is possible to 'distil the entire cosmos in a single image'.[76]

---

76. Lauweriks, 'Het nut en doel der kunst'.

6

Mies: The Correspondence of Thing and Intellect[1]

6.1 Classical *versus* anti-classical

Of all the great modern architects, Mies van der Rohe is the least known.[2]

Thus begins Philip Johnson's preface to the first edition of his 1947 Museum of Modern Art catalogue, *Mies van der Rohe*. At sixty-one, Mies had still built scarcely twenty buildings and – unlike Frank Lloyd Wright and Le Corbusier – published only a few terse statements about architecture and dry descriptions of his projects. By far the greater part of his work, including the Farnsworth house (1950), the apartment blocks at 860 Lake Shore Drive (1951), Crown Hall (1956), and the Seagram Building (1958), would be built in the last twenty years of his life. And it was only in these same twenty years, or after his death in 1969, that he would finally be recognized as one of the three or four major figures of the modern movement. Between 1955 and 1977 there appeared eleven monographs on Mies.[3]

The image of him that was built up in these works was an essentially static one. What was stressed was above all the unity of his total *œuvre*, the 'timeless perfection' of each individual building, the painstaking attention given to the refinement of every detail, and his delight in using durable and often luxurious materials – brick, travertine, onyx, ebony, glass, leather, raw silk, chromium plated steel, or bronze. The only strikingly different interpretation published in the 1950s was Bruno Zevi's pioneering work, *Poetica dell'architettura neoplastica* (*The Poetics of Neoplastic Architecture*, 1953).[4] In that book Mies, rather than Rietveld or Oud, emerges as the ultimate exponent of De Stijl architecture. Whereas most other critics at that time portrayed Mies' career as the patient refinement of a single idea – or in his own words, 'the slow unfolding'[5] of architectural form – Zevi sees it as a struggle between two conflicting ideas: on one hand the closed, delimited space of classicism, and on the other the open, continuous space of De Stijl.

For Zevi, the concepts of 'neoplasticism' and 'classicism' stand for opposite visions, not just of architecture, but of human society. The

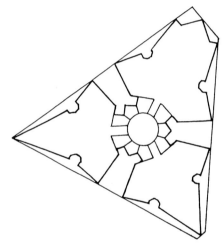

Figure 6.1 Ludwig Mies van der Rohe, Friedrichstrasse competition project, 1921: diagrammatic plan

1. This chapter is an edited and expanded version of an essay first published as 'Machines à Méditer', in the exhibition catalogue *Mies van der Rohe: Architect as Educator*, ed. Rolf Achilles, Kevin Harrington and Charlotte Myhrum, Illinois Institute of Technology University of Chicago Press, 1986.
2. P. Johnson, *Mies van der Rohe*, The Museum of Modern Art, New York, 1953, p. 7.
3. Max Bill (1955), Ludwig Hilbersheimer (1956), Arthur Drexler (1960), Peter Blake (1963), Werner Blaser (1965, 1977), A James Speyer (1968), Ludwig Glaeser (1969), Martin Pawley (1970), Peter Carter (1974), Lorenzo Papi (1975).
4. B. Zevi, *Poetica dell'architettura neoplastica*, Libreria Editrice Politecnica Tamburini, Milan, 1953.
5. L. Mies van der Rohe, 'Address to Illinois Institute of Technology' (1950), in P. Johnson, *Mies van der Rohe*, The Museum of Modern Art, New York, 1953, p. 40.

first represents freedom and democracy, the second, rigidity and despotism:

> The neoplasticist exploration emancipates us from the classicist, axial, over-structured and repressive vision that sees architecture as something to be contemplated rather than lived in, a symbol of theocratic, absolutist, state, bureaucratic or ideological power to which man must submit himself.[6]

This linking of architectural systems with political ones remained a central theme of Zevi's historical writing. Speaking in London thirty years later, and defending modernism against post-modernist criticism, he returns to the theme once more, citing its historical antecedents in the work of Alois Riegl and Georg Simmel and reminding his audience that Simmel had stated in 1896 that

> 'the tendency to symmetry, to a homogeneous arrangement of elements according to general principles, is typical of all despotic regimes,' while 'the form of the Liberal State tends to asymmetry,' to a recognition of the independent development of each element, and thus 'to free, wide-ranging relations' among them.[7]

Given his ideological stance, Zevi inevitably interprets Mies' development as a parabola. At its peak, around 1930 (Barcelona, Brno, Berlin), his work represents the final fulfilment of De Stijl, and the ultimate expression of democracy. The upward curve of the parabola represents, for Zevi, Mies' gradual self-liberation from the neoclassicism of his master Peter Behrens, and the downward curve after 1931 his slow sinking back into it:

> With the German pavilion at Barcelona of 1929 and the model house at the Berlin exhibition of 1931, the volumetric language of neoplasticism is transformed into a spatial one ... Neoplastic architecture finally discovers a protagonist who, overriding its grammatical and syntactic limitations, is able to raise it to the level of spatial poetry. Although extraneous to the history of De Stijl, Mies embodies its ideals and processes.[8]

Even though, according to Zevi, Mies finally 'betrayed' the De Stijl ideal by reverting to the closed and repressive forms of neoclassicism, it is nevertheless only in Mies that De Stijl achieved a mature and complete architectural expression. And paradoxically this very 'betrayal' serves to demonstrate still more clearly – by default as it

6. B. Zevi, *Poetica dell'architettura neoplastica*, 2nd edition, Giulio Einaudi, Turin, 1974, p. 210.

7. B. Zevi, 'Architecture versus historic criticism', RIBA Annual Discourse, London, 6 December 1983; reprinted in *RIBA Transactions*, no. 5, 1984, p. 40.

8. Zevi, *Poetica dell'architettura neoplastica*, 2nd edition, , p. 182.

were – the continued validity of those qualities that Mies suppressed in his later work:

> When, later, he abandons neoplasticism, he still demonstrates, by its absence, its continued validity. In fact, in the IIT blocks, the Chicago skyscrapers, the Farnsworth house, and above all in the Seagram Building in New York, he encloses himself in a world of formal inhibitions. Gone are the moving spatial ballets of Barcelona, of Berlin, of the Tugendhat house at Brno ... Rationalism on the point of relapsing into classicism: the Miesian parabola proves De Stijl to be an essential invariant in the language of modernism.[9]

An essential invariant: by all means. But the struggle between classicism and neoplasticism in Mies' work was a far more complex one than Zevi allows. It should be likened, not to a single parabola, but to a continual oscillation, the progress of which was marked by many uncertainties and shifts of position. And these uncertainties reflect the conflicting nature of modern architecture itself. That history – by which I mean the whole history of architecture since the enlightenment – has been one of struggle. But this struggle was not fought out (as Zevi believes) between a 'liberating' organicism or neoplasticism on one hand and a 'repressive' classicism on the other. Classicism has no intrinsic connection with either despotism or liberalism, though it has been employed – and exploited – by both.

Classicism, in its broadest sense, is simply the tendency of architecture to draw close to its essential type; the reverse of classicism is to move away from it. This classical type, to which all architecture must conform to a greater or lesser degree if it is to *be* architecture, arises from its inherent constructional nature and representational function ('representation' being here understood in the sense discussed in Chapters 2 and 3). The characteristics of this type are: the polarity of inside and outside; the concentricity of the inside space and of the solid elements that mark it out around the body of its occupant; materiality; and the mutual ordering and proportioning of the parts, and of the parts to the whole.

De Stijl was founded on a revolt against these principles and the attempt to replace them by opposite ones: spatial continuity, centrifugality, immateriality and the free association of contrasting elements. As we saw in Chapter 3, Van Doesburg, Van der Leck and especially Mondrian repeatedly identify materiality and enclosure in their writings as qualities intrinsic to architecture, and yet at the same time as obstacles that must first be annihilated before a 'neoplastic'

9. *Ibid.*, pp. 182–7.

architecture can become a reality: 'Architecture always presupposes enclosure: a building presents itself against space as a *thing*.'[10]

But this revolt can never be complete, and the confusing mixture of heterogeneous tendencies we habitually group together under the label 'modern movement' was derived in at least equal measure from broadly 'classical' traditions, notably the recovery of the vernacular initiated by the arts and crafts movement and the neoclassical revival associated with Adolf Loos, Peter Behrens and others.

This incompleteness was inevitable. Just as the classical type can never be identified with a single building but must be regarded rather as a kind of nucleus around which are gathered the innumerable variations to which building in general is susceptible, likewise the total reversal of the classical type can never be realized, because to do so would involve the denial of the very nature of building. Hence the anti-classical tendency in architecture has necessarily been accompanied by a pro-classical one. At intervals the dialectical struggle between classical thesis and anti-classical antithesis has resulted in a precarious synthesis: around 1800, 1900 and 1930. Chapter 4 showed this synthesis emerging in the Villa Savoye and the Barcelona Pavilion.

The tension between classical and anti-classical forces was constantly present in Mies' work and clearly reflected in the contrasting stages of his career. In the introduction to his book *The Artless Word* (1991) Fritz Neumeyer builds on and develops my first formulation of these ideas in 1984, pointing out that a reinterpretation of Mies is an important aspect of the fundamental revision needed of the history of modern architecture as a whole. The widespread misconception that modernism denied tradition, scale, variation and context is largely due, he writes, to a 'One-sided interpretation with a particular historical slant ... disseminated in such influential teaching texts as Sigfried Giedion's *Space, Time and Architecture*, in which the history of modernism is presented as unambiguous.'[11]

The case of Mies is particularly relevant in this reassessment, because contrary to the general assumption that his work was characterized above all by unity and consistency – even monotony – it is in fact full of conflict and barely resolved contradiction. For instance, Neumeyer points out that in the 1920s, at the time when he was most strongly influenced by De Stijl, 'Mies did not simply exchange old values for new ones, but continued the dialogue on successively new levels, as is evident from the simultaneity of neoclassical country houses and bold experiments.'[12]

In the last twenty years, several studies, notably Neumeyer's, have contributed further to the undermining of the magisterial image of

10. P. Mondrian, 'Het bepaalde en het onbepaalde', in *De Stijl*, vol. II, no. 2, December 1918, p. 16.

11. F. Neumeyer, *The Artless Word: Mies van der Rohe on the Building Art*, MIT Press, Cambridge, Mass., 1991, p. xx.

12. *Ibid.*, p. xviii.

Mies as a solitary thinker proceeding undeviatingly towards a single goal.[13] These studies show him as an altogether more interesting character. It is not that there is no truth whatever in the old monolithic image. That granite portrait of the architect is a true representation of an aspect of his career; but it shows only one side of him, like a carving in bas-relief. He did indeed move towards a goal, but his progress, especially in the early years, was full of ambiguities and changes of direction. He was not only closely involved with and influenced by the many conflicting movements that surrounded him; he was also a profoundly thoughtful architect who responded to the lessons of his own work. It was through building that he learnt how to build, and through thinking about his buildings that he learnt how to think. As he said: 'I want to examine my thoughts in action ... I want to do something in order to be able to think.'[14]

6.2 Mies, Aquinas and the definition of truth

The above statement implies a two-way relationship between the mind and things. We make things in order to think: our intellect not only *forms* the things we make, but these things in turn '*in-form*' the intellect. The idea that knowledge is a mutual relation or correspondence between things and the mind is contained in St Thomas Aquinas' famous definition of truth as *adaequatio rei et intellectus* – roughly translatable as the 'concordance', 'correspondence' or 'conformity' of thing and intellect. The Latin phrase has been quoted repeatedly in studies of Mies, yet until Franz Schulze published his biography in 1985 no critic seems to have inquired at what stage Mies first became interested in Aquinas; nor has anyone examined the meaning and context of the phrase, considered its specific relevance to Mies' work, or even taken the trouble to translate it. Peter Carter quotes Mies' own recollection of the matter:

It then became clear to me that it was not the task of architecture to invent form. I tried to understand what that task was. I asked Peter Behrens, but he could not give me an answer. He did not ask that question ... We searched in the quarries of ancient and medieval philosophy. Since we knew that it was a question of the truth, we tried to find out what the truth really was. We were very delighted to find a definition of truth by St. Thomas Aquinas: 'Adaequatio intellectus et rei' or as a modern philosopher expresses it in the language of today: 'Truth is the significance of fact.' I never forgot this. It was very helpful, and has been a guiding

13. W. Tegethoff, *Mies van der Rohe, Die Villen und Lanhaus-projekte*, Richard Bacht, Essen, 1981; F. Schulze, *Mies van der Rohe: A Critical Biography*, University of Chicago Press, Chicago, 1985; J. Zukowsky (ed.), *Mies Reconsidered: His Career, Legacy, and Disciples*, The Art Institute of Chicago and Rizzoli International, New York, 1986; D Dunster (ed.), *Mies van der Rohe: European Works*, Academy Editions, London, 1986; F Schulze (ed.), *Mies van der Rohe: Critical Essays*, The Museum of Modern Art, New York and MIT Press, Cambridge, Mass., 1989; F. Neumeyer, *The Artless Word*, MIT Press, Cambridge, Mass., 1991.
14. W. Blaser, *Mies van der Rohe, Furniture and Interiors*, Academy Editions, London, 1982, p. 10.

light. To find out what architecture really is took me fifty years – half a century.[15]

This suggests that Mies came across the phrase while he was still working for Behrens, that is between 1908 and 1912. In any case, one can fairly safely rule out the common assumption that he was exposed to scholastic teachings still earlier, as a pupil at the cathedral school at Aachen. Schulze cites the recollection of Mies' assistant Friedrich Hirz, who joined him in 1928 when he started work on the Barcelona Pavilion, that 'he read a lot of St Thomas Aquinas' while he was with him.[16] So what is certain is that Aquinas' definition became important for Mies at some time during the twenty years 1908–28.

In view of the frequent recurrence of the four Latin words in Mies' later writings and statements, and the great significance which he clearly attached to them for the understanding of his work ('I asked myself the question, "What is truth? What is truth?" until I stopped at Thomas Aquinas'),[17] surprisingly little attention has been given in architectural writing to their meaning or to their place in Aquinas' thought. The average architectural reader, baffled by the Latin, has been ready enough to accept the words of the 'modern philosopher' (in fact Max Scheler) as a satisfactory translation. But as Schulze points out, 'truth is the significance of fact' is not quite the same as 'truth is the correspondence of thing and intellect': 'Still, since Mies was not a trained philosopher, he evidently found the two statements close enough to his own view to be effectively identical.'[18]

This raises a doubt, which may as well be faced right away, as to whether Mies himself really understood what Aquinas meant, or bothered to seek further once he had hit on a maxim that seemed to reflect his own preconceptions. If that were the case the present investigation would be pointless. However, the recollections of Mies' friends and associates confirm that despite his lack of philosophical training his lifelong interest in philosophy was deeply serious, and certainly went far beyond a superficially learned dressing-up of his architectural rationale. Schulze describes how to the end of his life he would struggle to understand philosophical and scientific texts:

He read as he always had, and much the same philosophical fare, though his earlier preoccupation with morphological subjects shifted ... towards an interest in physics and cosmology. He laboured earnestly at this, poring over the same texts in German and English by Werner Heisenberg and Erwin Schrödinger and sometimes finding himself unable to understand what he had read.

15. P. Carter, 'Mies van der Rohe: an appreciation on the occasion of his 75th birthday', in *Architectural Design*, March 1961, p. 97.
16. Schulze, *Mies van der Rohe: Critical Biography*, p. 338.
17. L. Mies van der Rohe, interview with J. Peter, in The Oral History of Modern Architecture, Harry N. Abrams, New York, 1994, p.158.
18. Schulze, *Mies van der Rohe: Critical Biography*, p. 173.

Typically, he would go back to it again and again, insisting ... that it was imperative to learn the deeper truth he knew was there.[19]

This does not sound like the man who would seize on Aquinas' definition of truth as an impressive-sounding slogan, without probing further into what it meant.

The problem of the relation between the human intellect and things has engaged and divided philosophers since the Greeks. For Plato, reality lay in the immutable spiritual world of rational ideas or 'Forms' (such as the self-evident truths of geometry) and not in the flickering shadow of these Forms projected on the wall of the cave in which, so long as the soul remains imprisoned in the body, we are forced to lie chained. Before birth the soul existed in a spiritual world where it was in direct contact with the truth, and reasoning is the recollection of this latent knowledge. Hence true knowledge is to be sought in the mind and not in the perception of material things. Aquinas rejects Plato's doctrine, and instead, like Aristotle, identifies forms with their individual material manifestations. He writes:

According to Plato the forms physical matter takes on exist on their own account outside matter as actual objects of understanding called *Ideas* ... But according to Aristotle the forms of physical things exist only in matter and not as actually understandable. Since we can only understand what is actually understandable ... our minds need to make things actually understandable by abstracting their forms from their material conditions. Our ability to do this we call our *agent mind*.[20]

This has two consequences that are relevant to our understanding of Aquinas' definition, and perhaps also of Mies' architecture. First, it follows that our knowledge of these forms is not latent in the mind, but acquired through the perception of material things. As Aquinas expresses it, 'Our intellect draws knowledge from natural things, and is measured by them.'[21]

However, this poses a problem, which is the second consequence. If forms are embodied in the individual and the material, how does the mind, which is spiritual in nature, absorb them? Clearly, the thing itself, which we see in front of us, cannot be physically contained in the mind. According to Aquinas, the intellect cannot have direct knowledge of particular material things, but only of universal concepts which it abstracts from these individual objects. Therefore, to be intelligible, ideas must be universal; but reality consists in particular things.

19. *Ibid.*, p. 313.

20. T. Aquinas, *Summa Theologiae* (1267), ed. T McDermott, Methuen, London, 1991, p. 122

21. T. Aquinas, *De veritate* I.ii (1256), in *Quaestiones Disputatae*, P Lethielleux, Paris, 1925, vol. I, p. 6.

By identifying Forms with universal ideas existing independently of matter, Plato had avoided this paradox. But Aquinas, denying the separate existence of forms, is forced to postulate a special faculty, the 'agent mind', which has the power to convert sense-data into thinkable objects by abstracting universal essences from their material conditions. However, these universals, unlike Plato's Forms, have no existence outside the mind. Nor, being abstractions, can they be identical with the individual form of the thing in itself. That is why Aquinas defines truth as a concordance between things and the intellect; it is not a property of either, but a relationship between them. The full text of the definition of truth runs as follows:

> For true knowledge consists in the concordance of thing and intellect; not the identity of one and the same thing to itself, but a conformity between different things. Hence the intellect arrives at truth when it acquires something proper to it alone – the idea of the thing – which corresponds to the thing, but which the thing outside the mind does not have.[22]

6.3 Art as a way to knowledge

What role might works of art, and specifically Mies' architecture, play in this process of acquiring knowledge? Unfortunately for us, although Aquinas speaks of the intellect as *measuring* works of art (i.e. *forming* them) he makes no mention of its being also *measured by* them (i.e. *in-formed* by them) in the same way as by natural things. What concerns him is not art as such, but the analogy between the intellect of the artist and the divine intellect, in their creative function. Here is the translation of the whole passage:

> Our intellect draws knowledge from natural things, and is measured by them; but they are measured in turn by the divine intellect, which contains all created things, in the same way as works of art are contained in the mind of the artist. Therefore the divine intellect measures, but is not measured; natural things both measure and are measured; and our intellect is measured, but does not measure natural things, only artifacts.[23]

Although this says nothing specifically about art being a means to knowledge, it is far more in keeping with Aquinas' general world-view for the products of the human intellect to return to and perfect it, just as he regards the whole of creation as intended to return to God:

22. T. Aquinas, *De veritate* I.iii (1256), in *Quaestiones Disputatae*, vol. I, pp. 7–8.

23. T. Aquinas, *De veritate* I.ii (1256), in *Quaestiones Disputatae*, vol. I, p.6.

'The emanation of creatures from God would be imperfect unless they returned to Him in equal measure.'[24]

For the analogy that Aquinas draws between artistic creation and divine creation to be complete, the works of art which emanate from the human intellect must likewise return to that intellect in equal measure; otherwise the whole chain of dependence – from God, through nature and man, to art – would end in a blind alley. Therefore, just as the intellect forms the work of art, the work of art must in turn *in-form* the intellect.

Furthermore, as a concretization of human thought, placed 'out there' in the natural world, the work of art enables us, as Mies puts it, 'to examine our thoughts in action'.[25] The work of art is *more directly knowable* than natural things. They, originating from an infinite and uncreated intelligence, cannot be fully apprehended by our finite created intellect. But the work of art, which itself originates in that finite intellect, embodies the rational and universal forms of human thought, and is directly intelligible. Compared with the endless nuances, subtleties and complexities of nature, art is crude and primitive; but for the intellect it has a special immediacy and clarity. Jacques Maritain writes in *Art and Scholasticism* that

> The mind rejoices in the beautiful because in the beautiful it finds itself again: recognizes itself, and comes into contact with its very own light … It is important, however, to observe that in the beauty which has been termed connatural to man and is peculiar to human art this brilliance of form, however purely intelligible it may be in itself, is apprehended *in the sensible and by the sensible*, and not separately from it. The intuition of artistic beauty so stands at the opposite pole from the abstraction of scientific truth. For in the former case it is precisely through the apprehension of sense that the light of being penetrates the mind. The mind then, spared the least effort of abstraction, rejoices without labour and without discussion. It is excused its customary task, it has not to extricate something intelligible from the matter in which it is buried and then step by step go through its various attributes; like the stag at the spring of running water, it has nothing to do but drink, and it drinks the clarity of being.[26]

According to this view, the intelligibility of works of art allows them to mediate between us and the natural world, to which it gives, in our eyes, an added radiance, such as the Greek temple seems to bring to the landscape in which it is set. It is as though nature

24. T. Aquinas, *De veritate XX.iv* (1256), in *Quaestiones Disputatae*, vol. I, p. 499.

25. Blaser, *Mies van der Rohe, Furniture and Interiors*, p. 10.

26. J. Maritain, *Art and Scholasticism* (1923), Sheed & Ward, London, 1932, pp. 25–6.

demanded the sharp facets of our rational creations for its own completion. Mies observed that

> We must strive to bring nature, buildings and men together in a higher unity. When you see nature through the glass walls of the Farnsworth house, it takes on a deeper significance than when you stand outside. Thus nature becomes more expressive – it becomes part of a greater whole.[27]

The relevance of Aquinas' definition of truth to an understanding of Mies' architecture can be summarized, therefore, as follows. In opposition to Plato, Aquinas identifies truth, not with a pre-existing world of eternal ideas above and beyond the visible world, but with the products of human mental action: of a certain mutual relationship achieved between our mind and the world of real things. Much adverse criticism of Mies' work and philosophy has been based on the misconception that they were founded, on the contrary, on a platonist belief in a transcendental world of universal essences, of which his buildings were intended as symbols. Thus Charles Jencks writes in *Modern Movements in Architecture*:

> The problem of Mies van der Rohe for critics and inhabitants of his architecture alike is that he demands an absolute commit-ment to the Platonic world-view in order to appreciate his build-ings ... Hence in the best of Mies' work we are brought up to the question of belief, because, depending on our own beliefs in the existence of a transcendental world, we will experience this work as an adequate symbol of that world or, alternatively, as just a very exquisite farce. For instance, nominalist philosophers and pragmatists, who believe that universals do not in fact exist, would find the Platonic statements of Mies mostly just humorous, because they go to such terrific pains to project a non-existent reality.[28]

Attributing Mies' supposed platonism – unjustifiably, according to Franz Schulze's informants – to his 'neo-Thomist education at the Cathedral School at Aachen', Jencks completely overlooks the funda-mental contrast between Thomism and platonism:

> for it is likely that here he received the idea of intellectual clarity and the equation of beauty with truth. Beauty reveals truth or makes truth 'manifest'. Not only does Mies refer to Aquinas' formulation explicitly, but he also seems to uphold the further

27. L. Mies van der Rohe, in C Norberg-Schulz, 'Ein Gespräch mit Mies van der Rohe', in *Baukunst und Werkform*, Nov. 1958, pp. 615–6; reprinted in Neumeyer, *Artless Word*, p. 339.

28. C. Jencks, *Modern Movements in Architecture*, Penguin Books, Harmondsworth, 1973, pp. 95 & 105.

scholastic doctrine that all the apparent phenomena of this world are actually mere symbols for a greater reality lying behind them. To see the striking relevance of this Platonic belief in universals for Mies' work, one should remember that Plato put above the entrance to his Academy a sign that Mies might have placed above all his entrances: 'Nobody Untrained in Geometry May Enter My House' – because, it is implied, only geometry refers to the essential universals which lie behind the transient and multiform appearances.[29]

But as we have seen, for Mies, as for Aquinas, things are not mere appearances or symbols, but real; it is universals that exist only in the mind. Mies' buildings do not aim at universality in order to symbolize a 'greater reality lying behind them', but simply in order to be more completely intelligible to ordinary human beings. Their whole intent is to state, as lucidly as possible, what they are and how they are made. Moreover, the 'reductivism' of which Mies' critics accuse him is not a denial of the richness and complexity of nature, but intended to accentuate it: 'Nature, too, must lead its own life. We should take care not to disrupt it with the colourfulness of our houses and interior fittings.'[30] And:

> The Farnsworth house has never I believe been really understood. I myself was in that house from morning to evening. Up to then I had not known how beautiful the colours in nature can be. One must deliberately use neutral tones in interiors, because one has every colour outside. These colours change continuously and completely, and I can say that that simplicity is splendid.[31]

6.4 The impact of expressionism and De Stijl

The striving for structural clarity, and for that 'splendid simplicity' which found fulfilment in the Farnsworth house, was confirmed by Mies' reading of Aquinas; but it had first to contend with more immediate influences, which pulled in opposite directions. As has been said, the image built up in the Mies literature of the 1960s, of the granite monolith impervious to the battles that were going on around him, is one-sided. Against it must be set the fact that in his German years he was very much 'in the thick of it'[32] and shared fully in the intellectual and artistic conflicts of his time.

Despite the fact that up to 1926 most of Mies' commissioned designs and all his executed buildings – the Kempner, Feldmann, Eichstaedt and Mosler houses – continued the neoclassicism of his

29. *Ibid.*, p. 105.

30. L. Mies van der Rohe, in Norberg-Schulz, 'Ein Gespräch', in *Baukunst und Werkform*, Nov. 1958, pp. 615–6; reprinted in Neumeyer, *Artless Word*, p. 339.

31. L. Mies van der Rohe, 'Ich mach niemals ein Bild', in *Bauwelt*, Aug. 1962, pp. 884–5.

32. S. Honey, 'The office of Mies van der Rohe in America: the towers', in *UIA-International Architect*, 3, 1984, p. 44.

pre-war work, by 1921 he was already closely involved with avant-garde movements like expressionism and De Stijl. In that year he began sharing his studio with the expressionist (or organicist?) architect Hugo Häring, while at the same time he was in contact with the Swiss dadaist Hans Richter, and through him with Theo van Doesburg (in Berlin from late 1920) and El Lissitzky. In 1923 he collaborated with the last three named in the foundation of the magazine *G*, edited by Richter, Lissitzky and the ex-Bauhaus student Werner Graeff. *G* stood for *Gestaltung*, and *Neue Gestaltung* was the German translation of *Nieuwe Beelding*, which, lacking an exact English equivalent of *beelding*, I have here translated as 'new representation' (see Chapter 2).

These contacts were soon reflected in a series of speculative projects which Mies produced between 1921 and 1923. In the first two projects, his entry for the Friedrichstrasse competition (1921) (Figure 6.1) and the glass skyscraper project (1922) (Figure 6.3), the expressionist influence is most apparent. Franz Schulze remarks of Häring's own entry for the same competition (Figure 6.2), which he probably worked on literally side by side with Mies, that it is 'notable for fat, rolling exterior curves that readily bring the undulating volumes of Mies' second project to mind'.[33]

Mies' short article explaining the two glass tower projects begins with a statement about structural expression: 'Skyscrapers reveal their bold structural pattern during construction. Only then does the gigantic steel web seem impressive.'[34] It is therefore all the more surprising that the structural grid is absent from the published plans of both Mies' projects, and that in fact their irregular plan-form militates against the very quality that became the goal of Mies' later work: structural clarity. Schulze justly describes an unpublished plan of the second project in which Mies attempted to sketch in an arrangement of columns and beams, as

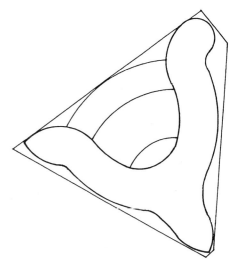

Figure 6.2 Hugo Häring, Friedrichstrasse competition project, 1922: diagrammatic plan

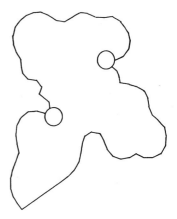

Figure 6.3 Ludwig Mies van der Rohe, glass skyscraper project, 1922: diagrammatic plan

a most unconvincing effort, in which a geometric system of piers is forced to take root in an amoeboid plan. The geometry itself collapses into irregularity and all trace of rational order is lost ... In the Glass Skyscraper Mies was preoccupied less with structure than with form.[35]

In his article Mies goes on to give three reasons for the 'at first sight arbitrary' outline of the 1922 skyscraper: 'sufficient illumination of the interior, the massing of the building seen from the street, and lastly the play of reflections'.[36] The functional justification is less convincing than the formal ones, and neither design is easy to reconcile with his

33. Schulze, *Mies van der Rohe: Critical Biography*, p. 103.

34. L. Mies van der Rohe, 'Two glass skyscrapers' (1922), in Johnson, *Mies van der Rohe*, p. 187.

35. Schulze, *Mies van der Rohe: Critical Biography*, p. 101.

36. Mies van der Rohe, 'Two glass skyscrapers', p. 187.

statement in *G* the following year, that 'Form is not the aim of our work, but only the result.'[37]

1922 seems to have been a turning point in Mies' development. Within a few months of the glass skyscraper, apparently in the winter of 1922–3,[38] he designed the concrete office building. An ideological and aesthetic gulf separates the two projects; there could be no better starting point from which to trace the story of Mies' gradual clarification of the structure of his buildings at the expense, if need be, of all other concerns. He acknowledged the self-denial – a sort of intellectual asceticism – that this involved, as well as its direct connection with Aquinas:

> I often throw out things I like very much – they are dear to my heart – but when I have a better idea – a clearer idea, I mean – then I follow that clearer idea ... Thomas Aquinas says that 'Reason is the first principle of all human work.' Now when you have once grasped that, then you act accordingly. So I would throw out everything that is not reasonable. I don't want to be interesting; I want to be good.[39]

Between 1922 and 1962, when he began work on the National Gallery in Berlin (Figure 6.4), Mies progressively simplified his plans, reducing them finally to a single vast square space, and articulated his structure so that each element was unmistakably distinct from every other. There is a striking, and not merely coincidental, parallel with the development of the classic gothic style over a similar forty-year period, about 1190–1230, and under the influence of the same scholastic demand for *claritas*. Then, too, the linked autonomous spaces of romanesque were reduced to the single uniform space of high gothic; and the structure was articulated so that each member was clearly identified. The classic Miesian corner detail (Figure 6.5) is comparable to the classic gothic compound pier with its central shaft surrounded by a cluster of slender colonnettes, each corresponding to a separate arch or vault rib (Figure 6.6). In *Gothic Architecture and Scholasticism* Erwin Panofsky argues that both scholasticism and gothic architecture were governed by the principle of transparency:

> Like the High Scholastic Summa, the High Gothic cathedral aimed, first of all, at 'totality' and therefore tended to approximate, by synthesis as well as elimination, one perfect and final solution ... Instead of the Romanesque variety of western and eastern vaulting forms ... we have the newly developed rib vault exclusively so that the vaults of even the apse, the chapels and the ambulatory no

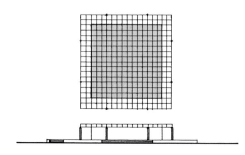

Figure 6.4 Ludwig Mies van der Rohe, National Gallery, Berlin, 1962–7: plan and elevation

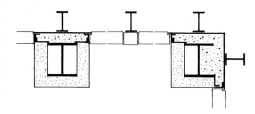

Figure 6.5 Ludwig Mies van der Rohe, 860 and 880 Lake Shore Drive, Chicago, 1949–51: plan details of typical column, corner column and mullion

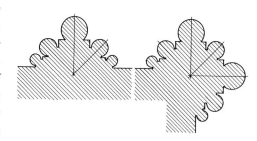

Figure 6.6 Chartres Cathedral, 1194–c.1224: typical pier and corner pier

37. L. Mies van der Rohe, *G*, no. 2, 1923; in Johnson, *Mies van der Rohe*, p. 189.

38. Schulze, *Mies van der Rohe: Critical Biography*, p. 106.

39. L. Mies van der Rohe, in *Conversations about the Future of Architecture*, Reynolds Metals Co. sound recording, 1958.

longer differ in kind from those of the nave and transept ...
According to classic Gothic standards the individual elements ...
must proclaim their identity by remaining clearly separated from
each other – shafts from the wall or the core of the pier, the ribs
from their neighbours, all vertical members from their arches; and
there must be an unequivocal correlation between them.[40]

I have argued elsewhere[41] that Panofsky's interpretation, which
implies that the architectural developments were either influenced
by the philosophical ones or shared with them a common 'spirit of
the age', rests on a flawed chronology. The designs of the classic
gothic churches cited by him pre-date – generally by about eight
decades – the scholastic treatises. Consequently, if there was indeed
an interaction between the rise of gothic architecture and that of
scholastic philosophy, it must have been architecture that influenced
philosophy, not the reverse: ideas first worked out in stone were only
later translated into abstract thought and writing in the philosopher's
study. This is quite contrary to our current preconception about how
such influences work, but it is perfectly in conformity with Mies'
dictum: 'I want to do something in order to be able to think.'

The comparison between scholasticism and Mies' architecture
coincides fairly closely with his own view of the matter. 'I was interested in structural architecture,' he recalls in an interview:

I was interested in Romanesque, I was interested in Gothic architecture. They are often misunderstood. You know, the profiles of
a pillar in a cathedral, that is still a very clear structure. The refine-
ments were to make it clearer, not to decorate it, but to make it
clearer.[42]

However, neither Mies nor the gothic builders arrived at the 'one
perfect and final solution' by a smooth progression. The development
of classic gothic, as Panofsky shows, was consistent, but not direct:

On the contrary, when observing the evolution from the beginning to the 'final solutions', we receive the impression that it went
on almost after the fashion of a 'jumping procession', taking two
steps forward and then one backward, as though the builders
were deliberately placing obstacles in their own way.[43]

Similarly, one has the feeling that Mies could quite logically have
gone straight from the concrete office project, the most prophetic of
his early designs, to the IIT Campus (Figure 6.7), leaving out all the

40. E. Panofsky, *Gothic Architecture and Scholasticism*, Thames & Hudson, London, 1957, pp. 43–50.

41. R. Padovan, *Proportion: Science, Philosophy, Architecture*, E. & F.N. Spon, London, 1999, pp.202–6.

42. L. Mies van der Rohe, interview by Peter, in *Oral History of Modern Architecture*, p. 165.

43. Panofsky, *Gothic Architecture*, p. 60.

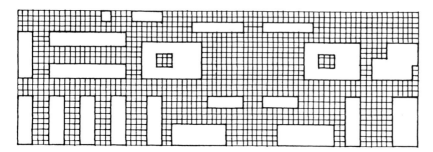

Figure 6.7 Ludwig Mies van der Rohe, IIT Campus, Chicago, 1940: plan

stages in between. For the concrete office contains all the characteristics of his later work: the reduction of the concept to its simplest, most essential statement; the clear, regular structure; and the universal, multi-functional space. But things are never that simple. Only by being open to contradictory influences, and resolving the resulting conflicts by what Bruno Zevi has called the 'spatial ballets' of Barcelona and Berlin, could Mies have arrived at the truly complex simplicity of the National Gallery.

With the two country house projects – in concrete (early 1923) and brick (winter 1923–4)[44] (Figure 6.8) – he veered off in a new direction, under the by now strong influence of Theo van Doesburg and De Stijl, through his close involvement with G. There was much about De Stijl to attract him. Here, finally, was a new art movement inspired primarily by philosophy; and its foundation manifesto had declared that the new consciousness of the age was 'directed towards the universal'.[45] But the philosophical bases of De Stijl were closer to platonism than to Aquinas' (and Mies') common-sense acceptance of the real existence of material things. As we saw in Chapter 2, De Stijl aimed at the representation (*beelding*), not of phenomena, but of an intelligible world of pure thought.

One of the central principles enunciated in Van Doesburg's architectural manifesto of 1924 was the elimination of the delimited interior space, enclosed on all four sides by load-bearing walls and further subdivided by partition walls into separate rooms, and their replacement by a continuous space within which walls and columns stood as isolated planes and lines:

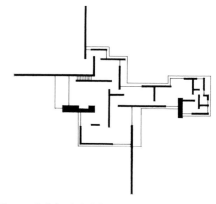

Figure 6.8 Ludwig Mies van der Rohe, brick country house project, 1923–4: plan

> The new architecture has *broken through the wall*, thus destroying the *separateness of inside and outside. Walls are no longer load-bearing*: they have been reduced to points of support. This gives rise to a new, open plan, totally different from the classical one, in that interior and exterior space interpenetrate.[46]

44. Schulze, *Mies van der Rohe: Critical Biography*, pp. 110 and 113.

45. 'Manifest I van "De Stijl", 1918', in *De Stijl*, vol. II, no. 1, November 1918, p. 2.

46. T. van Doesburg, 'Tot een beeldende architectuur', in *De Stijl*, vol. VI, no. 6/7, 1924, p. 80.

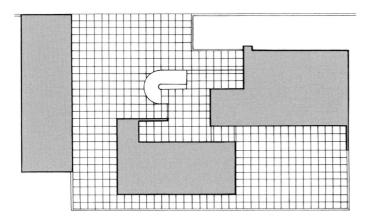

Figure 6.9 Ludwig Mies van der Rohe, Tugendhat house, Brno, 1928–30: block plan of upper floor

However, as we saw in Chapter 4, the three houses that Van Doesburg and Van Eesteren showed at the *L'Effort Moderne* exhibition consisted, not of a continuous space, but of interlocking spatial volumes. Only in Van Doesburg's analytical drawing of the second project were these volumes resolved into floating planes. And even Rietveld's Schröder house was in fact a single rectangular volume cleverly disguised by neoplasticist 'surface decoration': small projections and recessions and changes of colour designed to camouflage the flat planes of the box.

The reason for this lies in the problem of the relationship between wholes and parts. If architecture is reduced to a system of rectangular planes floating in a continuous space, no clearly delimited whole exists larger than these planes. So long as the scale remains small this does not matter, because the planes are still few enough and proportionately large enough to count in relation to the total composition. But as the scale increases these rectangular planes become so numerous, and their size in proportion to the whole so insignificant, that despite the variation of their dimension and direction the total impression is of a homogeneous 'soup' with innumerable 'bits' floating about in it. The effect is not that of a 'balanced relationship of unequal parts',[47] as Van Doesburg intended, but, paradoxically, of monotony and repetition. This can be seen in post-war attempts to apply De Stijl principles at an urban scale, such as Joost Baljeu's visionary project *It Can Be Architecture Tomorrow*.[48] To avoid this disintegration, a hierarchy of scale is needed, in which the smaller elements, such as wall-planes, become parts of larger discrete entities. One way of achieving this is to give a clearly recognizable form to the several spatial

47. *Ibid.*, p. 81.
48. J. Baljeu, *Morgen kan het architectuur zijn*, exhibition catalogue, Haags Gemeentemuseum, The Hague, 1975.

volumes defined by the walls, and in turn to whole buildings and urban spaces. This theme will be elaborated in the next chapter.

Mies' concrete country house project was also composed of such discrete volumes, arranged asymmetrically as an incomplete swastika around two C-shaped courts. This essentially neoclassical formula – which can be traced back through his Kröller project of 1912 to Schinkel's Charlottenhof – would be followed in several of Mies' designs of the 1920s and '30s: the first design for the Weissenhofsiedlung (1925), the Wolf house at Guben (1926), the Esters and Lange houses at Krefeld (1928), the upper floor of the Tugendhat house at Brno (1928–30) (Figure 6.9), the Gericke house project (1930), the Lemke house in Berlin (1932), and the first Ulrich Lange house project (1935). The brick country house project was therefore not only the first, but the only design to completely fulfil the De Stijl principle of total openness. As James Ingo Freed has observed in an interview with Franz Schulze,

> To begin with, I see that project as the most radical of all his works, and at the same time, the most modernist. The Brick Country House explodes the building and throws the pieces all over the countryside. In its unfixed, dynamic fragmentation it has definite affinities with modernist thought in other disciplines. How could it not have been so, with Mies so close in those days to the restless soul of Theo van Doesburg? Well, from that point onward, after doing the Brick Country House, Mies conceived no designs that were so totally freeflowing ... I see a significant intention here. It seems to me that the problem of the Brick Country House was that it led to many other possible organizations of the building. It isn't a reductive object ... There is no suggestion of a *way* of building, no minimalization, no intimation that such a design, if followed in other projects, could have provided him with some-thing he could hold up and say, '*This* is iconographic.' Or, alterna-tively – as he might later have said – 'Here we have, by contrast, the Farnsworth House. We have taken away from it everything we could take away, and what is left, sings.' ... But in the Brick Country House, as in most modernist designs, there are options left us. We end up with something variable, something additive. And here is where I think Mies broke with the modern move-ment.[49]

What Mies now aimed at, however, was no longer something additive or variable but an architecture that was as universal as possible: a universal architectural language. In this sense, while

49. I. Freed, 'Mies in America', in Schulze, *Mies van der Rohe: Critical Essays*, p. 193.

progressively abandoning the outward forms of De Stijl – the asymmetrical arrangements of shifting planes – he remained true to its central doctrine: the replacement of the individual and the particular by the universal and the general. He tried to forge an architecture that had the absolute generality of a scientific law. As he said in an interview with John Peter,

> You know, you often find in books, they have nothing to do with architecture, the very important things. Erwin Schrödinger, you know, the physicist, he talks here about general principles, and he said the creative vigor of a general principle depends precisely on its generality. That is exactly what I think when I talk about structure in architecture. It is not a special solution. It is the general idea.[50]

Presumably without knowing it, Mies was echoing what Ozenfant and Jeanneret had written nearly half a century earlier in *Après le cubisme*: 'Science and great Art have in common the ideal of generalizing, which is the highest goal of the spirit ... Art must generalize to attain beauty.'[51]

6.5 From Barcelona 1929 to Berlin 1962

Mies would only take up the planar theme of the brick country house once more in the 1920s, with the Barcelona Pavilion of 1929. Between 1924 and 1928 his work reflected the struggle between two approaches to architecture: on one hand the single, symmetrical block-form and clear, logically expressed structure of the concrete office project, and on the other the De Stijl-like composition of asymmetrically disposed volumes – *but not planes* – first seen in the concrete country house, but already latent in the abortive Kröller project of 1912. Both of these themes can be traced back to Schinkel – the first to the Altes Museum, the second to the Charlottenhof. But they also reflect the conflict in Mies' work between a *sachlich* concept of art as concerned with objective, practical realities, and the poetic De Stijl *beeldende* ideal of representing an immaterial world of pure thought.

To the first group belong the Afrikanischestrasse housing (1925), the Weissenhof apartment block (1927) and the replanning projects for the Leipzigerstrasse and Alexanderplatz in Berlin (1928). The second group includes, besides the concrete villa project, the first design for the Weissenhofsiedlung of 1925, the Liebknecht-Luxemburg monument of 1926, the Wolf house at Guben of the

50. Mies van der Rohe, in Peter, *Oral History of Modern Architecture*, p. 160.
51. A. Ozenfant and C.-E. Jeanneret, *Après le cubisme*, Paris, 1918, pp. 39–40.

same year and the Esters and Lange houses at Krefeld of 1928, as well as – so far as its exterior is concerned – the Tugendhat house at Brno, designed late in 1928 though not built until 1930.

Although the Wolf, Esters and Lange houses returned, therefore, to the principle of intersecting spatial volumes, as opposed to the brick country house solution of planes floating in free-flowing space, their plans reveal, nevertheless, their affinity with that project. All three houses have living rooms planned as series of interlocking rectangles, producing staggered garden elevations; and all wrestle unsuccessfully with the problem of structural clarity. Because the wall-planes of the brick country house were asymmetrically and irregularly disposed, but also load-bearing – thus anticipating Van Doesburg's rejection of repetition and symmetry, but not his demand that load-bearing walls be reduced to points of support – it was impossible to achieve a clear structure. Inevitably some walls carried loads and others not, while spans were unequal and varied in direction. Van Doesburg's manifesto had indicated a solution – the separation of the walls from the structure – but it took Mies five years to reach it. In the early days of the Barcelona project, he has recalled, 'One evening as I was working late on the building I made a sketch of a freestanding wall, and I got a shock. I knew it was a new principle.'[52]

This was the birth of the onyx wall that formed the core of the pavilion. Yet why did it constitute a new principle? Mies had already used free-standing walls, in the sense of isolated planes in space, in the brick country house project; what was new could only be the idea that the wall stood free of the structure, and loads were carried by columns.

The columns were slow to appear, however. The earliest surviving plans and sketches show quite recognizable versions of the design, with overhanging roof-slab, two courts containing pools, and a plinth approached by steps; but no columns. Then, late in 1928, they make their first appearance; but initially there are three rows, and their arrangement looks irregular. A later plan shows two rows, but of three columns only, one end of the roof still being supported by walls. Finally, a completely regular structure and the freely composed wall-planes are superimposed as independent but contrapuntal systems. It is as though the concrete office building and the brick country house had been overlaid upon each other: a synthesis of scholasticist clarity and neoplasticist spatial continuity.

However, by 1945–6, when he began to design the Farnsworth house, this synthesis was for Mies no longer good (that is, *clear*) enough. The rationality of the pavilion's structure was apparent only in plan; in three dimensions, the complete structural bay defined by

52. L. Mies van der Rohe, 'Six students talk with Mies', North Carolina State College, Spring 1952.

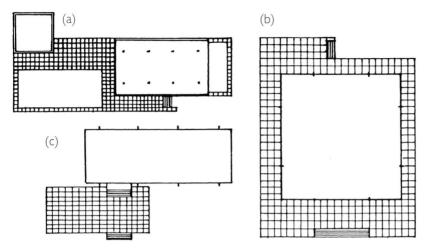

Figure 6.10 Comparative plans of (a) Barcelona Pavilion (1929), (b) Farnsworth house (1946–51), (c) Bacardi office project, Santiago de Cuba (1957)

four columns was nowhere visible. The walls played an ambiguous role, threatening to usurp that of the columns. Frank Lloyd Wright wrote to Philip Johnson: 'Some day let's persuade Mies to get rid of those damned little steel posts that look so dangerous and interfering in his lovely designs.'[53]

In the great works of around 1930, at Barcelona and Brno, the column structure is subordinate to the shifting wall-planes. Twenty years later, in Mies' American work, the position is reversed: the dominant theme is the classically regular, symmetrical trabeated structure, within which the asymmetrically disposed screens play a subordinate role. As suggested in Chapter 2, these later buildings come closer than anything else in modern architecture to realizing Arthur Schopenhauer's dream of an architecture stripped down to the purest possible expression of load and support:

> Its fundamental law is that no load may be without sufficient support, and no support without a suitable load ... The purest execution of this theme is column and entablature; hence the order of columns has become, so to speak, the thorough-bass of the whole of architecture.[54]

The Barcelona Pavilion (1929), the Farnsworth house at Plano, Illinois (1946–51) and the unbuilt Bacardi office project for Santiago de Cuba (1957) constitute as it were a set (Figure 6.10). Each consists of a pavilion raised above ground level, approached off-axis by flights of steps, and supported by eight columns. Each marks a breakthrough in

53. F.L. Wright, letter to Philip Johnson, 26 Feb. 1932, Archives of the Dept. of Architecture and Design, The Museum of Modern Art, New York; quoted in Schulze, *Mies van der Rohe: Critical Biography*, p. 158.

54. A. Schopenhauer, *The World as Will and Representation*, trans. E.F.J. Payne, Dover Publications, New York, 1969, vol. II, p. 411.

Mies' search for clarity and universality. And each is the model for subsequent designs.

Just as Mies' brick houses of the 1920s combine the intersecting volumes of the concrete house project with the staggered plan of the brick one, the houses of the 1930s, beginning with the Berlin Building Exhibition house of 1931, are variations on the Barcelona theme. In the same way, the Farnsworth house is the model for Crown Hall at IIT (1950–6), the Mannheim Theatre project (1952–3), Cullinan Hall, Houston (1954–8) and the Bacardi Building in Mexico City (1957–61). And finally, the unbuilt Bacardi project for Cuba, designed in 1957, is the first formulation – if one excludes the somewhat different Fifty-by-Fifty house and Chicago Convention Hall projects – of the Schaefer Museum project, Schweinfurt (1960–3) and the 'perfect and final solution' of the new National Gallery in Berlin, 1962–7 (Figure 6.4).

At Plano, the ambiguities of Barcelona are overcome by bringing the columns to the outer edge of the roof and floor planes, and stopping all interior divisions short of the ceiling. For Bacardi, the plan is reduced to a single great square bay, with two columns on each side. Less is more.

Thus Mies' career proceeded dialectically. It was not, as Zevi has described, a 'parabola' with its summit around 1930,[55] so much as a series of oscillations with an ultimate goal. It might be compared to the twisting course of a river which at last must flow into the sea. To pursue the simile, just as a river bears down to the sea sediment from its upper reaches, so, without the brick country house project, the Barcelona Pavilion and the Farnsworth house, Mies' final statement, the Berlin Gallery, would not have been possible.

6.6 The truth and its exposition

Aquinas' definition of truth suggests answers to the two most commonly raised criticisms of Mies' work: first, that despite all the talk about truth, his buildings are in fact false in their expression of structure; and secondly, that they make intolerable demands on those who use them.

The first objection is based chiefly on his practice, at Lake Shore Drive (1948–51) and elsewhere, of cladding the concrete casing of his steel columns with steel plates, and then applying to these plates H-section mullions which support no glazing (Figure 6.5). But Aquinas defined truth, as we have seen, as a correspondence between thing and intellect, that is between different things, and not as an identity between one and the other. He answered the objection that 'the

55. Zevi, *Poetica*, p. 187.

intellect is false if it understands an object otherwise than as it really is' by distinguishing between 'false' abstraction, which considers the form of the things as being separate from its matter, and 'true' abstraction, which merely considers the form of the thing separately from its matter:

> A man would falsely abstract the form of stone from matter if he denied its connection with matter, as Plato did; but there is nothing false about what a man understands existing immaterially in his mind, though materially in the thing understood. To understand natural things is not, as some have thought, to abstract their forms wholly from matter; for matter is part of the definition of natural things.[56]

Aquinas provides an architectural example which not only helps to clarify this principle, but also makes a direct comparison between architectural truth, rational truth and the absolute truth known only to the divine mind:

> Things essentially relate to the mind on which they depend for existence ... Thus man-made things are called true in relation to human minds (a house when it conforms to its architect's idea, a statement when it expresses true knowledge); whilst natural things are called true in relation to God's Idea of them. Truth then is primarily defined as a quality of mind: *truth reveals and makes clear what it is.*'[57]

The steel facings of Mies' columns are true, therefore, because 'they reveal and make clear' what the structure really is: namely a steel skeleton. In other words they correspond to, though they are not identical with, the actual steel structure, much as Aquinas justifies the intellect's abstract concept of a thing as corresponding to, though not identical with, the material individuality of the thing itself. The apparent steel structure is necessary to make the actual steel structure manifest; it does not try to present that structure as being otherwise than it really is: for instance, it would be false to apply the same steel facings to a structure of reinforced concrete. Panofsky sees the same kind of 'visual logic' in the classic gothic cathedral:

> We are faced neither with 'rationalism' in a purely functionalistic sense nor with 'illusion' in the modern sense of *l'art pour l'art* aesthetics. We are faced with what may be termed a 'visual logic' illustrative of Thomas Aquinas's *nam et sensus ratio quaedam est*

56. T. Aquinas, *Summa Theologiae* (1267), ed. T McDermott, Methuen, London, 1991, p. 133.

57. *Ibid.*, p. 45.

[i.e. 'for sense, too, is a sort of reason']. A man imbued with the Scholastic habit would look upon the mode of architectural presentation, just as he looked upon the mode of literary presentation, from the point of view of *manifestatio*. He would have taken it for granted that the primary purpose of the many elements that compose a cathedral was to ensure stability, just as he took it for granted that the primary purpose of the many elements that constitute a *Summa* was to ensure validity. But he would not have been satisfied had not the membrification of the edifice permitted him to re-experience the very processes of architectural composition just as the membrification of the *Summa* permitted him to re-experience the very processes of cogitation.[58]

6.7 The house as *machine à méditer*

The second criticism – that Mies' buildings make intolerable demands on those who use them – is more fundamental. It has been levelled against Mies since early in his career. In 1932 *Die Form*, the organ of the Deutsche Werkbund, whose vice-president Mies had become in 1926, published an article under the title 'Can One Live in the Tugendhat House?' The author, Justus Bier, claimed that 'personal life was repressed' by the 'precious' spaces and furnishings of the house, making it a 'showroom' rather than a home.[59] In the mid 1960s Lewis Mumford said much the same. Like Charles Jencks, he unjustly accuses Mies of 'Platonism':

Mies van der Rohe used the facilities offered by steel and glass to create elegant monuments of nothingness. They had the dry style of machine forms without the contents. His own chaste taste gave these hollow glass shells a crystalline purity of form; but they existed alone in the Platonic world of his imagination and had no relation to site, climate, insulation, function, or internal activity; indeed, they completely turned their backs upon these realities just as the rigidly arranged chairs of his living rooms openly disregarded the necessary intimacies and informalities of conversation.[60]

Two years later, Robert Venturi wrote that

Mies' exquisite pavilions have had valuable implications for architecture, but their selectiveness of content and language is their limitation as well as their strength. I question the relevance of analogies between pavilions and houses, especially analogies between

58. Panofsky, *Gothic Architecture*, pp. 58–9.
59. J. Bier, 'Kann man im Haus Tugendhat wohnen?', in *Die Form*, Oct. 1931, pp. 392–3.
60. L. Mumford, *The Highway and the City*, Secker & Warburg, London, 1964, p. 156.

Japanese pavilions and recent domestic architecture. They ignore the real complexity and contradiction inherent in the domestic program .... Forced simplicity results in oversimplification.[61]

Even Mies' biographer Franz Schulz recognizes that the Farnsworth house

is more nearly a temple than a dwelling, and it rewards aesthetic contemplation before it fulfills domestic necessity ... In cold weather the great glass panes tended to accumulate an overabundance of condensation ... In summer ... the sun turned the interior into a cooker ... Palumbo is the ideal owner of the house ... he derives sufficient spiritual sustenance from the reductivist beauty of the place to endure its creature discomforts.[62]

Of course that is just the point. Mies' buildings, before they are functional shelters or even objects of 'aesthetic contemplation', are sources of 'spiritual sustenance' – that is, food for the mind. Mies built, not only 'in order to be able to think', but in order to enable *others* to think. It is instructive to compare his attitude in this respect with that of Le Corbusier, which had an inherent ambiguity with regard to the status of architecture as an expressive art.

When Le Corbusier famously defines the house in *Towards a New Architecture* as 'a machine for living in',[63] and proceeds to list the various material comforts that it should provide ('Baths, sun, hot water, cold water, warmth at will ...') he is understandably regarded as preaching a gospel of pure utilitarian functionalism. This supposition is contradicted, however, on later pages, where he says that the merely practical house fails to touch the heart, and that architecture begins where the satisfaction of practical needs leaves off. The 'language of Architecture' is 'a mathematical creation of the mind'. As if to drive home the point, he repeats it identically in two places: 'By the use of inert materials and *starting from* conditions more or less utilitarian, you have established certain relationships which have aroused my emotions. This is Architecture.'[64]

As James Dunnett remarks, 'The anomaly was inevitably not wholly resolved.'[65] On one hand, in theory, Le Corbusier classified the house as a tool, and thus not as a work of art – a proper object of meditation in itself – but rather as the self-effacing container of that proper object, which for him, as we saw in Chapter 1, was the purist painting. The role of the dwelling was thus to serve as 'a vessel of silence and lofty solitude' in which the work of art could be contemplated in peace.[66] Elsewhere in his writings, on the other hand, and

61. R. Venturi, *Complexity and Contradiction in Architecture*, The Museum of Modern Art, New York, 1966, pp. 24–5.

62. Schulze, *Mies van der Rohe: Critical Biography*, p. 256.

63. Le Corbusier, *Towards a New Architecture*, The Architectural Press, London, 1946, p. 89.

64. *Ibid.*, pp. 141 & 187.

65. J. Dunnett, 'The Architecture of Silence', in *The Architectural Review*, vol. CLXXVIII, no. 1064, Oct. 1985, p. 72.

66. Le Corbusier, *The Radiant City* (1933), Faber & Faber, London, 1967, p. 67.

still more clearly in his practice, Le Corbusier obviously intends the house itself to be a work of art: an object of meditation in its own right.

The very phrase 'A house is a machine' can be properly understood, moreover, only by understanding what it is that Le Corbusier means by a machine. For him, at the time he wrote in the early 1920s, the machine was very much more than an inert implement. In *The Decorative Art of Today* he eulogizes the machine, not just as a labour-saving device, but as a 'mathematical creation of the mind' – as an entirely new, essentially spiritual phenomenon, quite different in nature from the hand tools of the past:

> Man has drawn himself up like a giant, he has forged himself a tool. He no longer works with his hands. His spirit gives the orders ... Freed, his spirit works freely. On squared paper he draws out the daring curves of his dreams. The machine gives reality to his dreams ... The machine, a modern phenomenon, is bringing about a reformation of the spirit across the world ... the machine is conceived within the spiritual framework which we have constructed for ourselves ... a framework which forms our tangible universe.[67]

Mondrian portrays the machine in similar terms – as a means of spiritual liberation – in a piece published five years earlier. Thanks to the machine, he writes in the fourth of his series of trialogues on 'Natural and Abstract Reality' (1919–20), the new man will be 'completely different from the old', because the machine will free him, not from the *necessity* of material labour, but from his *emotional involvement* with it. The machine *spiritualizes* man by detaching him from matter. Instead of concentrating on the material, he will be able to redirect his attention to the things of the mind:

> The 'new man' performs all the material operations, but he performs them out of 'necessity'. He performs them equally well, but his motivation is different. He lives in the material without enjoying it or suffering from it in the old way: he uses his physique as a perfect machine ... without *himself* being a machine. The difference lies *precisely* in this: formerly man was himself a machine, now he *uses* the machine, either his own body or a machine of his own making. To the machine he leaves so far as possible the heavy work while *he himself* concentrates on inwardness. On the highest level, his soul too is for him a 'machine'; *he himself* becomes *conscious spirit*.[68]

67. Le Corbusier, *The Decorative Art of Today*, The Architectural Press, London, 1987, pp. 106 and 110.
68. P. Mondrian, 'Natuurlijke en abstracte realiteit', in *De Stijl*, vol. III, no. 3, January 1920, p. 28.

But for Le Corbusier the machine can do more than liberate the spirit from the drudgery of manual labour; it can also be itself an object of contemplation – itself a source of spiritual sustenance – because it embodies the same pure geometrical forms – spheres, cylinders and so on – that are the primary truths of architecture, and indeed of the universe:

> If we pick up a polished pebble from the sea-shore, choosing the roundest among the millions of others ... it is because we aspire to the attainment of geometry. The machine thus appears to us the goddess of beauty ... But in place of the calcareous pebble ... the machine brings shining before us disks, spheres, the cylinders of polished steel, polished more highly *than we have ever seen before*: shaped with a theoretical precision and exactitude *which can never be seen in nature itself* ... The spirit of perfection shines out at points of geometrical perfection. It is essentially for this reason that man pauses before the machine to admire it. The beast and the divine in him eat their fill.[69]

Unlike Mondrian and Le Corbusier, Mies does not discuss the machine, but because the materials and craftsmanship of his houses are more precious, smoother and more precise than those of Le Corbusier's, they arguably come closer to Le Corbusier's vision of the machine as a highly polished geometrical product than do, say, the still rather peasant-like Villas Stein and Savoye. At the same time, one might expect the Tugendhat or Farnsworth houses, because of their minimal, recessive quality, to be better fitted to serve as neutral containers, 'vessels of silence', for the contemplation of art and other forms of meditation. And despite Justus Bier's objection that one could not hang pictures in the main space of the Tugendhat house, its owners maintained that it not only enhanced one's appreciation of objects, but of other people and of the experience of life itself. Replying in *Die Form* to Justus Bier's criticisms, Grete Tugendhat observed:

> I have ... never felt the spaces as precious, but rather as austere and grand – not in a way that oppresses, however, so much as one that liberates ... Just as in this space one sees each flower as never before, and every work of art (for instance the sculpture that stands before the onyx wall) speaks more strongly, so too the human occupant stands out, for himself and others, more distinctly from his environment.[70]

69. Le Corbusier, *Decorative Art of Today*, p. 112.
70. G. Tugendhat, 'Die Bewohner des Hauses Tugendhat äussern sich', in *Die Form*, Nov. 1931, pp. 437–8.

Mies liked to claim that by making his spaces 'universal' he enabled them to accommodate a wide variety of different uses (and presumably works of art) at different times, and thus to remain viable over a long period:

> The purposes for which a building is used are constantly changing and we cannot afford to tear down the building each time. That is why we have revised Sullivan's formula 'form follows function' and construct a practical and economical space into which we fit the functions ... I hope to make my buildings neutral frames in which men and artworks can carry on their own lives. To do that one needs a respectful attitude toward things.[71]

Nevertheless, both Mies' earlier, Stijl-like buildings (for instance Barcelona or Brno) and his later single-space, more neoclassical structures (such as the Farnsworth house or the Berlin National Gallery) do in fact impose a very strict discipline on the user and narrow restrictions on the sort of objects that can be displayed in the space. There does after seem to be some justice in Bier's remarks, as well as in those of Lewis Mumford and Robert Venturi quoted above. Provided the discipline and the restrictions are respected, the buildings may indeed be said to enhance experience, but when they are ignored, the reverse is the case. Mies' last great statement, the National Gallery, provides a salient example. There, as Maritz Vandenberg concludes:

> The lower galleries and sculpture garden fulfil their purposes admirably. However, the grand pavilion, whilst majestic and suitable for displaying large objects ... which stand up to the large scale and benefit from the modelling effect of side-lighting from the glass walls, fails badly as an exhibition space for smaller paintings.[72]

It is not just a matter of the size of the objects, however, or even of the different lighting and conservation requirements of paintings as opposed to sculpture. It is also a question of their *number*. The magnificent space should contain ideally only a very few, carefully chosen objects (such as the sculptures by Georg Kolbe and Wilhelm Lehmbruck that Mies selected for the Barcelona Pavilion and the Tugendhat house respectively). Perhaps, indeed, it would be best left entirely empty, as an extremely generous entrance hall.

For Le Corbusier, as for Mies, the house is not only a *machine à habiter* but also a 'pure creation of the mind'[73] – that is, in some sense

71. L. Mies van der Rohe, in C Norberg-Schulz, 'Ein Gespräch', in *Baukunst und Werkform*, Nov. 1958, pp. 615–6; reprinted in Neumeyer, *Artless Word*, p. 339.

72. M. Vandenberg, *New National Gallery, Berlin*, Phaidon Press, London, 1998, p. 22.

73. Le Corbusier, *Towards a New Architecture*, p. 185.

a *machine à méditer*. But in Le Corbusier's writings, more even than in his practice, there is an apparent conflict between his description of the house as a neutral container, an efficiently but unobtrusively functioning machine to meditate *in*, and his demand that it should at the same time establish certain relationships which arouse the emotions[74] – in other words, that it actively provoke particular mental states – that it be a machine to meditate *upon*. Is the real object of meditation the work of art normally stored in a dust-free closet until the moment comes for it to be brought out and hung on the wall for that purpose,[75] or rather the 'masterly, correct and magnificent play of masses brought together in light' of the architecture itself?[76]

For Mies there is no such contradiction between habitation and meditation: they are one and the same. The act of habitation is itself an act of meditation. Thus in his case the phrase 'machine for meditation' (which of course he did not use) means something at once more precise, more ambitious and more demanding of the user. The purpose of the Miesian house is to bring about a correspondence between thing and intellect: to act as a clear framework both for life and for thought.

74. *Ibid.*, p.187.
75. *Ibid.*, p. 109.
76. *Ibid.*, p. 31.

7

Figure and Ground

7.1 *Neue Gestaltung* and Gestalt psychology

Bruno Zevi accuses Van Doesburg of 'operating at a purely sculptural level':

> to animate the voids, he busied himself with the planes; he concentrated his attention on the two-dimensional elements in order to avoid a static three-dimensionality. Mies, on the contrary, creates fluid spaces and subordinates the plastic surfaces to them.[1]

What is at stake here, whether or not Zevi intended to say so, is the figure–ground status of the space as opposed to the coloured planes intended to animate that space. According to Zevi, Van Doesburg, by concentrating on the planes, gave them the status of figures, thereby reducing the space, by implication, to a formless background. Mies, in contrast, managed to 'create' fluid spaces, to which the planes were subordinate. This suggests that Mies succeeded in forming the spaces, not the planes, as the positive figure. It is not immediately obvious how this could be done.

Phenomena of visual perception, and notably the figure–ground problem, were an important area of study for the 'Gestalt' school of psychology, which arose in the early decades of the twentieth century. There is no adequate English equivalent of the German word *Gestalt*, any more than of the Dutch word *beeld* which it translates. (As mentioned in Chapter 6, *Neue Gestaltung* is the German translation of *Nieuwe Beelding*.) Consequently the German dictionary offers a vast range of alternative English meanings: *form, shape, figure, build, frame, stature, manner, character, configuration, design, construction*, and so on ... Common to all of these meanings is the idea of an *organized whole*, a *unity*. A central principle of Gestalt psychology is that an organized perceptual or behavioural whole has characteristic properties which cannot be reduced to those of its constituent parts.

One of the founders of Gestalt psychology, Wolfgang Köhler, gives the following account of the figure–ground phenomenon in his book *Dynamics in Psychology* (1942):

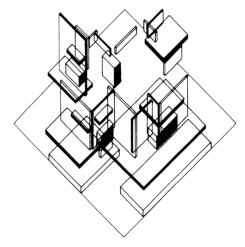

Figure 7.1 Theo van Doesburg, counter-construction based on private house project, 1923

Objects in visual space, but also circumscribed coloured surfaces, and areas which are merely surrounded by a contour, i.e., figures in the widest sense, have as a rule a dense and substantial appearance, while mere ground looks comparatively loose and empty. Figures also tend to stand out in space towards the subject. Moreover, only figures have, properly speaking, shapes; space between figures is for the most part shapeless. Thus the terms figure and ground refer to an essential perceptual difference.[2]

The concept applies most obviously to the traditional concept of sculpture as the art of moulding or carving solid figures – pre-eminently *human* figures – which stand *in* space. With sculpture conceived in this way, the figure–ground relation is relatively clear-cut: the sculpted image is unambiguously a *figure*, which 'stands out' against the 'loose and empty' space around it. With painting, on the other hand, both figure and ground occupy the same plane, and moreover both have to be 'made', in contrast to sculpture, where only the figure is made. Only by illusion can any part of the plane appear to stand out against the rest. In Chapter 1, section 1.13, I discussed Mondrian's exploitation of ambiguous figure–ground relations.

In the case of architecture the difficulties are still greater. The aim of architecture, it is widely assumed, is to create spatial form. But to perceive an architectural space as figure, our innate propensity to associate 'figure-character' with solid, sculptural objects, and to regard the surrounding space as ground, must somehow be overcome. The space is, by definition, not an object, it is not 'made', it is not dense or substantial, and it does not 'stand out towards the subject' but surrounds the observer on all sides. Yet, if architecture is essentially the 'creatrix of space' (*Raumgestalterin*) as August Schmarsow defined it in 1894,[3] then it must indeed be possible to perceive space as form, or more precisely, as *Gestalt*.

Among the De Stijl members who wrote on architecture, only Rietveld has much of a positive nature to say about space formation. Van Doesburg pays surprisingly little attention to space in his architectural manifesto, and when he mentions it at all, it is to deny it anything that resembles a *Gestalt*. The new architecture is to be *formless* (point 5) and *open* (point 9); there will be no separation between interior and exterior, i.e. universal, infinite space (points 5 and 8); and space will be considered, not in itself, but together with time within a four-dimensional space–time continuum (point 10). Insofar as one can make any sense out of these vague statements, they militate against any clear delimitation of a spatial form. Zevi's conclusion, that Van Doesburg failed to deal with space as such, seems to be justified.

2. W. Köhler, *Dynamics in Psychology*, Faber & Faber, London, 1942, pp. 23–4.

3. A. Schmarsow, *Das Wesen des Architektonischen Schöpfung*, Leipzig, 1894, p. 11.

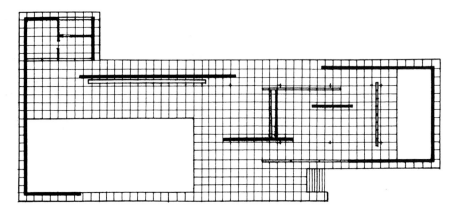

Figure 7.2 Ludwig Mies van der Rohe, Barcelona Pavilion, 1929: plan

The designs by Van Doesburg and Mies which Zevi is comparing in
the passage quoted above are the Van Doesburg/Van Eesteren 'private house' model exhibited in Paris in 1923–4, and the Barcelona
Pavilion. Of the former, his criticism seems to apply most obviously to
Van Doesburg's abstract 'counter-constructions' which reduce the
house to a composition of detached, floating planes (Figure 7.1). The
greatest differences between this and Mies' pavilion are, first, that the
pavilion really does consist of free-standing planes, whereas the house
model is in reality composed of interlocking cubes, and second, that
Mies allows the outer walls to fold around the corners so as to
contain the space (Figure 7.2).

The later design could be considered more radical in that it does
not suffer from the conflict between concept and realization shown
up by the contrast between Van Doesburg's axonometrics and the
house model itself. On the other hand, it is *less* radical to the extent
that the wall-planes, although thin, are expressed as solid slabs
composed of real materials (travertine, marble and onyx), and having
real thickness (about 175 mm). More important still, it accepts the
classical notion of spatial enclosure, contradicting the De Stijl principle of spatial continuity and Zevi's concept of the 'open corner' (see
Chapter 1, section 1.14). Are spatial enclosure and closed corners,
then, necessary conditions for space formation – *Raumgestaltung* –
and therefore for architecture as fundamentally a spatial art? The
answer to these questions is crucial to the debate about the validity
of the whole De Stijl project of creating an architecture of continuous
space defined by floating planes.

7.2 Rasmussen and the Rubin vase

The Danish architect Steen Eiler Rasmussen devotes the second, third and fourth chapters of his well-known book *Experiencing Architecture* (1959) to questions that relate directly to the argument just outlined. He already developed these ideas more than thirty years earlier, however, in a sixteen-page article dealing with Le Corbusier's La Roche-Jeanneret and Pessac houses – of all his designs, the ones that show most clearly the influence of De Stijl – which in 1926 he contributed to the German architectural magazine *Wasmuths Monatshefte für Baukunst*. In the article Rasmussen makes a more forthright and penetrating analysis of the architectural consequences of Le Corbusier's dematerialization of the built mass than he is prepared to do in the later book. There, he merely describes it a successful attempt to create by means of colour 'something poetic' and an illusion of weightlessness.[4] The following quotations are taken from the more outspoken original article.

In both versions of the text, Rasmussen begins by contrasting two ways in which architecture can be thought about: as solids assembled in space, or as voids carved out of a pre-existing mass. In the first, the solid elements are 'figure' and the space is 'ground', whereas in the second, the hollowed-out space is figure and the mass, ground. The first case is the more usual situation, since this is normally how buildings are built; but if one encounters the second type of space formation, one is 'forced to come to terms with the space-form as the datum: space itself becomes the material out of which the percipient must re-create in imagination the artistic process. These things are perhaps clearer in connection with two-dimensional images.'[5]

In 1921 – thus just five years before Rasmussen wrote – the Gestalt psychologist Edgar Rubin published in his book *Visuell wahrgenommene Figuren* a series of visual experiments involving figure–ground perception, of which the most striking is that known as the Rubin vase (Figure 7.3). Just as he would later in *Experiencing Architecture*, Rasmussen uses this diagram to illustrate the figure–ground problem in architecture:

> One recognizes the drawing as a picture of a black vase; one can also perceive it, however, as two white faces turned towards each other, against a black ground. But it is not possible to see both the vase and the faces simultaneously. And it is equally impossible to think spatially and plastically at the same time. One must go from the one perceptual form to the other by a complete change of representation ... That is not to say, however, that one and the

Figure 7.3 Rubin vase: alternative figure–ground relation of vase and heads

4. S.E. Rasmussen, *Experiencing Architecture*, MIT Press, Cambridge, Mass., 1964, p. 94.
5. S.E. Rasmussen, 'Le Corbusier: die kommende Baukunst?', in *Wasmuths Monatshefte für Baukunst*, 1926, pp. 378–9.

same building cannot equally well give rise to successive plastic (i.e. sculptural) and spatial representations. On the contrary.[6]

There exist, he says, rare examples of entirely concave spaces, such as caves, which can only be perceived as hollowed-out voids; but such extreme cases are exceptional:

> In most cases the perceptual image alternates from sculptural to spatial and back again ... In architecture there are a multitude of artistic means to achieve this. To arouse spatial images, the spaces are so far as possible made concave and have uniform boundaries which facilitate that interpretation, whereas the solid forms are made as convex as possible in form in order to reveal their corporeality.[7] (Figures 7.4–7.5)

Rasmussen opens the discussion of Le Corbusier with the great three-storey entrance hall of the La Roche house at Auteuil, completed a year or two before (see Chapter 4, section 4.10):

> When we look at the entrance hall of the house at Auteuil built by Le Corbusier and Pierre Jeanneret, we find that it is not conceived spatially, and still less plastically. We are most clearly conscious of the predominance of the lines and planes that delimit the spatial volumes and the solid bodies. Le Corbusier has explained to me how he designed this space: 'For me the window opening is here the most significant element, so I have made its upper edge continue the line of the upper edge of the adjoining parapet.' The illustration [Figure 7.6] shows that only the delimiting contours of the planes are continuous: the window has so to speak been transmuted into a wall-surface. In a traditional architecture of space and mass this would be false; here, however, it is not a defect, but expresses a fundamental conception. This conception is not really derived, I believe, from architecture, but belongs to the field of modern painting.[8]

Here Rasmussen breaks off to consider a still life by Ozenfant, in which the solid forms of bottles are similarly reduced to flat planes, producing an effect of ambiguity in which the bottles merge interchangeably with the spaces between them:

> So in Ozenfant's painting the optical impression becomes perspective-less and relief-less, the lines become merely the boundaries of planes, which themselves do not combine to

Figure 7.4 Concave and convex forms contrasted (after Rasmussen)

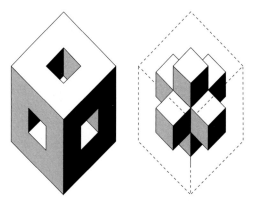

Figure 7.5 Concave (centripetal) and convex (centrifugal) compositions contrasted (after Van Doesburg)

---

6. *Ibid.,* p. 379.
7. *Ibid.*
8. *Ibid.,* p. 381.

Figure 7.6 Le Corbusier, La Roche-Jeanneret houses, Auteuil, 1923–4: view of entrance hall

produce a corporeal image. The same occurs in Le Corbusier's architecture, which produces neither a spatial nor a corporeal impression, while the separate planes are only used as abstract figures. Here in fact it is a question of false relations [falsche Beziehungen].[9]

To analyse more deeply this phenomenon Rasmussen now returns to the Rubin vase:

Besides the two possibilities already mentioned, of reading the drawing as either a black vase or two white faces, there exists a third: we can perceive the contours as such. To eliminate the reference to the vase and the faces, one need only rotate the image.[10]

This is not enough, however. As long as the vase remains black and the faces white, it remains impossible to see both kinds of figure as equivalent, and their mutual contours as the mutual separation between them. To destroy the figure–ground relation completely, it is necessary that the contours be reduced to meandering black lines against a continuous white ground (Figure 7.7). Applying the principle to three dimensions, these lines can now be compared to planes

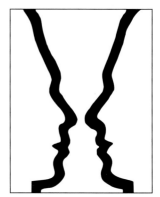

Figure 7.7 Rubin vase redrawn so that profiles become a linear figure against a white ground

9. *Ibid.*
10. *Ibid.*

which separate spatial volumes: the areas above, between and below the lines now represent both the exterior space and the interior space continuous with it. The effect must be imagined as similar to Van Doesburg's abstract reduction of the private house project of 1923 to a composition of floating planes in continuous space (Figure 7.1). Rasmussen again:

> In the same way one can conceive the three-dimensional space as defined by the surfaces that delimit it, rather than by masses, and the artist can suggest such a reading just as well as either a spatial or a sculptural interpretation.[11]

The description recalls Mondrian's statement, published four years before, that

> To see architecture as *form-making* is a traditional conception. It is the (perspective) vision of the past. In the neoplastic concept this is abandoned ... The new vision ... sees architecture as a *multiplicity of planes*: always the *plane*. This multiplicity is thus composed (abstractly) to form *a flat representation* ... Because it is essentially planar, neoplastic architecture demands *colour*, without which the plane cannot be for us a living reality. Colour is also necessary to remove the naturalistic appearance of materials.[12]

Thus for Mondrian the destruction of solidity and materiality is the great positive achievement of De Stijl. But for Rasmussen, in 1926, it holds great dangers:

> All surfaces thereby become equivalent, their materiality loses all significance, and only the lines that delimit the surfaces retain their value. We earlier concluded that the effect of masses arises from their evident materiality, profiling and corner-emphasis. Conversely, the absence of these elements destroys plasticity. When we look at Le Corbusier's architecture, we find that it increasingly renounces such means. Whereas his earlier buildings still had a hint of an entablature, his latest houses no longer have any mouldings at all; the walls appear to be made of paper. They are ... divested of all corporeality.[13]

Rasmussen draws similar conclusions from his analysis of Pessac (1925), and asks rhetorically, '*Ist dies nun die kommende Baukunst?*' – 'Is this then the architecture of the future?' (*Die kommende Baukunst* is the title of the German translation of *Vers une architecture*). He concludes that

11. *Ibid.,* p. 382.
12. P. Mondrian, 'De realiseering van het neo-plasticisme in verre toekomst en in de huidige architectuur', in *De Stijl*, vol. V, no. 5, May 1922, p. 68.
13. Rasmussen, 'Le Corbusier: die kommende Baukunst?', p. 382.

The value of Le Corbusier's architecture as the architecture of the future is wholly dependent on one's conception of what the lessons of this architecture are. If the programme is wrongly stated, it cannot give us the right expression for our time, no matter how skilful the solutions may be ... When we consider the single houses, the houses at Pessac, or those that Le Corbusier has published in *Vers une architecture*, we find conclusively that they rest upon few acceptable technical ideas ... The artist himself explained that his aim was 'to create something poetic'. And indeed these houses are poetic and beautiful with their luminous spaces, clear surfaces and whimsical outdoor rooms, and yet I honestly doubt that they represent the dwellings of the future.[14]

Rasmussen's final reservations about the enduring validity of Le Corbusier's architecture are mainly practical: the high cost of his more idiosyncratic design decisions, such as the provision of roof gardens; the poor standard of insulation; and the general unsuitability of the dwellings as the workers' housing for which they were intended:

In fact, at present the people on whose behalf that public-spirited man, M. Frugès, financed these houses, are still refusing to move in to them. That may be stupid ... Yet one might have thought that the design of a housing quarter like Pessac would have been based on a detailed study of the needs and wishes of the future inhabitants. The result would perhaps have been less 'poetic', but it would have made a more significant contribution to the solution of the pressing problem: the modern worker's dwelling.[15]

The houses remained empty, in fact, for five or six years, until after 1930, when the plots began to be sold off piecemeal. After that the settlement continued to be beset by problems, mostly not of Le Corbusier's making, such as the absence of shops and lack of public transport and other essential services. (Owing to the obstructiveness of the local authorities, water, gas and electricity connections were delayed.)[16]

In retrospect, however, such questions as the 'detailed study of the needs' of the 'modern worker's dwelling' seem to be of only passing importance, compared with Le Corbusier's own stated objective: 'to create something poetic'. The needs have long since changed, but the poetry remains. In fairness to Le Corbusier, I must quote Rasmussen's much rosier recollection of his visit to Pessac and of the magically dematerializing effect of the coloured planes, written thirty years after the original article:

14. *Ibid.*, p. 392.
15. *Ibid.*, pp. 392–3.
16. P. Boudon, *Lived-in Architecture*, Lund Humphries, London, 1972, pp. 14–15; and M. Ferrand, J.-P. Feugas, B. Le Roy, J.-L. Veyret (eds), *Le Corbusier: Les Quartiers Modernes Frugès*, Birkhäuser, Basel, 1998, p. 110.

Sitting in a garden on the roof of one of the houses, in the shade of a leafy maple tree, I could see how the sun dappled the Havana-brown wall with blobs of light. The only purpose of the wall was to frame the view. The buildings opposite could be perceived as houses only with great difficulty. The one to the left was simply a light-green plane without cornice or gutter. An oblong hole was cut out of the plane exactly like the one I was looking through. Behind and to the right of the green house were row-houses with coffee-brown façades and cream-coloured sides and behind them rise the tops of the blue 'sky-scrapers'.[17]

However, as Rasmussen writes in *Experiencing Architecture*, Le Corbusier later abandoned the style he had created in the 1920s: 'While at the time it was abstract painting that inspired him, today his buildings are more like monumental sculpture.'[18]

This transformation began in Le Corbusier's work as early as 1930. The Villa Savoye was his last 'purist' house. The projected Errazuris house in Chile, the Villa Mandrot near Toulon and the 'Clarté' apartment house in Geneva, all designed in 1930, establish a new principle which, despite changes, he would hold to throughout the rest of his career: a principle in which materials are shown 'as found' and the construction is exposed. One of the most beautiful examples of this new 'constructivism' is the 'maison de weekend en banlieue de Paris', designed in 1935.[19] With its concrete vaulted roofs covered in grass above and sheathed with unpainted plywood underneath, its walls of rubble or glass blocks and its unpainted plywood joinery, this little house looks forward to such post-war examples as the Fueter house on Lake Constance (1950)[20] and the Jaoul houses at Neuilly (1954–6).[21] Le Corbusier's description of the 'maison de weekend' emphasizes that the only architectonic means employed are the elements of the construction itself:

Here everything shows itself for what it is: the fairfaced stonework, natural externally, painted white internally; the wood of the ceiling and walls; the fairfaced brick of the fireplace; the white clay tiles of the floor; the 'Nevada' glass blocks; the cipolin marble table.[22]

The design points to a new, no longer abstract architecture: one which, having absorbed the lessons of De Stijl, seeks to integrate these with an exploration of the archaic principles of architecture as *Raumgestaltung*. This new architecture, which began to emerge from the 1930s onwards in the work of a handful of architects that included Le Corbusier, Wright, Alvar Aalto, Gunnar Asplund, Sigurd

17. Rasmussen, *Experiencing Architecture*, p. 95.
18. *Ibid.*, p. 103.
19. W. Boesiger, (ed.), *Le Corbusier 1929–34*, Les Editions Girsberger, Zurich, 1952, pp. 124–30.
20. W. Boesiger, (ed.), *Le Corbusier 1946–52*, Les Editions Girsberger, Zurich, 1953, pp. 64–6.
21. W. Boesiger, (ed.), *Le Corbusier 1952–57*, Les Editions Girsberger, Zurich, 1953, pp. 206–19.
22. W. Boesiger, (ed.), *Le Corbusier 1929–34*, Les Editions Girsberger, Zurich, 1952, p. 125.

Lewerentz and Louis Kahn, was, like much of the painting and sculpture of the same period, not so much 'classical' as 'primitive'.

7.3 Dom van der Laan and architectonic space

In the end Rasmussen leaves the question open of whether the alternating readings of solids and cavities that he attributes to traditional architecture can be replaced by a composition of floating and intersecting planes, or whether such a surface architecture must be an intrinsically impoverished one: merely an elegant novelty which we may admire for a season, but find shallow in the long run. It can also be argued, however, that *neither* of Rasmussen's analyses gives an adequate description of how architecture really works, or should work.

The problem with the Rubin vase as an analogy for architecture is that the diagram is intentionally ambiguous. The contour separating the faces from the vase is purposely a continuous undulation, in order that neither figure can be more convex, and thus more dominant, than the other. By applying the diagram to building, Rasmussen implies that architecture too is inherently ambiguous: that when we look at an interior, we constantly switch backwards and forwards between alternative readings, at one moment seeing it as a concave space hollowed out from a solid mass, and at the next, as convex masses standing in space. But is not such an alternation between two interpretations, each of which continually annihilates the other, bound in the long run to be disturbing and frustrating, like an illusion at a fun fair? Is not the architecture of planes, proposed by Van Doesburg and realized by Le Corbusier at Auteuil and Pessac, actually more satisfying, since the planes and volumes can coexist, as it were, in separate dimensions?

An alternative analysis is put forward by the Dutch Benedictine architect Dom Hans van der Laan in his treatise *Architectonic Space* (1977). In the 1940s Van der Laan (1904–91) set out to rediscover the primitive beginnings of architecture: the building of a wall, or the placing of a lintel upon two standing stones. As Geert Bekaert writes in his obituary of Van der Laan, 'The attraction of the work and life of Hans van der Laan lies in the radicalism with which he brings everything back to a primordial experience, as if he were the first (and only) man on earth.'[23]

Van der Laan deals with precisely the same questions that exercised Rasmussen half a century earlier, but arrives at more definite conclusions. Like Rasmussen, he begins by identifying two ways in which architectural space can come about: by digging materials out of the ground in order to build them up to enclose a habitable space, or

23. G. Bekaert, 'In memoriam Dom Hans van der Laan, in *Archis*, no. 9, 1991, p. 9.

conversely to throw the excavated material away and live in the resulting cavern. Only the first method, for Van der Laan, results in a truly human dwelling. It is true that

out of need or asceticism men have sometimes contented themselves with cave- or pit-dwellings of this kind. However, such a dwelling-form in no sense brings about the reconciliation of man and nature; by retreating into a cave man flees from nature instead of adapting it to his existence.[24]

A more convincing reason emerges later in the book, however, and it is of a purely formal and perceptual nature, which again involves figure–ground relationships. The Rubin vase could once more serve as an illustration. Van der Laan argues that an architectonic space (a space that genuinely conforms to the nature of architecture) is distinct from both the hollowed-out cave and the free-standing sculptural form. The surface of a free-standing mass clearly belongs to the form that it delimits. There is no ambiguity. Conversely, a hollowed-out spatial form readily 'borrows' the surface away from the mass within which it is formed, because we are unable to perceive the form of that mass when we are inside it (Figure 7.4). So in the first case we have a solid form set against a formless spatial ground (like the vase in Rubin's diagram), while in the second, we have a spatial form against a formless solid ground (like the two faces). According to Van der Laan, neither of these solutions results in an authentic architecture.

To be genuinely architectonic, a space must arise between solid forms that are unambiguous enough *as* forms to retain possession of their surfaces. For Rasmussen, such forms are convex; for Van der Laan, it is only necessary that they be revealed clearly as square-cut masses of sufficient thickness in proportion to their height and length, and to the width of the space. How is such a spatial form possible? Van der Laan acknowledges that it involves a paradox:

A mass owes its form to the correspondence between its opposite surfaces; in the case of a wall these are its inner and outer surfaces ... The space that arises between such walls cannot have a form in the same sense as does the solid wall; both the inside space and the wall would then owe their form to the same inner surface of the wall, which is impossible. A form can exist only against a formless ground, which means that a surface can only belong to one form.[25]

24. H. van der Laan, *Architectonic Space*, E J Brill, Leiden, 1983, p. 8.
25. *Ibid.*, p. 35.

The point corresponds exactly to the Rubin diagram, but translated from two into three dimensions. A two-dimensional figure can
only be perceived against a shapeless ground, so we can see either
the vase or the faces, but not both together. Similarly one can see a
solid form against a formless space, or a hollowed-out spatial form
against a formless mass, but not both at the same time. Van der Laan's
solution of the paradox is as follows:

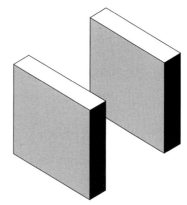

> So a space owes its form not to a bounding surface, but to the
> *form* of a bounding mass. Taken literally this is absurd, because it
> implies a fourth dimension. Lines are bounded by points, planes by
> lines and volumes by planes. We cannot imagine a reality bounded
> by volumes, because it does not exist. Nevertheless, from the
> formed solidity of its walls the space too acquires a certain form,
> though this is entirely different from that of a solid form.[26]

Figure 7.8 Dom Hans van der Laan: spatial form
constituted by the 'neighbourhood' between walls

In fact, it could be argued that Van der Laan's concept of spatial
form does depend on a kind of four-dimensionality, but of quite a
different sort from Giedion's or Van Doesburg's, since we are not
talking here of space–time. According to Van der Laan, the spatial
form is not constituted by a surface, but by the *mutual neighbourhood* of its opposite walls. This neighbourhood or rather 'nearness'
[*nabijheid*] is a proportion between the thickness of the walls and
their distance apart: walls twice as thick appear to be in each other's
neighbourhood at twice the distance apart. Therefore one could
say that four dimensions are needed to define the form of the
space: its length, height and width, together with the wall thickness
(Figure 7.8).

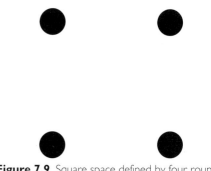

Figure 7.9 Square space defined by four round
forms

This principle is easier to grasp with the help of another familiar
Gestalt diagram, this time simply four black dots (Figure 7.9). Most
people seeing the dots will interpret them as defining a square. It is no
longer a question of having to choose between seeing either the dots
or the square space, as with the vase and the faces. The dots and the
square they define complement each other: the dots are necessary to
define the square, the square is necessary to determine the arrangement of the dots. By analogy, Van der Laan's 'architectonic' space is
marked out by solid masses which are co-present with the space they
demarcate. The interpretation is strengthened by the fact that the
masses are squared off, just as it would be if the dots in the diagram
were made square instead of round (Figure 7.10).

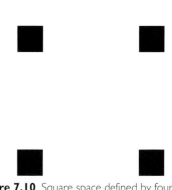

Figure 7.10 Square space defined by four
square forms

The correct proportion of the wall thickness to the width of the
space is crucial to the spatial form: the walls must be neither too thick
nor too thin for the space. If they are too thick the space appears

26. *Ibid.*

hollowed out, like a cave; it borrows the surface from the wall, destroying its form. Conversely, if the wall thickness is negligible in proportion to the width of the space, as happens in many modern buildings, including Le Corbusier's houses of the 1920s, the walls appear, according to Van der Laan, as formless membranes wrapped around a space-bubble. In both cases the effect is much the same: the spatial form is expressed as a 'pseudo-solid form' contained within its surfaces. And in both cases the architecture is impoverished, being deprived of one of its dimensions.

The two-dimensional diagram again illustrates this phenomenon. If the square dots are too much enlarged with respect to the space between them, they cease to appear as four black figures against a white ground, and instead we see a white cross against a black ground (Figure 7.11). The cross so to speak 'robs' the black squares of their outline, destroying them as figures and becoming itself the dominant figure. Note that whereas the original square was superposed over the dots and included them in its surface (Figures 7.9–7.10), the cross now appears to stand in front of a continuous black background. The corresponding diagram for an architecture of thin planes is one in which the black squares are replaced by eight separate lines, so that the white cross is absorbed into a continuous white ground (Figure 7.12), just as, in architecture, Van Doesburg demanded the continuity of interior and exterior space.

Whereas in Rasmussen's description of traditional and classical architecture the viewer alternates between spatial and sculptural interpretations, with Van der Laan, provided the proportion of mass to space is right, the need to alternate is done away with. In his view, the experience of architecture is enriched precisely by the fact that we can see the two kinds of form simultaneously, overlaid upon each other – as it were in separate dimensions.

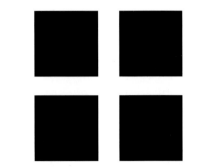

Figure 7.11 White cross as figure against black ground

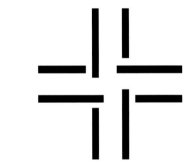

Figure 7.12 Linear figures against continuous white ground

7.4 Towards a deeper perspective

However, Van der Laan's theory, that an architectonic space can be delimited only by permanent wall-masses that stand in each other's neighbourhood, applies only to very simple spaces, such as a room or a gallery contained between two parallel walls. In the case of even slightly more complex buildings like his own abbey church at Vaals (1956–68), and still more when he applies the principle to urban design, all spaces wider than seven times the wall thickness must derive their form either directly or indirectly by way of the proportion between their width and that of a basic gallery space formed between walls. In order to reveal this proportion, a court or small square needs to be surrounded by an open colonnade,[27] and larger squares surrounded by public buildings which themselves are planned around courts.[28] Such demands are not only extremely restrictive, one doubts also if they are effective – that is, whether the proportions in question can be perceived by an observer on the ground.

Because the effect of foreshortening increases with the dimensions, it is very difficult to gauge such proportional relations. Standing in a large square, one can judge the relative heights and widths of the surrounding buildings far more exactly than the size or shape of the square itself. In reality, an urban space is perceived, not just as a horizontal extension, but as a play between vertical, horizontal and diagonal dimensions. The ratios between exclusively horizontal measures, which serve more or less adequately to explain the relations between walls and spaces in the primitive cell or gallery, need to be replaced by a more flexible principle which takes account of the real complexity of perceived spatial relationships at the larger scale.

This is precisely what Van der Laan proposed and began to map out in the last years of his life. In 1987, four years before he died, he described how, since completing his book *Architectonic Space* in 1977, he had arrived at a new, 'deeper perspective' on the problem of architectonic space. This new insight replaced the former theory, by which urban spaces are derived from a basic space-cell by a chain of superpositions of larger upon smaller spaces, with a new one, in which complete building volumes are placed directly in relation to each other within a continuous natural space:

> by the placing together of building volumes, I come into direct contact with the space of nature, and as it were make natural space visible, by a certain play of its dimensions, between these volumes ... You see the deeper perspective in which architecture is now gathered up ... Now architecture is absorbed into the whole world of ordered arrangements of forms, amongst which it takes the foremost place. Still-life paintings are an authentic response to this phenomenon, as are the placing of furniture in a room, the planting of trees and shrubs in a garden, or even the setting of a table for a meal. By all these means, architectonic space, which begins by being removed from nature, is returned to it.[29]

Thus architectonic space is no longer cut out from natural space and separated from it by a wall, but becomes itself part of that space, momentarily halted and held in suspension within a field of forces set

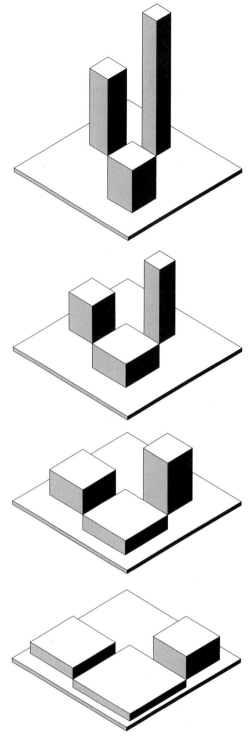

Figures 7.13–16 Dom Hans van der Laan: examples of spaces generated by arrangements of three forms in varying proportions

27. *Ibid.*, p. 162.
28. *Ibid.*, p. 168.
29. H. van der Laan, letter to the author, 18 March 1987, pp. 3–4.

up by the interrelations of solid, or virtually solid, volumes. These volumes are differentiated, no longer merely by the contrasting scale of their horizontal dimensions, but by their 'posture'. They are distinguished as 'standing', 'sitting' or 'lying' forms. The emphasis on the contrasting posture, proportion and placing of these forms seems to echo Van Doesburg's statement in the twelfth point of his architectural manifesto:

> Against symmetry the new architecture sets the *balanced proportion of unequal parts* – that is, of parts which because of their contrasting functional character differ in posture, measure, ratio and position.[30]

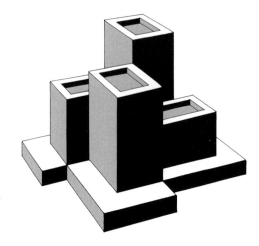

Figure 7.17 Theo van Doesburg, garden sculpture (flower vase), 1919

Van der Laan demonstrated the new theory with a set of abstract models, each composed of three equal volumes of contrasting proportion, ranging from tall, narrow, standing forms to broad, low, lying ones (Figures 7.13–7.16). These compositions closely resemble certain De Stijl constructions (Figure 7.17) or a suprematist design for an ideal city by Kasimir Malevich. There is also a close affinity with the late urban projects of Mies van der Rohe, such as the Chicago Federal Center (1959–73) or the Toronto-Dominion Centre (1963–9) (Figure 7.18), both of which combine two towers of contrasting heights with a low, square hall to define between them a central plaza.

However, Van der Laan himself disowned any De Stijl or other modernist influence on his thought, insisting that all his work had been

> built up and brought to completion quite independently of our entire modern western civilization ... I realize that some traces of all those cast-offs might here and there be discovered in it, but you must never regard my work as merely an echo of all those theorists who did no more than hazard a guess at one or another aspect of it; I know this sounds opinionated, but facts are facts.[31]

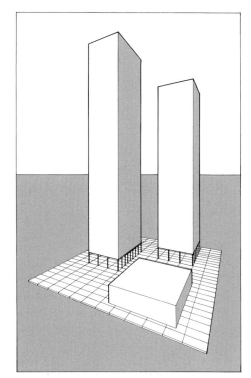

Figure 7.18 Mies van der Rohe, Federal Center, Chicago, 1959–73

This denial sounds, however, not only 'opinionated' but disingenuous. Admittedly, there is a fundamental difference between De Stijl's reduction of solid form to planes without depth and Van der Laan's reliance on three-dimensional mass as the basis of architectonic space formation. Similarly, there is a distinction between the De Stijl concept of the continuity of interior and exterior space and Van der Laan's final vision in which *external* architectonic space is continuous with natural space, but brought into being by building volumes comprising envelopes within which the *internal* spaces are contained

30. T. van Doesburg, 'Tot een beeldende architectuur', in *De Stijl*, vol. VI, no. 6/7, 1924, p. 81.

31. H. van der Laan, letter to the author, 25 August 1988, p. 2.

in the traditional way. However, Van der Laan was exposed to the De Stijl doctrines at an impressionable age, as an architectural student at Delft in 1923–6. The De Stijl publications were debated by the student discussion group, the BSK, which Van der Laan founded during his second year and presided over until he abandoned his architectural studies in order to become a monk in 1926. One of the former members of that group, the architect S.J. van Embden, sums up as follows the confusing but stimulating architectural climate that surrounded Van der Laan and his fellow students in those years:

> First of all, engaged in a rearguard action, were the last of the historicising traditionalists. Next came the recently formed estab-lishment composed of the 'moderns' of the turn of the century, led by the great Berlage. But making their influence felt at the same time, and enjoying much success with the public, were the men of the 'Amsterdam School', in revolt against the rationalism of the older moderns ... Finally, contributing greatly to the violence of the general tumult, was the latest phenomenon: the Stijl move-ment's recent breakthrough from the world of the fine arts into the field of architecture.[32]

De Stijl's radicalism and its claim to stand for higher, more spiritual values could hardly be ignored. And even though Van der Laan had no direct contact with the De Stijl members at that time, the friend-ship and mutual respect that grew up between him and the greatest De Stijl architect, Gerrit Rietveld, in Rietveld's last years, is evidence that the two were pursuing a common goal. Furthermore, Van der Laan's final, 'deeper' perspective gives rise to a concept of architec-ture fundamentally different, as he himself admitted, from that set out in *Architectonic Space*. There, vertical walls had created a separate 'shell-space', a formed 'inside', divided off from the spatial continuum of nature. Now, that continuum is itself 'made visible' by the placing of forms within it, much as the placing of magnets imposes a pattern on a scattering of iron filings. It now becomes a question, not of enclosing a separate space within the space of nature, but of arranging objects within that space, by means of which it is revealed in its own right. And these objects are no longer walls, but – though Van der Laan never used the phrase – 'virtual masses', that is, ensembles of walls and spaces which, like people conversing in a room, take up contrasting positions and postures in the space:

> It is therefore no longer just a matter of defining the forms of things by their height, length and breadth – that is, by imposing

32. S.J. van Embden, 'Herinneringen aan Dom Van der Laan', in *Architectuur/Bouwen*, no. 9, 1991, p. 12.

upon them the three dimensions of our bodies. We now impose our standing, sitting, or lying posture upon the things themselves, in this case upon buildings, which rise up, as towers, houses and galleries, within the space of nature.[33]

Unlike Van Doesburg's demand for total spatial continuity, Van der Laan's deeper perspective acknowledges that exterior (urban) and interior space are bound to remain separate. (The inevitability of this is now all the greater because of the tendency towards ever higher standards of thermal insulation.) However much one may try to complicate the shape of the external envelope by means of projecting bays and inset porches (as Van Doesburg and Van Eesteren did with their three house models of 1923), it remains a sharp boundary between indoor and outdoor space. Nor can this boundary be dissolved simply by making the envelope a glass box, as Mies did in his American work.

It has to be recognized that interior and urban space exist on separate, mutually superposed levels, just as, at a smaller scale, in Van der Laan's earlier theory, the wall and the space it brings into being are overlaid upon each other. Between interior and exterior, the building envelope acts as what Le Corbusier in his criticism of the De Stijl projects calls 'the shield of pure form ... the pure envelope which covers abundance with a mask of simplicity'.[34]

As I argued in Chapter 4, Le Corbusier's Villa Savoye and Mies' Barcelona Pavilion are ideal examples of this principle. Within the villa's four-square envelope, or the pavilion's clamp-like U-shaped walls with their closed corners, the free play of wall-planes and flowing space is possible. Externally, the building as a whole becomes in turn a potential element in the corresponding play of 'virtual masses' at an urban scale, by which, as Van der Laan says, 'natural space is made visible, by a certain play of its dimensions, between these volumes'. At a still larger scale, the city as a whole can be conceived as a figure set against the surrounding countryside. Thus as Christian Norberg-Schulz writes in *Existence, Space and Architecture* (1971):

In general, the levels form a hierarchy. The house, for instance, is essentially interior space but, in relation to the urban level, it functions as a private or public 'landmark' or *Mal*, that is, its properties as a *mass* become relevant. The same holds true for the town itself, which although easily characterized as 'public interior space', in relation to the landscape becomes a concentrated 'form'. Even a whole continent appears as a figure or mass at a geographical

33. H. van der Laan, 'Instruments of order', in W. Graatsma (ed.), *Ter ere van Dom Hans van der Laan, 1904–1991*, Rosbeek, Nuth, 1992, p. 78.

34. Le Corbusier, 'L'exposition de l'Ecole spéciale d'architecture', in *L'Esprit Nouveau*, no. 23, May 1924.

level. (A figure, in general, has a higher density than its surround-ings.)[35]

Norberg-Schulz brings us back, finally, to the question of figure and ground. At each level, as Wolfgang Köhler puts it in the passage quoted near the start of this chapter, 'figures ... have as a rule a dense and substantial appearance', and they 'tend to stand out in space towards the subject'. The lesson of this chapter is that such figure-character is relative. A given form can appear as 'ground' in the context of a stronger, denser form, while at a larger scale it may appears as 'figure' with respect to a more open background. And this phenomenon can be repeated several times, at different levels of insideness and outsideness.

35. C. Norberg-Schulz, *Existence, Space and Architecture*, Studio Vista, London, 1971, p. 98.

8

The Unchanging and the Changeable

8.1 Three kinds of simultaneity

We can begin this concluding chapter by turning once more to the central idea of Sigfried Giedion's *Space, Time and Architecture*: the necessary connection between the theory of relativity in physics and concepts of simultaneity in art and architecture. Giedion implies that the revolutions which took place in art around 1910 – he mentions cubism, purism, constructivism, neoplasticism and futurism – were a historical necessity: the inevitable and obligatory expression of Einstein's discovery of relativity at about the same time:

> In many places, about 1910, a consciousness that the painter's means of expression had lost contact with modern life was beginning to emerge. But it was in Paris, with cubism, that these efforts first attained a visible result ... Cubism breaks with Renaissance perspective. It views objects relatively: that is, from several points of view, no one of which has exclusive authority. And in so dissecting objects it sees them simultaneously from all sides – from above and below, from inside and outside ... The presentation of objects from several points of view introduces a principle which is intimately bound up with modern life – simultaneity. It is a temporal coincidence that Einstein should have begun his famous work ... in 1905 with a careful definition of simultaneity.[1]

As will have become clear from previous chapters, I do not return to Giedion's analysis because I agree with it, but because his use (or misuse) of the term 'simultaneity' provides an ideal vantage point from which to explore the aims and the failings of modernism. The concept of simultaneity is employed by Giedion in two entirely different senses. Not only do science and art, according to him, share the new awareness of simultaneity; they do so *simultaneously*. Since the principle of simultaneity is 'intimately bound up with modern life', no authentic (or 'constituent') modern art or architecture can afford to lag behind in reflecting that principle. Giedion speaks of the 'coincidence' of Einstein's 1905 paper with the invention of cubism three or four years later, but his whole thesis becomes meaningless if this is

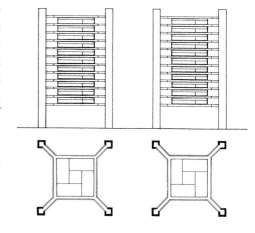

Figure 8.1 Theo van Doesburg, 'circulation city', 1929: diagrammatic elevation and plan

1. S Giedion, *Space, Time and Architecture*, Harvard University Press, Cambridge, Mass., 1941, pp. 355–7

taken to mean that the two events merely coincided, as it were by accident. A causal connection is implied; art is obliged to synchronize with and give expression to other developments in modern life, notably the latest discoveries in science.

Both aspects of simultaneity were inherent in the modernist approach to urban design. On the one hand, the principle of simultaneity, in the sense of the compression of the time dimension, was interpreted literally as the ability to travel very quickly from one part of the city to another, and to experience many sensations in rapid succession. On the other hand, it was a dogma of modernism that the only authentic or valid architecture was that which was 'of its time', that is, simultaneous with advances in other fields.

Thus, in the first place, rapid transport came to be regarded as the next best thing to absolute instantaneity: at the heart of Le Corbusier's *ville contemporaine* of 1922 is the aerodrome built over the central station, to which pilots are expected to descend perilously between the surrounding glass skyscrapers. The fast autoroute that forms the central artery of the city also passes under the airfield:

> This is the ideal city. A model city for commerce! Is it the mere fancy of some neurotic passion for speed? But, surely, speed lies on this side of mere dreams; it is a brutal necessity. One can only come to this conclusion; that the city which can achieve speed will achieve success – and this is an obvious truth.[2]

Le Corbusier's exposition of the *ville contemporaine* in his book *Urbanisme* of 1924 provoked from Van Doesburg a series of critiques and counter-proposals, culminating in 1929 with his design for a *ville de circulation* or 'transport city' (Figure 8.1). The very name of this proposal expresses its main purpose:

> Centralization or dispersal: this is the essential difference between the ancient and the modern city, and one must ask oneself whether the change from the one to the other can be achieved simply by disembowelling, in the manner of Haussmann's boulevards. Radical innovations have been proposed: development of aerial and underground transport, construction of multi-level cities, separation of vehicle and pedestrian traffic ... The city must be an efficient mechanism, a machine for movement in all directions.[3]

The *ville de circulation* is a direct rebuff to the *ville contemporaine*. As early as January 1925, in an article on the latter in the Dutch

2. Le Corbusier, *The City of Tomorrow* (1924), The Architectural Press, London, 1971, pp. 190–91.

3. T. van Doesburg, unsourced quotation in B. Zevi, *Poetica dell'architettura neoplastica*, Libreria Editrice Politecnica Tamburini, Milan, 1953, pp. 134–5.

journal *Het Bouwbedrijf*, Van Doesburg criticizes Le Corbusier's plan as still rooted in the essentially centralized town planning of Haussmann:

> Le Corbusier takes Haussmann's system of opening up as starting point for his new urban plan. That this is not a *basic* solution to the problem of urbanity is evidenced by that fact that he does not get to a radical *decentralization*, but simply relocates the traffic axes.[4]

The same emphasis on traffic appears in four urban projects created in 1924–6 by Doesburg's close collaborator Cor van Eesteren. These comprise his competition entries for the filling in of the Rokin canal in Amsterdam (1924), for Unter den Linden in Berlin (1925) – for which he won first prize – and for the centre of Paris (1926), and a more abstract project for a business district in Paris (1924). The main themes of all four projects are the need to liberate traffic, and the practical and aesthetic necessity of high buildings to compensate for the inevitable street widening. Van Eesteren's exposition of the Rokin project, published in *De Stijl* in 1925, makes both points:

> In the first place the Rokin must serve traffic. The nearer the great traffic routes which serve a great city approach the centre, the narrower they become. Thus contrary to what one might expect, the breadth of a city's main arteries is not in direct but in inverse proportion to the intensity of the traffic ... THE SCALE OF THE CITYSCAPE MUST CHANGE. The old beauty of Amsterdam was built upon a particular pattern of life with its own dimension and scale. The beauty that we can achieve will be based upon today's attitude to life, *and upon its scale and dimension* ... Only *a new element*, and in fact *an element of height*, can once more restore a definite proportion of breadth to height.[5]

Nevertheless, all four projects, while far more open and larger in scale than the classical cityscape, preserve to some degree the very elements that Van Doesburg attacks: the street and the continuous street-façade. And much the same can be said, despite its arrangement of parallel slab-blocks perpendicular to the street axis, of Mies van der Rohe's only large-scale city-centre project of the 1920s, his proposed remodelling of the Alexanderplatz in Berlin (1928). Both Van Eesteren's and Mies' plans fall far short of Van Doesburg's radical demand that 'the *street* will have to disappear first of all, for it is

---

4. T. van Doesburg, 'Le Corbusier's *ville contemporaine*', in *Het Bouwbedrijf*, vol. II, no 1, Jan 1925, pp. 32–8; in *Theo van Doesburg on Modern Architecture*, Birkhäuser, Basel, 1990, p. 33.

5. C. van Eesteren, 'Moderne stedebouwbeginselen in de practijk', in *De Stijl*, vol. VI, no. 10/11, 1925, pp. 162–7.

exactly these tubes formed by the classic street walls that are causing the increasing traffic congestion'.[6]

More radical were the 1924 proposal of Mies' collaborator Ludwig Hilbersheimer (1885–1967) for a *Hochhausstadt* (high-rise city), his 1927 plan for a *Wohlfahrtsstadt* (welfare city), and above all his project of 1933–5 for a linear 'decentralized city' with tall towers dispersed among low buildings in a park-like landscape. This last would later become the model for Mies' and Hilbersheimer's joint design for the 1955 Lafayette Park development in Detroit – appropriately, a city famous for car manufacture. It is described by Alison and Peter Smithson as the purest expression of

> The ideal of a calm, open-space-structured urban pattern ... certainly the most civilized dwelling-quarter of this century. A place full of potential, and of lessons – in its discrete means of traffic separation – its to-the-whole-city-scaled urban structure. It brings to Detroit an amazing other idea of how life can be lived with machines.[7]

Lafayette Park is perhaps the closest realization of Van Doesburg's vision of a decentralized, open city of smooth, unhindered circulation.

The second sense in which the concept of simultaneity was interpreted by the modern movement of the 1920s showed itself in the idea that in order to be contemporary, 'of its time', the whole city must be rebuilt at a blow: *simultaneously*. In his article on the Rokin project Van Eesteren demands that 'The beauty that we can achieve will be based upon today's attitude to life, *and upon its scale and dimension*.' In his 1926 competition entry for Paris, the Madeleine sits squashed between two skyscrapers. Apart from this, none of the above-mentioned proposals of Van Eesteren, Le Corbusier, Hilbersheimer or Mies incorporates a single existing building.

Still more extreme in the ruthlessness with which it would have sacrificed so much beauty to the necessity of the *Zeitgeist* and the purity of the *tabula rasa* is Le Corbusier's *Plan Voisin* for the centre of Paris (1925). The whole area north of the Rue de Rivoli and stretching from the Elysée to the Gare de l'Est was to have been flattened and replaced by a grid of cruciform skyscrapers surrounded by lower buildings in a continuous parkland traversed by fast motorways. Around the edges of this sea of glass and grass, and occasionally floating like jetsam within it, only the principal monuments are preserved: the Louvre, the Palais Royal, the Bourse, the Place Vendôme.

---

6. Van Doesburg, 'Le Corbusier's *ville contemporaine*', in *Het Bouwbedrijf*, vol. II, no 1, Jan 1925, pp. 32–8; in *Theo van Doesburg on Modern Architecture*, p. 35.

7. A. and P. Smithson, 'Mies van der Rohe', in *Architectural Design*, vol. XXXIX, no. 7, July 1969, p. 365.

The spirit of the *Plan Voisin* set the pattern for the 'slum clearances' and 'comprehensive redevelopments' carried out throughout the world in the 1940s, 1950s and 1960s. Two contrasting features of such plans are worth highlighting: the principle that *everything must be wiped clean and renewed at the same time* (the principle of simultaneity), and its converse, the idea that where an individual building is 'protected' on account of its outstanding artistic or historic importance, *it is preserved as a 'museum piece'*, a dead survival from the past, embalmed and cut off from the life of today.

From the 1960s onwards, however, architectural theory reacted against the utopianism of the early modern movement. Already at the CIAM '59 conference in Otterlo, Aldo van Eyck proclaimed: '*The time has come to gather the old into the new; to rediscover the archaic principles of human nature*'.[8] It began to be realized that city building must be a gradual, dynamic process rather than an instantaneous, static product. Among the books and essays that signalled the start of this new way of thinking – of which some have already been mentioned in earlier chapters – are:

1961	Jane Jacobs	*The Death and Life of Great American Cities*
1963	Joseph Rykwert	*The Idea of a Town*
1965	Christopher Alexander	*A City is not a Tree*
1966	Aldo Rossi	*L'architettura della città*
1966	Robert Venturi	*Complexity and Contradiction in Architecture*
1973	Herman Hertzberger	*Huiswerk voor meer herbergzame vorm*
1975	Rob Krier	*Stadtraum*
1975	Colin Rowe and Fred Koetter	*Collage City*

Too often, however, when the lessons of these publications began to be applied in practice, the 'old' continued to be seen only as something to be conserved from the past, and not as an essential ingredient of the present. The number of buildings thought worthy of preservation grew, but attitudes to them did not fundamentally change. In the words of the Flemish architect bOb (*sic*) Van Reeth,

From the moment that we began to see that the old city was something of value and not something that must be torn down, it

8. A. van Eyck, in O. Newman, *CIAM '59 in Otterlo*, Karl Krämer Verlag, Stuttgart, 1961, p. 27.

nevertheless continued to be seen as an old city. In other words, the old city was still looked upon as a construction that had served its time, and which could no longer be useful … But a built environment is not like a vintage car that requires you to dress up in knickerbockers when you take it out for a ride. You don't have to behave anachronistically just because you live in an old house. Once you realize this – once you understand the real meaning of simultaneity – then everything recovers an almost incredible freshness. Buildings together make up the city, simultaneously and not separately.[9]

Here, simultaneity is understood in a third, quite different way, entirely opposed to the utopian modernist conception that everything must be either 'of its time' or 'preserved as a relic of the past'. Old buildings are now regarded as contemporaneous with new ones, since both exist simultaneously and both can be equally useful. The corollary of this is that the old fabric of the city is not scrupulously 'preserved' like an antique car kept in a motor museum and brought out, if at all, on ceremonial occasions; it is regarded as a functioning tool, which one is not afraid to convert to new uses or update as needed. It is respected and valued, not nostalgically or merely as 'heritage', but as a useful part of our everyday environment.

A consequence of this third, 'post-modern' concept of simultaneity is that buildings should be built *generously*. On one hand, their dimensions must be generous: they must not be so tightly tailored to their original function that they quickly become obsolete, but have a *loose fit* which allows them to be adapted to other uses. On the other hand, their specification must also be generous: they must be built to last a long time, *to extend generously through time* as well as space.

Just as the third conception extends the role in architecture of *time* by so to speak 'lengthening the duration of the present', it also enlarges the importance of *space*. Old buildings are no longer seen as museum pieces to be preserved as objects of art, but as functional containers of space. One considers oneself free to alter their physical structure and construction in order to extend the usefulness of that space. Apart from its service to the space, the building as object has no value. The solid walls, floors and roofs of buildings are necessary solely to bring into being interior spaces, and the solid forms of building-masses to give rise to urban spaces. More abstractly one can say, as in the last chapter, that both mass and space occur simultaneously as positive 'figures', but the role of the mass is supportive. It does not exist for its own sake, but in order to enable the space to come into existence.

9. B. Van Reeth, in W. Koerse and B. Van Reeth, *Architectuur is niet interessant*, Hadewijch, Antwerp, 1995, p. 81.

8.2 An alternative manifesto

Although this book deals mainly with events that took place in the 'heroic period' – the fourteen years 1917–31, between the foundation of *De Stijl* and the death of its founder, Theo van Doesburg – its aim is not to be a purely historical study, but to learn lessons from the events and theories of that time which may be relevant to the problems of today. Chapters four and seven speculated that the permeation of the De Stijl idea brought with it dilemmas which were brilliantly but temporarily resolved at Poissy and Barcelona, but that these dilemmas are still 'fundamental to the debate about the validity of the modern movement as a whole'.

The principles identified in the previous section with 'a third kind of simultaneity' are at first sight the antithesis of everything that Le Corbusier, Mies and De Stijl stood for. But are they? This chapter will argue that the buildings and writings of the heroic period contain many clues to and intimations of the new insights which only came to prominence fifty years later, in the 1960s and 1970s. Let us first try to summarize these insights. The following twelve points might be placed beside the sixteen points of Van Doesburg's 1924 manifesto, 'Towards a Representational Architecture'.

1. We build in order to delimit habitable spaces. I say 'delimit' rather than 'enclose', because the habitable space created by buildings includes outdoor spaces such as porticos, colonnades, interior courts and, above all, urban spaces.

2. Architectural space cannot, however, be formed directly. Space can only be 'made' by *forming* its opposite: solid elements. So platforms are levelled, walls and columns erected, roofs laid upon them, and so on.

3. This raises the problem of figure and ground, discussed in the last chapter. Just as a space can only be made by forming solids, it only becomes *visible* at the point where it ceases to exist: where it is interrupted by the surface of a solid. We do not see the form of the room we are in; we see the surfaces of the floor, walls and ceiling. As Rietveld points out, it is impossible to perceive 'universal space' until it has 'some kind of boundary: clouds, trees, or something else that gives it measure ... In fact, the concept "universal space", which we presuppose as always existing, can be manifested only as a continuation of that little piece of realized space which has come into being by virtue of its delimitation.'[10]

10. G. Rietveld, 'Levenshouding als achtergrond van mijn werk', in T M Brown, *The Work of G Rietveld, Architect*, A.W. Bruna & Zoon, Utrecht, 1958, p. 163; see chapter 1, section 1.6.

4. The problem is not merely sensory, but conceptual. Human beings have a natural tendency to perceive whatever is *made directly* as a positive form, and that which *arises indirectly* from that making as a formless background. Since buildings are normally made by putting together pieces of solid matter, and the space inside and outside the building 'arises', the latter tends to be seen merely as 'void', emptiness, nothingness. Therefore we find it much easier to think of and visualize solid things rather than spaces. It takes a special aptitude and a conscious effort to begin to visualize the shape of a space as a positive thing. Architects, too, often suffer from this 'spatial myopia'. They are so preoccupied with the material elements of building, the design of which demands most of their energies (and the cost of which is often the basis for the calculation of their fees), that they ignore the end towards which these elements are only the means: interior space and exterior, urban space.

5. But while it is important to be aware of space, our natural inclination to perceive solid forms – the structural and constructional elements of building – is not groundless. The essence of architecture is *con-struction*: the putting together or piling up of solid elements to make a structure.

6. This brings us from the problem of space to that of time. If we exclude the cost of the site, the cost of building is equal to the cost of procuring and assembling the constructional materials. This is not just a question of money, but of precious, mostly non-renewable energy and other natural resources. It is therefore desirable that the building, once built, should last as long as possible. Building structures need to have *long life*.

7. On the other hand the uses of buildings are constantly changing. A building planned exactly to fit a precise functional programme stands a good chance of being obsolete by the time the builders have left the site. Furthermore, in the case of speculative building, there can be no precise programme, because the eventual tenants and their needs are unpredictable. Either way, there is a mismatch between permanent construction and temporary space-use.

8. The way to overcome this mismatch is to separate, in some way, the quasi-permanent physical structure of the building from the shaping of its spaces, so that the latter can change while the former endures. Our structures can only have *long life* if they also have *loose fit*.

9. Borrowing an analogy from the theatre, the terms 'shell' and 'scenery' have been coined to describe this separation. The permanent *shell* of a theatre is designed to fit every production put on in the life of the building. These productions include plays that have not yet been written, and their staging may involve radical changes in theatrical style undreamed of when the theatre was built. The *scenery*, on the other hand, is designed specifically for each new production by a specialist set designer (not the architect of the building). It is intimately bound up with the plot and mood of the play, the interactions of the various characters, the creative aims of the director, and the precise movements of the actors. This is self-evidently the most practical arrangement; yet outside the theatre we persist generally in designing and building the scenery once and for all, as part of the permanent shell, and are taken aback when we inevitably find ourselves forced to tear down and rebuild that shell to satisfy needs that we had failed to anticipate in the design.

10. The first thing we must do if we want to solve these problems of architectural space – particularly urban space, which is the most neglected – and of what might be called 'architectural time', is to focus our attention on the rather intangible 'space–time' or spatio-functional aspect of architecture; that is, on the interactions between shifting space-use, semi-permanent spatial form and more or less fixed structure. To focus on space-use and space-form does not mean, therefore, that we can afford to pay less attention to the structural shell; only that we must look at it in a different way. We must consider the structure not only as a means, but also as an end.

11. The second thing we need is a more positive attitude to planning. At present – notably in Britain – the planning of cities is mainly directed to the negative prevention of undesirable new building. As a result, town planners are in a weak position when presented with demands for development. Their role is seen as that of obstruction. Unable to act, they can only react. Lack of a positive vision of the future form of the city produces either stasis or chaos: in selected areas, rigid preservation of the 'historic heritage', and elsewhere, surrender to pressure not to stand in the way of 'progress'.

12. Development proposals should instead be regarded as opportunities to complete a pre-existing 'model'. This model is not something that can be fixed, but must evolve with time, like

the city itself. It must also vary in concreteness, according to the scale involved: the larger the scale, the more abstract and diagrammatic the model must be, and the less precisely it can specify the appearance of individual buildings and spaces. The planning of baroque Rome under Sixtus V (1585–90), the purposeful development of central Paris over the last four centuries, and Ildefonso Cerdá's plan for Barcelona (1859) are examples of such large-scale diagrammatic models.

8.3 Particular functions and universal construction

The above twelve points have formal, functional and constructional implications. Here, however, I shall concentrate on the purely formal aspect: the legibility of architectural spaces, and their relation to their complement, architectural masses. This is not a simple matter, because as stated above, it is easier for us to read and conceive the formed masses, and to overlook the resulting spaces.

Once structure is regarded as both an end in itself and as a means of achieving our still somewhat vaguely defined objective, 'an architecture that changes in space and time', some difficult questions arise. What form should the permanent shell and impermanent scenery take? Which shall be the dominant element? Which is figure and which ground? Which constitutes the 'real' architecture?

Two opposed strategies can be distinguished. In the first, the scenery is dominant and the shell recedes into the background. The permanent structure is conceived as a purely utilitarian system of supports, a ground against which the scenery appears as figure. The visible architecture is all contained in the exterior and interior cladding of the shell, not the shell itself. In the second strategy, the shell plays the major role. It forms the enduring monumental background against which the scenery is allowed to play a subordinate though still important part, completing and modifying the structure in various important ways. These two strategies are most clearly epitomized on one hand by the anti-structuralism of Van Doesburg and Mondrian, and on the other, paradoxically, by the late work of the greatest heir of De Stijl, Mies van der Rohe.

The concluding chapter of my earlier book *Proportion* deals with a related territory: the relation between 'necessary' and 'essential' functions in architecture.[11] The distinction between the necessary and the essential is taken from Marc-Antoine Laugier's *Essai sur l'architecture* (1753), in which he distinguishes the essential parts of architecture – the four columns and roof of his hypothetical primitive hut, which do

11. R. Padovan, *Proportion: Science, Philosophy, Architecture*, E. & F.N. Spon, London, 1999, pp. 336-354.

little more than define a habitable space – from those necessary features that are added to make the hut comfortable or convenient for a particular purpose. The beauty of architecture, he says, resides entirely in the former, while the latter is merely a concession. The third category – the ornamental conventions of the academic architecture of Laugier's time – is simply a defect, being neither useful nor beautiful.[12] Building on this distinction, I argue that the distinction between the necessary and the essential does not lie, as is widely assumed, in the contrast between the physical and mental functions of architecture – its uses and meanings – but in that between the particular and the universal. The particular is necessary; the universal is essential. But the essence of architecture, as I have said, is construction: the putting together of discrete parts to make an articulate whole. The construction is therefore that part of architecture which most closely approaches the universal: it is that which has no other function than the provision of a habitable enclosure, in the most universal sense of the word. It may comprise no more than a roof that gives no protection from the cold, or four walls that delimit an urban space but give no shelter from the rain. In chapter one I quoted Rietveld's observation:

> The means of bringing an undefined space to a human scale can consist of a line on a road, a floor, a low wall, a ceiling, a combination of vertical and horizontal planes, curved or flat, transparent or solid. It is never a question of shutting off, but always one of defining what is here and what is there, what is above and what is below, what is between and what is around.[13]

The enclosure embodies only one idea: the elementary principle of human habitation, the demarcation of a habitable space within the open space of nature. All the particular, 'necessary' uses and meanings that buildings and cities can serve or embody are elaborations of, and depend upon, that essential function and that essential meaning. Schopenhauer remarks in *The World as Will and Representation* that:

> Unlike the works of the other fine arts, those of architecture are very rarely executed for purely aesthetic purposes. On the contrary, they are subordinated to other, practical ends that are foreign to art itself. Thus the great merit of the architect consists in his achieving and attaining purely aesthetic ends, in spite of their subordination to ends foreign to them.[14]

12. M.-A. Laugier, *Essai sur l'architecture*, Pierre Mardaga, Brussels, 1979, p. 10.

13. G. Rietveld, unreferenced remark quoted in *G. Rietveld Architect*, exhibition catalogue, Stedelijk Museum, Amsterdam, 1971 and Hayward Gallery, London, 1972.

14. A. Schopenhauer, *The World as Will and Representation*, trans. E.F.J. Payne, Dover Publications, New York, 1969, vol. I, p. 217.

When these practical ends are removed – for instance, when a building no longer serves its original function, or has become disused – we still appreciate it for its intrinsic aesthetic or architectonic properties. A building does not cease to be architecture when it becomes a ruin; in fact, its architectural qualities may even be enhanced, or at least appear more clearly. And this is purely because, when the uses are removed, only the construction remains.

The aim of this discussion is to show that the distinction between shell and scenery is not just a matter of economic expedience – a way of extending the useful life of a structure. It is inherent in the very nature of architecture. The shell is that 'universal' character of a building which endures through all the particular changes and adaptations it may be subjected to; the scenery comprises the changes and adaptations themselves.

The two ideas can thus be related to the theme that runs through this book: the struggle between the universal and the individual. The evolution of humanity towards the universal is the central argument, for instance, of Mondrian's essay 'Neoplasticism in Painting', serialized in the first twelve numbers of *De Stijl*, and of the foundation manifesto published in the thirteenth issue. In the essay Mondrian writes that

> All historical styles have striven towards one common goal: to give expression to the *universal*. Thus every *style* has a *timeless content* and a *transitory appearance*. We can call the timeless (universal) content the *universality of the style*, and the transitory appearance its *distinguishing or individual character*. The style in which the individual aspect is most subordinated to the service of the universal will be the greatest; the purest style will be that in which the universal content is *represented most determinately*.[15]

Just as for Mondrian it is the transitory appearance that gives each style its individual character, one might argue that it is the changing scenery that gives an individual character to the neutral shell at a particular time. A streetscape constantly changes, for instance, as shop fronts are replaced, yet the street has also a universal aspect which persists through all these changes, and which is embodied in its general alignment and proportions and its place in the structure of the city as a whole. If this analysis is correct, then according to Mondrian the best architecture would be that in which the individual scene changes are subordinated to the discipline of the universal shell, rather than one that is determined by these temporary changes. However, let us first explore this second alternative.

15. P. Mondrian, 'De nieuwe beelding in de schilderkunst', in *De Stijl*, vol. I, no. 2, December 1917, p. 13

8.4 The utilitarian support system

In the case of the 'utilitarian support system' the aim is to make the construction so far as possible entirely recessive and passive: a purely utilitarian support system whose design may safely be left to the engineers. It is generally imagined as comprising a series of floor-planes supported by slender or widely spaced steel or reinforced concrete columns, with vertical service-ducts at strategic intervals. One of the earliest intimations of this principle comes not from an architect or engineer but from Mondrian himself – in apparent contradiction of his statement about style in painting quoted above – in his essay on the future of architecture (1922):

> Colour extends *over the whole architecture* ... so that ... each element annihilates the other. But in this way one also comes in collision with the *traditional conception* of 'structural purity'. There still exists the idea that the structure must be 'shown'. The latest technology has already dealt this notion a damaging blow, however. For instance, in reinforced concrete construction, what was defensible in brickwork is no longer valid. If the representational concept requires the structure to be visually suppressed, then the means must be found to satisfy both structural necessity and the demands of representation ... Technology itself is already working hand in hand with the new representational concept ... Whereas brickwork required rounded forms to span spaces, concrete construction produces the flat roof. Steelwork also offers many possibilities.[16]

Mondrian's relegation to the past of the idea that 'the structure must be shown' is almost identical with Le Corbusier's contemporaneous statement:

> One commonplace among Architects (the younger ones): *the construction must be shown* ... But ... to show the construction is all very well for an Arts and Crafts student who is anxious to prove his ability. The Almighty has clearly shown our wrists and our ankles, but there remains all the rest![17]

For Mondrian the traditional structural and constructional nature of architecture is a barrier to the achievement of his neoplastic or 'new representational' architecture. But more interesting than this negative point is his tantalizingly brief allusion to the fitting out of the interior itself: 'In the interior, the empty space will be "given

16. P. Mondrian, 'De realiseering van het neo-plasticisme in verre toekomst en in de huidige architectuur', in *De Stijl*, vol. V, no. 5, May 1922, pp. 69–70.
17. Le Corbusier, *Towards a New Architecture*, The Architectural Press, London, 1946, p. 102.

definition" by so-called "furniture elements", and these in turn related to the articulation of the space, since *the one will be determined simultaneously with the other.*[18]

Mondrian's description anticipates by almost forty years, and in certain respects advances beyond, the more detailed formulation of the concept of 'support structures', developed in the 1950s and 1960s by N.J. Habraken and the Dutch Foundation for Housing Research (SAR). In his book *Supports: An Alternative to Mass Housing* (published in Holland in 1961) Habraken describes support structures as

> not in themselves dwellings or even buildings, but ... capable of lifting dwellings above the ground; constructions which contain individual dwellings as a bookcase contains books, which can be removed and replaced separately; constructions which take over the task of the ground, which provide building ground up in the air, and are permanent like streets.[19]

The necessary complement of the support structure, barely mentioned by Habraken, is some system of light, flexible 'scenery' manufactured to fit the structure, with which the individual inhabitants can subdivide and equip their own houses: something like Mondrian's space-articulating 'furniture elements', or his evocation of the dwelling as '*a construction of coloured and colourless planes, combined with furniture and equipment, which must be nothing in themselves but constituent elements of the whole.*'[20] Note that here the coloured planes and other elements are described as 'nothing in themselves but constituents of the whole'. This begins to expose an inherent conflict in Mondrian's theory: the empty space will be articulated and 'given definition' by the furniture elements, but these, like the coloured planes, are not autonomous elements but must be subordinated to the whole. How can they be subordinated to the whole and yet at the same time bring the whole into being?

In the early 1960s the architectural journals were inundated by a spate of utopian projects for unbuilt, probably unbuildable and almost certainly uninhabitable 'space-cities'. Usually these consisted of endless mega-structures. Examples are:

1960	Erik Friberger	'deck house', Kallebäck, Göteborg[21]
1960	Arato Isosaki	'space city'
1960	Kisho Kurokawa	'agricultural city'

18. Mondrian, 'De realiseering', in *De Stijl*, vol. V, no. 5, May 1922, p. 70.

19. N.J. Habraken, *Supports: an alternative to mass housing*, The Architectural Press, London, 1972, p. 59.

20. P. Mondrian, 'Neo-plasticisme: de woning – de straat – de stad', in *i10*, vol. 1, no. 1, 1927, p. 18.

21. C. Caldenby, J. Lindvall, W. Wang (eds), *20th Century Architecture, Sweden*, Prestel-Verlag, Munich, 1998, p. 145.

1960	Constant Nieuwenhuys	'New Babylon', hanging sector[22]
1961	Kenzo Tange	Tokyo plan
1961	Candilis, Josic and Woods	project for Toulouse-Le Mirail
1962	Yona Friedman	'urbanisme spatiale'
1964	Archigram	'plug-in city'

Finally, rather belatedly, came Superstudio's 'continuous monument', and their proposal, in 1972, to cover the earth with a virtual cartesian grid representing the total evanescence of architecture and its replacement by some form of 'cyber-network' (a fairly accurate anticipation of the World Wide Web), populated by wandering tribes of people carrying banners and trophies, recalling a film by Federico Fellini:

> We can imagine a network of energy and information extending to every properly inhabitable area. Life without work and a new 'potentialized' humanity are made possible by such a network … Naked humanity, walking along the highway with banners, magic objects, archaeological objects, in fancy dress … Nomadism becomes the permanent condition … The model constitutes the logical selection of these developing tendencies: the elimination of all formal structures, the transfer of all designing activity to the conceptual sphere. In substance, the rejection of production and consumption, the rejection of work, are visualized as an aphysical metaphor: the whole city as a network of energy and communications.[23]

The need to build permanent three-dimensional structures – buildings and cities – will thus disappear altogether. Rooms and urban spaces will be defined purely by the spontaneous gathering of greater or lesser numbers of people in any given place. At any moment, a particular part of the continuous gridded platform can become a temporary 'city', while at the next it reverts to being a 'room' occupied by a single person:

> The distances between man and man … generate the ways in which people gather, and therefore 'the places': if a person is alone, the place is a small room; if there are two together, it is a larger room; if there are ten, it is a school; if a hundred, a theatre; if

22. S. Sadler, *The Situationist City*, MIT Press, Cambridge, Mass., 1998, p. 128.
23. Superstudio, 'Description of the microevent/microenvironment', in E. Ambasz (ed.), *Italy: The New Domestic Landscape*, The Museum of Modern Art, New York, 1972, p. 242–4.

a thousand, an assembly hall; if ten thousand, a city; if a million, a metropolis ... The tendency to the spontaneous gathering and dispersing of large crowds becomes more and more detached from the existence of three-dimensional structures.[24]

The reduction of the support structure to a boundless, amorphous, utopian condition of universal harmony could hardly go further. Mondrian would have approved of it, one imagines. Just as he envisaged nearly half a century earlier, the noble human savage is here pictured as 'a part of the whole ... no longer conscious of his individuality ... happy in this earthly paradise that he has himself created'.[25]

The snag is that, as Colin Rowe and Fred Koetter would soon point out in *Collage City*, 'around the corner we may be pretty certain about the superior restaurant and the Lamborghini which is waiting to take us there'.[26] Superstudio's vision of a workless paradise in which electronics has dispensed with the need of production or consumption has the same air of unreality as Jean-Jacques Rousseau's description of the rural retreat he dreams of, where

> I would gather round me ... a band of friends who know what pleasure is ... Every meal will be a feast, where plenty will be more pleasing than any delicacies. There will be no such cooks in the world as mirth, rural pursuits, and merry games ... Our meals will be served without regard to order or elegance; we shall make our dining-room anywhere, in the garden, on a boat, beneath a tree ... No tedious flunkeys to listen to our words, to whisper criticisms on our behaviour ... We shall be our own servants, in order to be our own masters.[27]

Here again, one feels sure that nevertheless, as with Superstudio's Lamborghini, there are servants lurking at a discreet distance to do the cooking and the washing up (not to mention producing the food), and that a comfortable room awaits the picnickers in Rousseau's 'little white house with green shutters' if it should start to rain.

Unfortunately, it seems that we shall continue after all to need shelter, and therefore physical structures of some kind; and unless we are prepared like Superstudio to cover the whole habitable land surface of the globe with a concrete grid, it is likely that our living-platforms will still need to be stacked up in vertical tiers, and these will require structural supports. Two years after Mondrian published his urban utopia, Theo van Doesburg made his more concrete and

24. *Ibid.*, p. 243–4.

25. Mondrian, 'Neo-plasticisme: de woning – de straat – de stad', p. 18.

26. C. Rowe and F. Koetter, 'Collage City', in *The Architectural Review*, vol. CLVIII, no. 942, August 1975, p. 74.

27. J.-J. Rousseau, *Emile*, J.M. Dent & Sons, London, 1911, pp. 317–8.

down-to-earth proposal for the *ville de circulation* or 'circulation city', the aims of which he explained as follows:

> First of all, independence of buildings from structure. In the system of construction I developed from 1924 onwards, such independence is made possible by means of external columns integrated organically into the mechanisms of internal and external circulation. I have used these columns, which are four metres square, to house lifts, plumbing, refuse chutes – in short all the functional mechanisms of the building. Externally, they act as supports for electric cables and streetlighting ... So finally we have replaced the existing system of corridor traffic by an open space ... in which the traffic circulates freely in all directions, both vertically and laterally.[28]

Van Doesburg's 4 m^2 structural towers are about 64 m high and spaced at roughly 36 m and 26 m centres. A vertical stack of 24 m^2 platforms is suspended in the middle of each 36 m space, leaving the ground level almost entirely free for traffic (Figure 8.1). The structural intentions are ambiguous, however. A pinwheel arrangement of columns and beams is shown within the platform areas, but although the ground level is entirely free of columns no suitably dimensioned girders are shown at roof level from which the pinwheel structure might be suspended. Apart from this, the proposal is a perfectly sound one, and extremely advanced for its time. Its urbanistic potential would be greatly enhanced if a regular grid were substituted for Van Doesburg's alternating tartan (Figures 8.2–8.3). Assuming no reduction in density, this would require the towers to be equally spaced at 31 m centres. It would make possible a variety of layouts, including diagonal rows or zigzags (Figure 8.4), clusters (Figure 8.5), or large open squares (Figures 8.6–8.7).

It is in fact very similar to the concept of 'served' and 'servant' spaces that Louis Kahn would develop in the mid-1950s and would realize most clearly in his Richards Medical Research Building at the University of Philadelphia (1957–60). His unexecuted project for a city tower for Philadelphia (1956–7) has an even more striking, though presumably fortuitous, resemblance to Van Doesburg's circulation city of towers and suspended platforms. Kahn's idea that 'a street might want to be a building', and his affirmation of those aspects of architecture that transcend function and circumstance, are pertinent to the kind of shell–scenery relationship we are exploring. He writes:

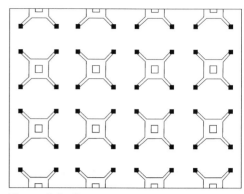

Figure 8.2 'Circulation city': diagrammatic plan

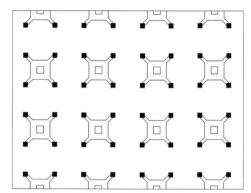

Figure 8.3 'Circulation city': plan at same density on regular 31 m grid

28. T. van Doesburg, 'Die Verkehrstadt', in *Architektur der Gegenwart*, no. 3, 1929; quoted in Zevi, *Poetica*, pp. 135–6.

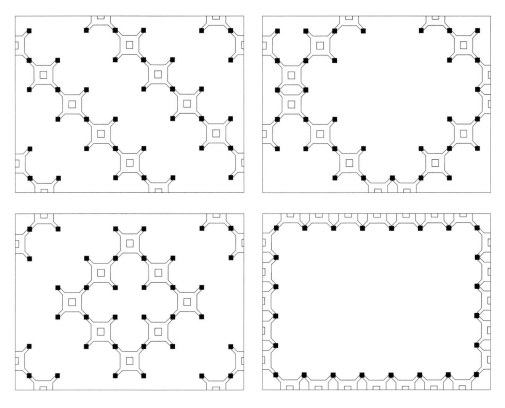

Figure 8.4–8.7
'Circulation city':
alternative layouts
with regular grid

The continual renewal of architecture comes from changing concepts of space. Long ago, when the walls parted and became columns, architecture began. Are there signs of another transformation, equally far reaching? ... Does not a street want to be a building? What does development of our cities mean without an order-concept of movement which gives architectural form and logical position to the harbours of stopping? I believe firmly that we will become ever more attuned to qualities that exist in the spaces that 'want to be' – qualities that transcend function and circumstances.[29]

Nevertheless, the most striking graphic image of such a permanent, 'street-like' support structure dates from only three years after Van Doesburg devised his 'circulation city', and about thirty years before Habraken developed his theory of 'building sites in the air'. In *Le Corbusier and the Tragic View of Architecture*[30] Charles Jencks draws attention to the similarity between Habraken's theory and Le Corbusier's serpentine 'viaduct housing' which forms part of his 'Plan A' for Algiers (1931–2). In *The Radiant City* he describes it as follows: 'The artificial lots are created first: highway + floorings for the

29. L. Kahn, quoted in *The Architectural Review*, vol. CXXI, no. 724, May 1957, p. 344.
30. C. Jencks, *Le Corbusier and the Tragic View of Architecture*, Allen Lane, London, 1975, pp. 122–3.

substructures. And these sites are put up for sale as villas with garden and limitless view.'[31] The structure is literally both a highway and a building. Le Corbusier's sketch shows the vast undercroft structure that supports the motorway infilled by the inhabitants themselves with dwellings in a variety of styles, resembling a vertical casbah.

The picturesque effect of these folkloristic insertions recalls the fate of his own earlier housing at Pessac, which I discussed in chapters four and seven. Were these efforts at self-expression on the part of the occupants at Pessac a marvellous demonstration of human freedom and the principle of permanent support structure and flexible infill, or a criminal desecration of the architect's original vision? In his fascinating study of the Pessac scheme, based on interviews with the inhabitants, Philippe Boudon's conclusion is largely positive:

> One's immediate impression of Le Corbusier's Pessac project in its present state is that it must have been an architectural failure, since otherwise it would never have been transformed to such an extent. In point of fact, however, we see ... that ... the alterations are an entirely positive feature ... Clearly, the range of possible and actual combinations is very wide. But then, according to one of the occupants, the architect's task is to provide an infrastructure, a basic framework, within which the occupants would be able to give a more or less free rein to their own ideas.[32]

But although Le Corbusier's eventual, rather philosophical response to the fact that his purist colony had been almost unrecognizably altered by the residents was 'You know, it is always life that is right and the architect who is wrong',[33] at the time he protested vigorously and tried to have the alterations stopped. In 1931 he wrote angrily to the engineer Vrinat, who had succeeded Le Corbusier's client, Henry Frugès (who became bankrupt in 1929), that

> I cannot begin to understand how you, who are aware of the spirit in which Pessac was created, have allowed the villa no. 14 to fall into such a ruinous state, taking on the appearance of the sort of gewgaw architecture seen in pseudo-modern seaside resorts, or that the bricking up of the arcades has been permitted, or the repainting of the staggered rows ... It is an absolute horror, a most unappealing kind of boorishness ... I had thought that after all the sacrifices that Pessac has involved, one would at least have prevented the people from laying their disastrously incompetent hands on it.[34]

31. Le Corbusier, The Radiant City (1933), Faber & Faber, London, 1967, p. 247.
32. P. Boudon, Lived-in Architecture', Lund Humphries, London, 1972, pp. 114 & 120.
33. Le Corbusier, quoted in Boudon, Lived-in Architecture, p.1.
34. Le Corbusier, letter to M. Vrinat, 16 June, 1931, quoted in M. Ferrand, J.-P. Feugas, B. Le Roy, J.-L. Veyret (eds), Le Corbusier: Les Quartiers Modernes Frugès, Birkhäuser, Basel, 1998, pp. 110–12.

In comparison, Van Doesburg's despairing outcry at the 'improvements' made to his Café Aubette is at once resigned and dismissive: 'the public wants to live in mire and shall perish in mire'.[35]

None of these examples, however – neither Van Doesburg's 'circulation city' nor Kahn's 'streets that want to be buildings', nor Le Corbusier's designs for Algiers and Pessac, nor for that matter any of the 1960s megastructures – is a true example of the support system. In order to fulfil its multiple functions of structural support and housing of services, the support system inevitably acquires a dominant presence. Conversely, if the structure is as purely utilitarian and recessive as the theory implies, it will fail to serve as an ordering principle, and the final outcome will be visual chaos – disguised in Superstudio's collages by the spurious discipline of the all-pervading cartesian grid.

In Le Corbusier's Algiers sketch, the grand sweep and sheer mass of his viaduct is more than strong enough to master aesthetically all the little variations introduced by the freeholders. The architect of the structure still determines the ultimate form of the urban space, just as he does in the space-city projects of the 1960s. And at Pessac, although the purist architecture seemed too fragile to stand up to the owners' assault on it, Le Corbusier certainly aimed to provide more than a merely technical support for their interventions. He intended his houses to be 'poetic': to 'establish certain relationships which aroused the emotions'.[36] Habraken, on the contrary, holds that 'Dwelling is too ordinary a matter to be called art … A detail, a certain dwelling, a given building, may be a work of art, but housing is not architecture.'[37] But in that case, why need architects get involved? Housing that is not architecture already happens almost everywhere, and happens most spectacularly, as both Charles Jencks[38] and Superstudio point out, in shanty towns, *barriadas* and *bidonvilles*. But Superstudio pursue such logic still further, questioning the need to build at all, beyond making provision for basic services:

> Bidonvilles, drop-out city, camping sites, slums, tendopoles, or geodetic domes are all different expressions of an analogous attempt to control the environment by the most economical means. The membrane dividing exterior and interior becomes increasingly tenuous: the next step will be the disappearance of this membrane and the control of the environment through energy (air-cushions, artificial air-currents, barriers of hot or cold air, heat-radiating plates, radiation surfaces, etc.).[39]

35. T. van Doesburg, letter to Adolf Behne, November 7, 1928, quoted in N. Troy, *The De Stijl Environment*, MIT Press, Cambridge, Mass., 1983, p. 176.
36. Le Corbusier, *Towards a New Architecture*, p. 141.
37. Habraken, *Supports*, p. 32.
38. Jencks, *Le Corbusier and the Tragic View*, p. 122.
39. Superstudio, 'Description of the microevent', p. 244.

It is obvious that this was written before we became energy-conscious or aware of global warming. Apart from such technical drawbacks, however, the support system concept fails to provide an adequate ordering principle. In order to build a real city, it seems that the support structure must play a more significant architectural role than Habraken's theory allows. It must become a monumental framework. Within the context of the frame the transitory elements can enjoy a relative freedom. The monument will be intentionally left unfinished. It will constitute, as it were, a 'habitable ruin'.

8.5 The habitable ruin (1): Rossi and Mies

By a habitable ruin I mean something equivalent to the ancient monuments cited by Aldo Rossi as offering the best model for town building: ruins like the amphitheatre at Lucca or Diocletian's palace at Split, which have proved adaptable to completely different functions, and which precisely because of their monumental, 'functionally indifferent' forms offer, in the words of Aldo Rossi, 'potentially the greatest freedom of arrangement, and more generally the greatest functional freedom'.[40] The monumental ruin is building from which all the 'necessities' – in the sense defined in section 8.3 – have been removed. It is architecture stripped down to its essence, the delimitation of space.

It is interesting that in *The Radiant City* Le Corbusier cites as a precedent for his habitable viaduct an existing structure in Algiers occupied in a similar way to Rossi's re-inhabited Roman monuments: the so-called 'Arcades des Anglais', a viaduct constructed in about 1850, under the arches of which a population of fishermen had installed themselves: 'Heavy traffic goes by above their heads: the biggest boulevard in Algiers ....'[41]

Architecture, Rossi maintains, is inherently unconcerned with function, and *for that very reason*, paradoxically, ideally responsive to changes of function. Le Corbusier's viaduct might, like the Arcades des Anglais, make a good framework for housing precisely because it is not designed for housing, but to support a roadway. 'A building that has become a ruin,' says Louis Kahn, 'is again free of the bondage of use.'[42] The same applies to a building designed for a different function than its eventual one, or for no function at all. Like Zen archers, architects must lean to strike the target by *not* aiming at it.[43]

In *L'architettura della città*, Rossi deals directly with the central issue of this chapter. He begins his discussion with the still basically medieval Palazzo della Ragione in Padua (1425). When one visits such a monument, he writes,

40. A. Rossi, 'Two Projects', in *Lotus*, no. 7, 1970.

41. Le Corbusier, *Radiant City*, p. 241.

42. L. Kahn, lecture, Yale University, October 30, 1963, publ. as 'Remarks' in *Perspecta*, no. 9/10, 1965, p. 305.

43. E. Herrigel, *Zen in the Art of Archery*, Routledge & Kegan Paul, London, 1953.

one is struck by the multiplicity of functions that a building of this type can contain over time and how these functions are entirely independent of the form. At the same time, it is precisely the form that impresses us; we live it and experience it, and in turn it structures the city.[44]

Elaborating on the French historian Marcel Poète's theory of persistences or 'permanences',[45] Rossi argues that cities tend to develop along certain axes which are established by their major monuments and other artefacts (such as bridges and streets). These form the backbone of the city plan, and continue to determine and rejuvenate the city's life long after they have outgrown their original purpose. Sometimes they are retained simply because their artistic and historic value *as* monuments is recognized, but more often they survive because of their continuing adaptability and ability to absorb and generate new uses. Again, Rossi cites the Palazzo della Ragione in Padua as an example:

I remarked on its permanent character before, but now by permanence I mean not only that one can still experience the form of the past in the monument but that the physical form of the past has assumed different functions and has continued to function, conditioning the urban area in which it stands and continuing to constitute an important urban focus. In part this building is still in use; even if everyone is convinced that it is a work of art, it still functions quite readily at ground level as a retail market. This proves its vitality.[46]

In a search for an equivalent modern example we could do worse than start with Mies van der Rohe, whom Rossi so much admired:

I have always loved a few modern architects, principally Adolf Loos and Mies van der Rohe, and I still consider myself their student. They are the architects who have done most to establish a thread of continuity with their history and hence with human history ... Mies ... is the only one who knew how to make architecture and furniture which transcend time and function.[47]

And 'transcending time and function' is a good description of the nature of the permanent structure we are trying to define. Just as Rossi speaks of the monument as offering the greatest functional freedom, Mies, in his 1958 interview with Christian Norberg-Schulz, speaks of 'clear structure' as the necessary complement of the 'free

44. A. Rossi, *The Architecture of the City*, MIT Press, Cambridge, Mass., 1982, p. 29.
45. M. Poète, *Introduction à l'urbanisme: l'évolution des villes, la leçon de l'antiquité*, Boivin, Paris, 1929.
46. Rossi, *Architecture of the City*, p. 59.
47. A. Rossi, *A Scientific Autobiography*, MIT Press, Cambridge, Mass., 1981, p. 74.

ground plan'. The structure, he says, 'is the backbone of the whole and makes the variable ground plan possible. Without this backbone, the ground plan would not be free, but chaotically blocked.'[48]

For Mies, the structure provides a clear and positive framework which although functionally 'neutral' can serve both functionally and aesthetically as 'the backbone of the whole', a backbone strong enough to hold the building together not only physically but also formally. A frequent subject of debate between Mies and his friend Hugo Häring, when the two shared Mies' Berlin studio in the early 1920s, was the question whether buildings should be 'universal' or tailored to particular functions. Interviewed forty years later, he recalled urging Häring to

> 'Make your spaces big enough, man, that you can walk around in them freely, and not just in one predetermined direction! Or are you all that sure of how they will be used? We don't know at all whether people will do with them what we expect them to. Functions are not so clear or so constant; they change faster than the building.[49]

Against this, in chapter six I concluded that the problem with Mies van der Rohe's idea – that by making his spaces 'universal' he could enable them to accommodate a wide variety of uses at different times and thus remain viable over a long period – was that his spaces actually impose extreme restrictions on the way the spaces are used. However much he might wish to regard them as 'neutral frames in which man and artworks can carry on their own lives',[50] the fact remains that they are far from neutral. He was more interested in the enduring properties of his buildings than their day-to-day flexibility. As Peter Blundell-Jones remarks,

> Ironically, Mies' claims about flexibility had less to do with the accommodation of change than with the assurance of permanence, for only by providing buildings of neutral elegance to fulfil a wide range of demands could he be sure that he would transcend the great changes he saw in modern life. His buildings have rightly been called monumental, for it is precisely in buildings celebrating the dead that humanity has tried hardest to pursue an architecture of transcendence – transcendence of mortality.[51]

In itself the fact that Mies' structures are monumental rather than strictly neutral is not necessarily a disadvantage. The last thing architecture should aim at is a negative neutrality; it must react positively

48. L. Mies van der Rohe, in C. Norberg-Schulz, 'Ein Gespräch mit Mies van der Rohe', in *Baukunst und Werkform*, Nov. 1958, pp. 615–6; reprinted in F. Neumeyer, *The Artless Word*, MIT Press, Cambridge, Mass., 1991, pp. 338–9.

49. L. Mies van der Rohe, in 'Mies in Berlin', interview by H. Eifler and U. Conrads, RIAS recording, Berlin, Bauwelt Archiv, Berlin, 1966; quoted in F. Schulze, *Mies van der Rohe*, University of Chicago Press, Chicago, 1985, p. 109.

50. L. Mies van der Rohe, in Norberg-Schulz, 'Ein Gespräch', p. 339.

51. P. Blundell-Jones, *Hugo Häring*, Edition Axel Menges, Stuttgart, 1999, p. 156.

with people and objects, in order that a dialogue can arise between the building and its contents. If this view is correct, then whatever its purpose, a building should 'bring about a correspondence between thing and intellect'; it should provide 'a clear (i.e. not entirely neutral) framework for life and thought'.

But there is a second and more serious problem with Mies' solution, and that is the lack of any geometrical or directional inflection of the frame. As we saw in chapter six, Mies' late buildings evolved towards an every greater spatial uniformity. In the new National Gallery in Berlin (Figure 8.8), not only is every point on the floor plan so far as possible identical with every other point, but even directionality is given up. Columns are distributed equally, two on each of the four sides, and the roof structure consists of equally spaced beams running in both directions, forming square coffers. The building no longer has a front or sides, and no 'place' within it, not even the entrance, is distinguished from any other, beyond the fact that the space closest to the windows is over-lit (at least for showing paintings), and the space in the middle under-lit. Consequently no genuine choices are offered to the designer who has to arrange an exhibition in the space. Where all alternatives are the same, no real choice exists. There is minimal dialogue between the building and its contents. Michael Brawne's observation, directed to museum design, is equally relevant to architecture in general: he argues that the pursuit of 'limitless flexibility and undifferentiated space' is founded on a profound misunderstanding of the nature of art and architecture. A work of art is valued for its uniqueness, and architecture (as Kahn said) is the thoughtful making of unique places: 'Neither art nor architecture is anonymous ... It is, therefore, not a matter of competition between art and its environment ... in which one or other aspect has to be negated but of arriving at a working relationship between the two.'[52]

Lastly, despite the permissive undertones of his statement that 'we don't know whether people will do with our spaces what we expect them to do', Mies' 'neutral' style is in fact so insistent that it is unthinkable that anyone would subdivide his spaces otherwise than with the familiar self-effacing screens that are invariably used for the purpose in all his buildings. There is none of the easy informality one finds even in Le Corbusier's houses, where all sorts of apparently heterogeneous objects can be brought in without suggesting that a sacrilege has been committed. Ingo Freed points out, however, that in Mies' brick country house, in contrast to his later works, 'there are options left us. We end up with something variable, something additive.'[53]

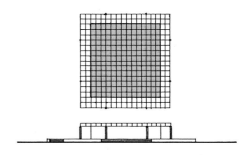

Figure 8.8 Ludwig Mies van der Rohe, National Gallery, Berlin, 1962–7: plan and elevation

52. M. Brawne, *The New Museum*, The Architectural Press, London, 1965, p. 10.

53. I. Freed, 'Mies in America', in F Schulze (ed.), *Mies van der Rohe: Critical Essays*, The Museum of Modern Art, New York and MIT Press, Cambridge, Mass., 1989, p. 193.

8.6 The habitable ruin (2): Hertzberger and the necessity of differentiation

At the opposite end of the spectrum from Mies stands Herman Hertzberger, for whom the permanent structure, while still clear and coherent, must be strongly differentiated in its various parts – hierarchically and in other ways. Thanks to this variation and to the fact that it is left unfinished, it can offer the user hints and opportunities for its completion in many different directions. Hertzberger begins with a forthright condemnation of the activity of the architectural profession as at present constituted, for producing an alien and alienating environment far inferior to the shanty town. A complete reversal of the architect's mindset is needed to overcome this:

> We could set out by assuming, as many do, that all of what architects do is unnecessary, since people, left to themselves, could provide for their own needs better than we can ... Wherever the architect effectively determines the environment of people on a large scale, and gives it form in word and deed, he in fact contributes ... to the perpetuation and extension of a world where everything is too cold, and too large: a grim underworld of gravestone skyscrapers, passages, lifts, tunnels, and pipes through which people circulate and are transported ... In order to make any real contribution, architects have to use everything they influence or create to support the people in the struggle against alienation from their surroundings, from each other, and from themselves.[54]

In contrast to designing permanent structures that are either neutral and recessive (as Habraken envisages) or uniform and generalized (like Mies' late buildings), Hertzberger recommends us to create incidents which allow users to make particular choices: to attach their lives to them, much as molluscs attach themselves to rocks. The aim is not to offer unlimited choice, but a manageable range of suggestions:

> 'Irregularities', such as differences of level and unevenness of the building line, occur frequently, and instead of trying hard to iron these out, we should direct ourselves to forming them consciously in such a way that they can be exploited ... One might assume that in fact we only have to make unemphatic empty cartridges, as neutral as possible, so as to allow the occupants optimal freedom to fulfil their specific wants. However paradoxical it may seem, it is very questionable whether such a degree of freedom might not

54. H. Hertzberger, 'Huiswerk voor meer herbergzame vorm', in *Forum*, vol. XXIV, no. 3, 1973, sections 0.3 & 0.4.

have a paralysing effect ... like the sort of menu that offers such an endless array of dishes that instead of making you hungry it dulls your appetite.[55]

Nevertheless, these incidents, these suggestions, though particular, must be unspecific:

Things which offer themselves explicitly and exclusively for a specific use – to sit on, for instance – are probably not capable of playing other roles when those are asked of them ... It has as it were been too clearly worked out what is expected of the user; what is, or is not, permitted ... What we have to aim at is to form the material of the things we make in such a way that ... it will be suitable for more purposes, and thus be able to play as many other roles as possible in the service of the various individual users, so that each will then be able to react to it for himself, interpreting it in his own way, annexing it to his familiar environment, to which it will then make a contribution.[56]

Thus it is necessary to leave buildings unfinished: to leave room for the inhabitants to complete them themselves. New buildings should be something like ruins that have been taken over and appropriated by a population of squatters:

What matters then is that the occupants have to go and build their own accommodation, and in this process architects cannot do more than hand them the tools by which they will be moti-vated to thinking and working for themselves ... The more some-body is personally able to influence his surroundings the more involved and attentive he becomes, and also the more likely he will be to give them his love and care.[57]

This sounds remarkably similar to what happened to Le Corbusier's Cité Frugès, as described by Henri Lefèbvre:

Perhaps it was because he was a genius and because (for better or worse) men of genius never do precisely what they set out to do, but the fact of the matter is that in Pessac Le Corbusier produced a kind of architecture that lent itself to conversion and sculptural ornamentation. And what did the occupants do? Instead of installing themselves in their containers, instead of adapting to them and living in them 'passively', they decided that as far as

55.   *Ibid.*, sections 2.3 and 4.4.
56.   *Ibid.*, section 2.2.
57.   *Ibid.*, sections 6.3 and 7.1.

possible they were going to live 'actively'. In doing so they showed what living in a house really is: an activity.[58]

On the other hand, the architect is obliged to do more than just 'handing the user the tools' and leaving him to finish the job. He has to make a start. And that is where the difficulties begin. The problem with Hertzberger's own buildings is that the conditions and purposes for which they are designed – especially the larger and more institutional ones – too often require them to be over-specific. The rough concrete surfaces, meant to imply non-completion, merely appear uncongenial, a sort of calvinistic denial of sensual pleasure. They invite not participation but vandalism; they offer too nearly the same cold, grim, over-sized, deterministic environment of 'passages, lifts, tunnels, and pipes' that Hertzberger himself condemns. Furthermore, his geometry is too intricate: he cannot resist playing the ingenious maker of interlocking patterns. In short, one must try to do as Hertzberger says, not as he does. It is true that the architect should embody in the framework he provides a certain degree of complexity and variety. But though varied, these built-in incidents should be general; though complex, they should nevertheless be simple. In chapter three I quoted Judd: *'Complicated* is the opposite of *simple*, not *complex'*.[59]

The aim, therefore, is an unfinished structure, yet paradoxically one that is satisfying and inspiring in its present as well as in its future state: a folly, a *beautiful, habitable ruin*. Now, Mies van der Rohe's Barcelona Pavilion is unlikely to be a building that Hertzberger would cite as a model of the 'more hospitable form' that he is seeking. Yet it is really an elemental house, reduced to its essential nature as a basic shelter, so to speak 'unfinished', being free of the usual bondage to the utilitarian requirements and circumstantial demands normally made of a completed domestic dwelling.

At the same time, though 'basic', it is also relatively complex. Unlike the Berlin National Gallery and other late works, it is far from being just a glass box containing so many identical square metres of floor space. Like an ancient monument, but unlike the 'space city' projects of the sixties, it embodies what Hertzberger calls 'irregularities'. If for some reason it were ever decided to 'finish' it by adding a bathroom and a kitchen to convert it into a 'real' house, it would provide many differentiated kinds of space, hooks on which the designers and occupants could hang their own contributions. When we build shells which we intend to last a long time, and to serve many, unpredictable functions during their life, the spaces defined by the structure should, like those of the Barcelona Pavilion, vary from

58. H. Lefèbvre, preface, P Boudon, *Lived-in Architecture*, Lund Humphries, London, 1972.
59. D. Judd, 'On furniture', in *Donald Judd, Complete Writings 1975–1986*, Van Abbemuseum, Eindhoven, 1987, p. 107.

expansive to intimate, elongated to square, low to high, dark to bright.

8.7 The necessary and the essential: Oud and Le Corbusier

The advantage of the ruin as a model for architecture is as I have said not just that it is incomplete but that it presents us with an architecture stripped down to its essentials. Like Laugier's primitive hut, the ruin, too, reveals the distinction between the essential and the necessary. Paradoxically it is often only when a utilitarian building, such as a barn or warehouse, falls into disuse that we become aware of its *architectural* qualities. This is because, as Louis Kahn points out, it is 'again free of the bondage of use'; the necessities are stripped away and its essential, architectonic properties are revealed – properties which (to quote Kahn again) 'transcend function and circumstances'. A monument is merely a building which has been designed to serve the essential functions exclusively. A building that once served but has since lost the *necessary* functions, and has become a ruin, acquires the character of a monument, because it retains only the essential.

Once more, Le Corbusier's Quartiers Modernes Frugès provides us with an ideal example. As Philippe Boudon discovered, one of the reasons why Le Corbusier's houses proved so adaptable is that the plans are highly generalized; the functions of spaces are not made too specific. Boudon compares the Pessac plans instructively with those of Oud's five similarly dimensioned row houses at the Weissenhofsiedlung (1927) (Figures 8.9–10). In the latter, every available square metre is designed to function in only one way. But Le Corbusier, the formalist, asks each element to serve several roles. He exposes the staircase, for instance, so that it functions not only as a circulation device but also as a visual incident – a 'stage-set' – in the living room, which is thereby incorporated in the whole 'architectural promenade' of the house. Oud, the functionalist, encloses the staircase in an entrance hall, so that it can serve only one function:

> It is interesting to note that the theory of separate functions in urban development formulated by Le Corbusier is not reflected in his architecture, least of all at Pessac. His theoretical insistence on separate spheres for 'living', 'working' and 'communications' has no tangible effect as far as the Q.M.F. [Quartiers Modernes Frugès] were concerned. There we find virtually no corridors, no clear areas designed to serve exclusively as communication links.

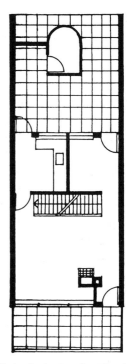

Figure 8.9 Le Corbusier, Quartiers Modernes Frugès, Pessac, 1925: house plan

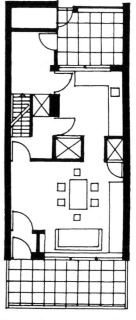

Figure 8.10 J.J.P. Oud, Weissenhofsiedlung, Stuttgart, 1927: house plan

Oud's design, on the other hand, allowed for numerous elements of this kind.[60]

Despite Le Corbusier's definition of the house as purely a tool or a machine for living in, at Pessac and elsewhere he approached it, on the contrary, as a question of form; he set out, as he said, to make poetry. In 1923, in the same year that he published *Vers une architecture*, and well before the Neue Sachlichkeit had properly got under way in Germany, a most penetrating and prophetic book was published by Theo van Doesburg's close friend, the German art critic Adolf Behne. In *Der moderne Zweckbau* or *The Modern Functional Building* Behne contrasts 'functionalism', exemplified by Hans Scharoun, with 'rationalism', represented, entirely appropriately, by Le Corbusier:

> If every building is part of a built whole, then it recognizes from its aesthetic and formal requirements certain universally valid rules, rules that do not arise from its individual functional character *[Zweckcharakter]* but from the requirements of this whole … The functionalist prefers to exaggerate the purpose to the point of making it unique and momentary (a house for each function!) but the rationalist takes the purpose broadly and generally as readiness for many cases, simply because he gives thought to the enduring qualities of building, which perhaps see many generations with changing requirements and therefore cannot live without leeway … As the functionalist looks for the greatest possible adaptation to the most specialized purpose, so the rationalist looks for the most appropriate solution for many cases. The former wants what is absolutely fitting and unique for the particular case; the latter wants what is most fitting for general need, the norm.[61]

According to Behne, the rationalist recognizes '*universally* valid rules … that do not arise from its *individual* functional character'; he considers the '*enduring* qualities of building' (i.e. *long life*), which require '*leeway*' (i.e. *loose fit*); he is concerned with the '*general*' rather than the '*particular*'. Note the recurrence (highlighted by my italics) of ideas and oppositions that have been the leitmotiv of the present chapter, and indeed of this whole book: polarities such as *individual–universal, particular–general, unique–normal, specialized–multipurpose, temporary–permanent*, and so on.

60. Boudon, *Lived-in Architecture*, pp. 31–2.

61. A. Behne, *Der moderne Zweckbau*, 1923; English edition, *The Modern Functional Building*, The Getty Research Institute, Santa Monica, Calif., 1996, pp. 137–8.

8.8 Collage and contradiction

In *Collage City*, Rowe and Koetter propose that buildings and cities should be assembled piecemeal, as 'collages'. They compare this to the method of *bricolage* by which Picasso, for example, incorporates incongruous items such as scraps of wallpaper or cane seating in a cubist painting, or bicycle handlebars and saddle into a sculpture of a bull's head. Pointing to the propensity of the first half-century of modern architecture to offer only the once-for-all solution – 'the *single central vision*' – which, like Le Corbusier's *ville radieuse* or Wright's Broadacre City, offers either absolute integration or total atomization, and is thus inherently static – the authors propose instead one that is composite and even contradictory, an agglomeration of fragmentary utopias:

> it is better to think of an aggregation of small, and even contradictory, set pieces (almost like the products of different régimes) than to entertain fantasies about total and 'faultless' solutions which the condition of politics can only abort ... [Because] collage is a method deriving its virtue from irony ... it is also a strategy which can allow Utopia to be dealt with as an image, to be dealt with in *fragments* without our having to accept it *in toto* ... [and thus] fuel a reality of change, motion, action and history.[62]

At present the architect is still employed almost exclusively to provide a product: the finished building. In the hard struggle to survive in the commercial world, everything encourages us to concentrate on the product and forget that this is only a means to an end: the provision of living space. What is needed is a new machinery of patronage geared, not to a product, but to a *process*. We must learn to focus, not on erecting buildings, but on adapting them.

The past is rich in examples. For economic and technical reasons, the medieval cathedrals were built by generations of master builders employed by successive ecclesiastical clients with constantly changing requirements. In his book *The Contractors of Chartres* John James describes how the vast enterprise of constructing, within a century and a half, '50 major religious buildings and 400 minor churches, abbeys and retreats' in northern France was undertaken by a population of two and a half million people – 'an incredible and magnificent effort that has few parallels among unindustrialized countries in the history of the world'.[63] All this was achieved by mobile crews, and despite 'inadequate long term supervision, and *ad hoc* solutions'.[64]

62. Rowe and Koetter, 'Collage City', pp. 81 and 90.

63. J. James, *The Contractors of Chartres*, Mandorla Publications, Wyong, N.S.W., 1981, p. 11.

64. Ibid., p.13

James asks us to imagine

> a modern building designed successively by Walter Gropius, Frank
> Lloyd Wright, Le Corbusier, Alvar Aalto and others. Our reaction
> might be to say 'what a mess'. But no ... each newly arrived archi-
> tect would be forced by the difficulties of the problems posed
> earlier, and of the alien conceptions already begun, to think much
> more carefully and deeply about the job ... That is why one often
> finds that additions are an architect's best work: the complexities
> of the problem squeeze a better solution out of us. Once we
> understand that there is no reason why great architecture cannot
> be created in this additive way, working unhurriedly over genera-
> tions, then the apparent chaos in organization of these giant struc-
> tures begins to reveal an underlying order.[65]

Such additive, organic ways of making buildings and cities did not
cease with the end of the middle ages; they continued through the
renaissance and baroque periods. The greatest achievements of
European architecture from the fifteenth to the eighteenth century
are often urban spaces defined by façades added to existing buildings,
or interiors created within existing structures. Examples that come to
mind are Alberti's external and internal refacing of San Francesco in
Rimini (1440–61); Michelangelo's transformations of the
Campidoglio in Rome (1537–64) and of the Baths of Diocletian to
create the church of Santa Maria degli Angeli (1561–4); Palladio's
alterations and additions to the medieval Palazzo della Ragione at
Vicenza – a structure very similar to the one in Padua cited by Rossi –
to create the Basilica (1546–9); and finally, the growth of the basilica
and piazza of St Peter in Rome between 1506 and 1656, to the
successive designs of Bramante, Perruzzi, Raphael, Giuliano da
Sangallo and the younger Antonio da Sangallo, Michelangelo, Della
Porta, Maderno and Bernini.

Since the mid-1960s architectural theory has moved away from
the utopianism of the earlier modern movement and towards a
revaluation of the medieval, renaissance and baroque approach to
city building as a dynamic process rather than a final, static product. In
1966, the year in which Rossi's *L'architettura della città* was published,
there also appeared another work which marks the symbolic beginning of this new way of thinking: Robert Venturi's *Complexity and
Contradiction in Architecture*. Venturi's viewpoint is essentially similar
to Rossi's, although he differs in his approach and his choice of examples. He redirects us to the principle with which this chapter began:
that the creation of urban space demands a recognition that the

65. *Ibid.*, p. 14.

requirements of the exteriors and interiors of buildings must be kept separate. He points out that this contradicts the concept of spatial continuity advocated by De Stijl and other early modern movements:

> Contrast between the inside and the outside can be a major mani-festation of contradiction in architecture. However, one of the powerful twentieth century orthodoxies has been the necessity of continuity between them: the inside should be expressed on the outside ... The idea has been emphasized by historians ranging from Vincent Scully's discovery of its early evolution in Shingle Style interiors to its flowering in the Prairie House and its culmina-tion in De Stijl and the Barcelona Pavilion. Flowing space produced an architecture of related horizontal and vertical planes ... Such cornerless architecture implied an ultimate continuity of space.[66]

(Note, incidentally, Bruno Zevi's advocacy of the 'open corner', and his pinpointing of this as the salient architectural achievement of De Stijl: see chapter one, section 1.14.)

Venturi points out that to make interiors which look like exteriors is nothing new: 'The Renaissance church interior, for instance, has a continuity with its exterior; the interior vocabulary of pilasters, cornices, and drip mouldings is almost identical in scale and some-times material with its exterior vocabulary.'[67]

Such continuity of outside and inside space and surface allowed Giambattista Nolli to draw the plan of Rome in 1749 as a continuity of public 'interiors', either roofed or unroofed. However, this conti-nuity applies only to the major *public* interiors, such as churches and theatres, which Nolli equates with the streets and squares as *figure*, against the formless, undifferentiated ground constituting the mass of private building, with its hundreds of smaller rooms serving particular functions. The separation of private from public, of transitory from permanent, of spaces that serve specific uses from those that are 'just for people to *be* in', is the key to architecture's flexibility. To make this possible, as Venturi points out, the inside must in general be able to differ from the outside, and therefore the intervening structure must adapt to the separate requirements of both:

> Designing from the outside in, as well as the inside out, creates necessary tensions, which help make architecture. Since the inside is different from the outside, the wall – the point of change – becomes an architectural event. Architecture occurs at the meeting of interior and exterior forces of use and space. These interior and environmental forces are both general and particular,

66. R. Venturi, *Complexity and Contradiction in Architecture*, The Museum of Modern Art, New York, 1966, p. 71.

67. *Ibid.*

generic and circumstantial. Architecture as the wall between the inside and the outside becomes the spatial record of this resolution and its drama. And by recognizing the difference between the inside and the outside, architecture opens the door once again to an urbanistic point of view.[68]

8.9 Both that which is unchangeable and that which is in change

It is a common human tendency to seek a single big idea that will explain everything. In his study of Tolstoy's view of history, Isaiah Berlin borrows a metaphor from the Greek poet Archilochus:

'The fox knows many things, but the hedgehog knows one big thing'. Scholars have differed about the correct interpretation of these dark words, which may mean no more than that the fox, for all his cunning, is defeated by the hedgehog's one defence. But, taken figuratively, the words can be made to yield a sense in which they mark one of the deepest differences which divide writers and thinkers, and, it may be, human beings in general. For there exists a great chasm between those, on one side, who relate everything to a single central vision, one system more or less coherent or articulate, in terms of which they understand, think and feel — a single, universal, organizing principle in terms of which alone all that they are and say has significance — and, on the other side, those who pursue many ends, often unrelated and contradictory ... related by no moral or aesthetic principle; these last lead lives, perform acts, and entertain ideas that are centrifugal rather than centripetal, their thought is scattered or confused, moving on many levels, seizing upon the essence of a vast variety of experiences and objects for what they are in themselves.[69]

Berlin applies this analogy to the classification of thinkers and writers: Plato and Dostoevsky, for instance, are 'hedgehogs', Aristotle and Pushkin, 'foxes'. Of his subject, Tolstoy, he concludes, however, that he

was by nature a fox, but believed in being a hedgehog; that his gifts and achievement are one thing, and his beliefs, and consequently his interpretation of his achievement, another; and that consequently his ideals have led him, and those whom his genius for persuasion has taken in, into a systematic misinterpretation of what he and others were doing or should be doing.[70]

---

68. Ibid., pp. 88–9.
69. I. Berlin, *The Hedgehog and the Fox*, Weidenfeld & Nicolson, London, 1953, p. 1; partly quoted in Rowe and Koetter, 'Collage City', p. 80.
70. Berlin, *Hedgehog and Fox*, p. 4.

Rowe and Koetter transfer Berlin's metaphor to architecture. They lament the apparent shortage of foxes among the leaders of modern architecture; and it is undeniable that all the principal subjects of this book – Le Corbusier, Mies, Van Doesburg, Mondrian – seem at first sight to have more of the hedgehog than the fox about them. Despite their obvious differences, they all professed to believe in one big idea: the universal, as opposed to the individual or the particular. Le Corbusier tirelessly restated his universal solution for the housing of mankind, with the *Ville Contemporaine* of 1922, the *Ville Radieuse* of 1933 and the various *unités d'habitation* of 1945–65. Mies, throughout the same four decades, gradually eliminated from his work 'everything that is not reasonable',[71] coming finally to the ultimate distillation, the 'universal space' of his National Gallery in Berlin (1962–7). Van Doesburg and Mondrian endlessly refined and elaborated the idea that humanity was moving inevitably away from the individual and towards the universal.[72]

When one looks more closely, however, things are not so one-sided. What Berlin says of Tolstoy – that he was by nature a fox, but believed in being a hedgehog – can be applied with at least equal force to each of them. Van Doesburg's constantly changing allegiances are reflected in his adoption of alter egos and pseudonyms (such as the Dutch dadaist poet I.K. Bonset and the Italian futurist anti-philosopher Aldo Camini) to express the tumult of mutually conflicting ideas that possessed him. Mondrian, too, was continually evolving. Having arrived at the ultimate expression of the 'universal' around 1931, he set about destroying it. First, the lines were multiplied and duplicated (1932–42), and finally the lines themselves dissolved away. Yve-Alain Bois describes the process as follows:

> The next stage is to abolish line itself (as form) by means of 'mutual oppositions,' which Mondrian explicitly attempts in his New York work ... But this last destruction only becomes possible when repetition is openly accepted; and the acceptance of this possibility – whose exclusion is the point of departure for neo-plasticism – prepares the way for another radical transformation in Mondrian's theoretical machine; he discovers a need to destroy the entity known as the 'surface' ... 'I think', he said at the end of his life, 'the destructive element is too much neglected in art'.[73]

Rietveld, for his part, was obviously more fox than hedgehog, and scarcely bothered to disguise himself as the latter. But even Mies, the most outwardly hedgehog-like of all, had much of the fox about him, as is demonstrated by the uncertain, meandering course he followed

71. L. Mies van der Rohe, in *Conversations about the Future of Architecture*, Reynolds Metals Co. sound recording, 1958.

72. 'Manifest I van "De Stijl", 1918', in *De Stijl*, vol. II, no. 1, November 1918, pp. 2–5.

73. Y.-A. Bois, 'The Iconoclast', in Bois, Joosten, Rudenstein, Janssen, *Piet Mondrian 1872–1944*, Little, Brown & Co., Boston, 1994, p. 316.

between the expressionistic glass skyscrapers of 1921–2 and the Farnsworth house of 1946–51 (see chapter six, sections 6.4 and 6.5). Finally, the ever-contradictory Le Corbusier must be classed, as Rowe and Koetter themselves conclude, as 'a fox assuming hedgehog disguise for the purpose of public appearance',[74] because while the large public world of his urban plans is simple, straightforward and dictatorial, the small private world of his villas is witty, complex and convoluted.

Venturi emphasizes that many of the greatest masterpieces of the modern movement – notably Le Corbusier's Villa Savoye – deny modernism's theoretical continuity of space in subtle ways, by means of built-in complexities and contradictions. His interpretation of the Villa Savoye is the almost complete antithesis of Giedion's description of 'inner and outer space penetrating each other inextricably (see chapter one, section 1.10):

> The Villa Savoye with its wall openings which are, significantly, holes rather than interruptions, restricts any flowing space rigidly to the vertical dimension ... Its severe, almost square exterior surrounds an intricate interior configuration glimpsed through openings and from protrusions above. In this context the tense image of the Villa Savoye from within and without displays a contrapuntal resolution of severe envelope partly broken and intricate interior partly revealed. Its inside order accommodates the multiple functions of a house, domestic scale, and partial mystery inherent in a sense of privacy. Its outside order expresses the unity of the idea of house at an easy scale appropriate to the green field it dominated and possibly to the city it will one day be part of.[75]

In fact, the Villa Savoye can be considered as a highly wrought essay in the concept of support structure and infill. The principle of the 'free plan' made possible by a regular column grid was proposed by Le Corbusier as early as 1915 with the 'domino' system, and first clearly demonstrated in the second design for the villa at Carthage (1929).[76] It might be defined as 'Habraken + art'. It so happens that in these cases the architect of the support system was also the architect of the intricate interior. But when in the 1960s the villa had actually become a ruin, threatened with demolition, and Le Corbusier was campaigning to save it, his intention was not to restore it to its original state but to transform it. To his intense annoyance he was prevented from doing this by the official designation of the building as a historic monument.[77] Having embraced the third, post-modern, meaning of 'simultaneity', he

74. Rowe and Koetter, 'Collage City', p. 81.
75. Venturi, *Complexity and Contradiction*, pp. 72–3.
76. *Le Corbusier et Pierre Jeanneret, 1910–1929*, Girsberger, Zurich, 1956, pp. 178–9.
77. J. Sbriglio, *Le Corbusier: La Villa Savoye*, Birkhäuser, Zurich, 1999, pp. 162–9.

found himself the prisoner of the second, modernist one, according to which an old building can be preserved only as a dead monument, not as a living piece of useful space. Likewise, in the conflicts of individual *versus* universal and private *versus* public, Le Corbusier stood again for both/and, not either/or. As André Wogensky puts it, 'he sought to reconcile the protection of privacy with the collective life, to resolve the individual/society dilemma by integrating the dwelling units into a community – what he called the vertical village'.[78]

In conclusion, the lesson of the handful of artists and thinkers discussed in this book is that we must seek, not one simple thing, but many complex and contradictory things. In art and architecture, the universal cannot exist without the individual, the simple without the complex, the structure without the habitable space, and so on. In each of the pairs of opposites, or apparent opposites, that have been our themes, we must choose not one side or the other, but both together. One half of the pair needs and complements the other:

universal	+	individual
simple	+	complex
one	+	many
shell	+	scenery
permanent	+	transitory
unchanging	+	changeable
general	+	special
regular	+	irregular
sameness	+	difference
collective	+	private

Mondrian realized this from the start. In section 8.2 I quoted his statement in the second instalment of 'Neoplasticism in Painting' that 'In painting, although it has a timeless content ... style can only be *manifested in the domain of appearances* ... The universal in style must be expressed through the individual, that is, *by means of* representation.'[79] At the cost of distorting the meaning of Mondrian's essentially abstract statement, intended to refer only to painting, I have applied it by analogy to the concrete problem of the polarity in architecture of universal shell and specialized scenery, comparing the former to the 'timeless content' and the latter to the 'transitory appearance'

The hedgehog-like pursuit of the absolute and the universal is often described as 'platonic', and Berlin names Plato as the first of his

78. A. Wogensky, foreword to R. Walden (ed.), *The Open Hand*, MIT Press, Cambridge, Mass., 1977, pp. ix–x.
79. Mondrian, 'De nieuwe beelding', in *De Stijl*, vol. I, no. 2, December 1917, p. 13.

hedgehogs; but it was none other than Plato who wrote that the philosopher

> must refuse to accept from the champions either of the One or the many Forms the doctrine that all Reality is changeless; and he must turn a deaf ear to the other party who represent Reality as everywhere changing. Like a child begging for 'both', he must declare that Reality or the sum of things is both at once – all that is unchangeable and all that is in change.[80]

80. Plato, *The Sophist*, in F.M. Cornford, *Plato's Theory of Knowledge*, Routledge & Kegan Paul, London, 1960, p. 242.

Bibliography

Alexander, C. 'A city is not a tree', in *Architectural Forum*, April–May 1965.

Ambasz, E. (ed.). *Italy: The New Domestic Landscape*, The Museum of Modern Art, New York, 1972.

Apollonio, U. *Futurist Manifestos*, Thames & Hudson, London, 1973.

Aquinas, T. *De veritate* (1256), in *Quaestiones Disputatae*, P. Lethielleux, Paris, 1925.

Aquinas, T. *Summa Theologiae*, ed. T. McDermott, Methuen, London, 1991.

Auping, M. (ed.). *Abstraction – Geometry – Painting*, Harry N. Abrams, New York, 1989.

Baljeu, J. *Theo van Doesburg*, Studio Vista, London, 1974.

—— *Morgen kan het architectuur zijn*, exhibition catalogue, Gemeentemuseum, The Hague, 1975.

Banham, R. *Theory and Design in the First Machine Age*, The Architectural Press, London, 1960.

Behne, A. *The Modern Functional Building*, The Getty Research Institute, Santa Monica, Calif., 1996.

Bekaert, G. 'In memoriam Dom Hans van der Laan', in *Archis*, no. 9, 1991.

Berlage, H.P. 'Normalisatie in woningbouw', 1918.

Berlin, I. *The Hedgehog and the Fox*, Weidenfeld & Nicholson, London, 1953.

Bier, J. 'Kann man im Haus Tugendhat wohnen?', in *Die Form*, October 1931.

Blaauw, C.J. 'J L M Lauweriks', in *Bouwkundig Weekblad*, no. 53, 1932.

Blaser, W. *Mies van der Rohe, Furniture and Interiors*, Academy Editions, London, 1982.

Blijstra, R. *C van Eesteren*, Meulenhoff, Amsterdam, 1971.

Blotkamp, C. *Ad Dekkers*, Staatsuitgeverij, The Hague, 1981.

—— 'Mondriaan ↔ architectuur', in *Wonen TABK*, nos. 4–5, March 1982.

—— *Mondrian: The Art of Destruction*, Reaktion Books, London, 1994.

Blotkamp, C. et al. *De Beginjaren van De Stijl 1917–1922*, Reflex, Utrecht, 1982.

Blundell-Jones, P. *Hugo Häring*, Axel Menges, Stuttgart, 1999.

Boccioni, U. 'Technical manifesto of futurist sculpture', in *Poesia*, Milan, 11 April 1912, reprinted in U. Apollonio, *Futurist Manifestos*, Thames & Hudson, London, 1973.

Boekraad, C.; Bool, F.; Henkels, H. *De Stijl: De Nieuwe Beelding in de Architectuur*, Delft University Press, Delft, 1983.

Boesiger, W. (ed.). *Le Corbusier, œuvre complète*, Les Editions Girsberger, Zurich, 1952.

Bois, Y.-A. 'Mondrian et la théorie de l'architecture', in *Revue de l'Art*, Paris, 1981.

—— *Painting as Model*, MIT Press, Cambridge, Mass., 1993.

Bois, Y.-A. and Troy, N. *De Stijl et l'architecture en France*, Pierre Mardaga, Brussels, 1985.

Bois, Y.-A.; Joosten, J.; Rudenstine, A.Z.; Janssen, H. *Piet Mondrian 1872–1944*, Little, Brown & Co., Boston, 1994.

Boudon, P. *Lived-in Architecture*, Lund Humphries, London, 1972.

Boyd White, I. and Wit, W. de (eds). *Hendrik Petrus Berlage: Thoughts on Style 1886–1909*, The Getty Center, Santa Monica, Calif., 1996.

Brawne, M. *The New Museum*, The Architectural Press, London, 1965.

Brooks, H.A. *Le Corbusier's Formative Years*, University of Chicago Press, Chicago and London, 1997.

Brown, T.M. *The Work of G Rietveld, Architect*, A.W. Bruna & Zoon, Utrecht, 1958.

Cache, P. 'A plea for Euclid', in *ANY*, no. 24, 1999.

Caldenby, C.; Lindvall, J.; Wang, W. (eds). *20th Century Architecture, Sweden*, Prestel-Verlag, Munich, 1998.

Carter, P. 'Mies van der Rohe: an appreciation on the occasion of his 75th birthday', in *Architectural Design*, March 1961.

Casciato, M.; Panzini, F.; Polano, S. (eds). *Funzione e Senso: Architettura – Casa – Città. Olanda 1870–1940*, Electa, Milan, 1979.

Cohen, J.-L. *Le Corbusier and the Mystique of the USSR*, Princeton University Press, Princeton, N.J., 1992.

Doesburg, T. van. 'Fragmenten I', in *De Stijl*, vol. I, no. 4, 1918.

—— 'Denken – aanschouwen – beelden', in *De Stijl*, vol. II, no. 2, 1918.

—— 'Fragmenten III: Beelding van innerlijkheid en uiterlijkheid', in *De Stijl*, vol. II, no. 4, 1919.

—— 'Moderne wendingen in de kunstonderwijs', in *De Stijl*, vol. II, no. 9, 1919.

—— 'Slotbemerkingen', in *De Stijl*, vol. II, no. 10, 1919.

—— 'Schilderkunst van Giorgio de Chirico en een stoel van Rietveld', in *De Stijl*, vol. III, no. 5, 1920.

—— 'Rondblik', in *De Stijl*, vol. IV, no. 6, 1921.

—— 'The significance of colour for interior and exterior architecture', in *Bouwkundig Weekblad*, vol. 44, no. 21, 1923.

—— 'Tot een beeldende architectuur', in *De Stijl*, vol. VI, no. 6/7, 1924.

—— *Grundbegriffe der neuen gestaltenden Kunst* (1925); English translation: *Principles of Neo-Plastic Art*, Lund Humphries, London, 1969.

—— 'Le Corbusier's ville contemporaine', in *Het Bouwbedrijf*, vol. II, no. 1, 1925; in *Theo van Doesburg on Modern Architecture*, Birkhäuser Verlag, Basel, 1990.

—— 'Van kompositie tot contra-kompositie', in *De Stijl*, vol. VII, no. 73/74, 1926.

—— 'Schilderkunst en plastiek', in *De Stijl*, vol. VII, no. 7, 1927.

—— '10 jaren Stijl', in *De Stijl*, vol. VII, nos. 79 & 84, 1927.

—— 'Der Kampf um den neuen Stil', in *Neuer Schweizer Rundschau*, 1929.

—— 'Die Verkehrstadt', in *Architektur der Gegenwart*, no. 3, 1929.

—— 'From intuition towards certitude' (1930), in *Réalités Nouvelles*, no. 1, 1947.

—— 'Towards White Painting', in *Art Concret*, April 1930.

—— 'elementarisme', in *De Stijl*, last issue, 1932.

—— 'Stuttgart-Weissenhof 1927', in *On European Architecture*, Birkhäuser Verlag, Basel, 1990.

Doesburg, T. van and Eesteren, C. van. 'Vers une construction collective', in *De Stijl*, vol. VI, no. 6/7, 1924.

Doesburg, T. van; Hoff, R. van't; Huszar, V.; Kok, A.; Mondrian, P.; Vantongerloo, G.; Wils, J. 'Manifest I. van "De Stijl", 1918', in *De Stijl*, vol. II, no. 1, 1918.

Doig, A. 'De architectuur van De Stijl en de westerse filosofische traditie', in *Wonen TABK*, no. 15–16, 1982.

—— *Theo van Doesburg: Painting into architecture, theory into practice*, Cambridge University Press, Cambridge, 1986.

Doorman, M. *Steeds mooier: over vooruitgang in de kunst*, Ooivaar, Amsterdam, 2000.

Dunnett, J. 'The architecture of silence', in *The Architectural Review*, vol. CLXXVIII, no. 1064, October 1985.

Dunster, D. (ed.). *Mies van der Rohe: European Works*, Academy Editions, London, 1986.

Eddington, A.S. *The Nature of the Physical World*, J.M. Dent, London, 1935.

Eesteren, C. van. 'Moderne stedebouwbeginselen in de practijk', in *De Stijl*, vol. VI, no. 10/11, 1925.

Embden, S.J. van. 'Herinneringen aan Dom Van der Laan', in *Architectuur/Bouwen*, no. 9, 1991.

Fechner, G.T. *Vorschule der Aesthetik*, Georg Holms, Hildesheim, 1978.

Ferrand, M.; Fergas, J.-P.; Le Roy, B.; Veyret, J.-L. (eds), *Le Corbusier: Les Quartiers Modernes Frugès*, Birkhäuser, Basel, 1998.

Friedman, A.T. *Women and the Making of the Modern House*, Harry N. Abrams, New York, 1998.

Friedman, M. (ed.), *De Stijl: 1917–1931, Visions of Utopia*, Phaidon, London, 1982.

Georgiadis, S. *Sigfried Giedion: An Intellectual Biography*, Edinburgh University Press, Edinburgh, 1993.

Giedion, S. *Space, Time and Architecture*, Harvard University Press, Cambridge, Mass., 1941.

Gleick, J. *Chaos*, Sphere Books, London, 1988.

Gombrich, E.H. *Art and Illusion*, Phaidon, London, 1959.

—— *Meditations on a Hobby Horse*, Phaidon, London, 1963.

—— *The Story of Art* (1950), Phaidon, London, 1966.

Habraken, N.J. *Supports: an alternative to mass housing*, The Architectural Press, London, 1972.

Hegel, G.W.F. *The Philosophy of History*, Dover Publications, New York, 1956.

Heidegger, M. *Vorträger und Aufsätze*, Günther Neske Verlag, Pfullingen, 1954.

Herrigel, E. *Zen in the Art of Archery*, Routledge & Kegan Paul, London, 1953.

Hertzberger, H. 'Huiswerk voor meer herbergzame vorm', in *Forum*, vol. XXIV, no. 3, 1973.

Hesse-Frielinghaus, H. *Briefwechsel Le Corbusier – Karl Ernst Osthaus*, Karl Ernst Osthaus Museum, Hagen, 1977.

Holly, M.A. *Panofsky and the Foundations of Art History*, Cornell University Press, Ithaca, N.Y., 1984.

Honey, S. 'The office of Mies van der Rohe in America: the towers', in *UIA-International Architect*, no. 3, 1984.

Hume, D. *A Treatise of Human Nature*, J.M. Dent, London, 1911.

Ikonomou, E. and Mallgrave, H.F. (eds.), *Problems of Form and Space in Nineteenth Century German Aesthetics: Vischer, Fiedler, Wölfflin, Göller, Hildebrand, Schmarsow*, The Getty Center, Santa Monica, Calif., 1993.

Jacobs, J. *The Death and Life of Great American Cities*, Random House, New York, 1961.

Jaffé, H.L.C. *De Stijl*, Thames & Hudson, London, 1970.

—— *Mondrian*, Thames & Hudson, London, 1970.

—— *De Stijl 1917–1931*, Harvard University Press, Cambridge, Mass., 1986.

James, J. *The Contractors of Chartres*, Mandorla Publications, Wyong, N.S.W., 1981.

Jencks, C. *Modern Movements in Architecture*, Penguin Books, Harmondsworth, 1973.

—— *Le Corbusier and the Tragic View of Architecture*, Allen Lane, London, 1975.

—— *The Language of Post-Modern Architecture*, Academy Editions, London, 1984.

Johnson, P. *Mies van der Rohe*, The Museum of Modern Art, New York, 1953.

Judd, D. 'Art and Architecture' (1987), in *Donald Judd: Architektur*, Westfälischer Kunstverein, 1989.

—— *Donald Judd, Complete Writings 1975–1986*, Van Abbemuseum, Eindhoven, 1987.

—— 'It's hard to find a good lamp', in *Donald Judd Furniture*, Museum Boymans-Van Beuningen, Rotterdam, 1993.

Kahn, L. 'Remarks', in *Perspecta*, no. 9/10, 1965.

Kant, I. *Prolegomena to every future metaphysics that may be presented as a science*, Open Court Publishing, La Salle, Ill., 1902.

Kaufmann, E. *Architecture in the Age of Reason*, Dover Publications, New York, 1955.

—— *Da Ledoux a Le Corbusier*, Gabriele Mazzotta, Milan, 1973.

Koerse, W. and Reeth, B. Van. *Architectuur is niet interessant*, Hadewijch, Antwerp, 1995.

Köhler, W. *Dynamics in Psychology*, Faber & Faber, London, 1942.

Küper, M. and Zijl, I. van. *Gerrit Th. Rietveld 1888–1954*, Centraal Museum, Utrecht, 1992.

Laan, H. van der. *Architectonic Space* (1977), E.J. Brill, Leiden, 1983.

—— 'Instruments of Order', in Graatsma, W. (ed.), *Ter ere van Dom Hans van der Laan, 1904–1991*, Rosbeek, Nuth, 1992.

Laporte, P. 'Cubism and relativity – with a letter of Albert Einstein', in *Art Journal*, vol. XXV, no. 3, 1966.

Laugier, M.-A. *Essai sur l'architecture*, Pierre Mardaga, Brussels, 1979.

Lauweriks, J.L.M. 'Het nut en doel van der kunst', in *Theosophia*, no. 15, 1906–7.

Le Corbusier. *Towards a New Architecture* (1923), The Architectural Press, London, 1946.

—— *The City of Tomorrow* (1924), The Architectural Press, London, 1971.

—— 'L'Exposition de l'Ecole spéciale d'architecture', in *L'Esprit Nouveau*, no. 23, May 1924.

—— *The Decorative Art of Today* (1925), The Architectural Press, London, 1987.

—— *Précisions* (1930), MIT Press, Cambridge, Mass., 1991.

—— *The Radiant City* (1933), Faber & Faber, London, 1967.

—— *The Modulor* (1950), Faber & Faber, London, 1961.

Le Corbusier and Pierrefeu, F. de. *The Home of Man*, The Architectural Press, London, 1948.

Leck, B. van der. 'De plaats van het moderne schilderen in de architectuur', in *De Stijl*, vol. I, no. 1, 1917.

Maritain, J. *Art and Scholasticism* (1923), Sheed & Ward, London, 1932.

Mies van der Rohe, L. 'Ich mach niemals ein Bild', in *Bauwelt*, August 1962.

Milner, J. *Mondrian*, Abbeville Press, New York, 1992.

Mondrian, P. 'De nieuwe beelding in de schilderkunst', in *De Stijl*, vol. I, nos. 1–12, 1917–18.

—— 'Het bepaalde en het onbepaalde', in *De Stijl*, vol. II, no. 2, 1918.

—— 'Natuurlijke en abstracte realiteit', in *De Stijl*, vols. II–III, 1919–20.

—— 'De realiseering van het neo-plasticisme in verre toekomst en in de huidige architectuur', in *De Stijl*, vol. V, nos. 3–5, 1922.

—— 'Neo-plasticisme: de woning – de straat – de stad', in *i10*, vol. I, no. 1, 1927.

Mumford, L. *The Highway and the City*, Secker & Warburg, London, 1964.

Neumeyer, F. *The Artless Word*, MIT Press, Cambridge, Mass., 1991.

Newman, O. *CIAM '59 in Otterlo*, Karl Krämer Verlag, Stuttgart, 1961.

Norberg-Schulz, C. *Existence, Space and Architecture*, Studio Vista, London, 1971.

Oud, J.J.P. 'Het monumentale stadsbeeld', in *De Stijl*, vol. I, no. 1, 1917.

—— 'Architectuur en normalisatie bij den massabouw', in *De Stijl*, vol. I, no. 7, 1918.

Overy, P. *De Stijl*, Studio Vista, London, 1969.

—— *De Stijl*, Thames & Hudson, London, 1991.

Overy, P.; Müller, L.; Oudsten, F. den. *The Rietveld Schröder House*, Butterworth Architecture, London, 1988.

Oxenaar, R.W.D. *Bart van der Leck 1876–1958*, Rijksmuseum Kröller-Müller, Otterlo/Stedelijk Museum, Amsterdam, 1976.

—— 'Van der Leck and De Stijl', in Friedman, M. (ed.), *De Stijl: 1917–1931, Visions of Utopia*, Phaidon, London, 1982.

Ozenfant, A. and Jeanneret, C.-E. *Après le cubisme*, Paris, 1918.

Padovan, R. 'The pavilion and the court', in *The Architectural Review*, December 1981.

—— 'Mies van der Rohe reinterpreted', in *UIA-International Architect*, no. 3, 1984.

—— 'Machines à méditer', in Achilles, R.; Harrington, K.; Myrhum, C. (eds), *Mies van der Rohe: Architect as Educator*, Illinois Institute of Technology/University of Chicago Press, Chicago, 1986.

—— *Dom Hans van der Laan and the Necessity of Limits*, Stichting Manutius, Maastricht, 1989.

—— *Dom Hans van der Laan, Modern Primitive*, Architectura & Natura Press, Amsterdam, 1994.

—— *Proportion: Science, Philosophy, Architecture*, E. & F.N. Spon, London, 1999.

Panofsky, E. *Gothic Architecture and Scholasticism*, Thames & Hudson, London, 1957.

—— 'Der Begriff des Kunstwollens', in *Aufsätze zu Grundfragen der Kunstwissenschaft*, Berlin, 1964.

Paul, J. 'German neo-classicism and the modern movement', in *The Architectural Review*, London, vol. CLII, no. 907, September 1972.

Pawley, M. *The Private Future: Causes and consequences of community collapse in the West*, Thames & Hudson, London, 1973.

Peter, J. (ed.). *The Oral History of Modern Architecture*, Harry N. Abrams, New York, 1994.

Petit, J. *Le Corbusier lui-même*, Geneva, 1970.

Plato, *Timaeus*, in Cornford, F.M., *Plato's Cosmology*, Routledge & Kegan Paul, London, 1937.

—— *The Republic of Plato*, trans. and ed. F.M. Cornford, Oxford University Press, Oxford, 1941.

—— *The Sophist*, in Cornford, F.M., *Plato's Theory of Knowledge*, Routledge & Kegan Paul, London, 1960.

—— *Theaetetus*, in Cornford, F.M., *Plato's Theory of Knowledge*, Routledge & Kegan Paul, London, 1960.

—— *Laws*, Penguin Books, Harmondsworth, 1970.

Poète, M. *Introduction à l'urbanisme: l'évolution des villes, la leçon de l'antiquité*, Boivin, Paris, 1929.

Pommer, R. and Otto, C.F. *Weissenhof 1927 and the Modern Movement in Architecture*, University of Chicago Press, Chicago, 1991.

Pound, E. *Literary Essays of Ezra Pound*, Faber & Faber, London, 1954.

Rapoport, A. *House Form and Culture*, Prentice-Hall, Englewood Cliffs, N.J., 1969.

Rasmussen, S.E. 'Le Corbusier: die kommende Baukunst?', in *Wasmuths Monatshefte für Baukunst*, 1926.

—— *Experiencing Architecture*, MIT Press, Cambridge, Mass., 1964.

Richardson, J. *A Life of Picasso*, Jonathan Cape, London, 1996.

Riegl, A. *Die Spätrömische Kunstindustrie* (1901), Vienna, 1927.

Rietveld, G.T. 'Aanteekening bij kinderstoel', in *De Stijl*, vol. II, no. 9, 1919.

—— 'Nut, constructie (schoonheid: kunst)', in *i10*, vol. I, no. 3, 1927.

—— 'Inzicht', in *i10*, no. 17/18, 1928.

—— 'New functionalism in Dutch architecture' (1932), in Küper, M. and Zijl, I. van, *Gerrit Th. Rietveld 1888–1954*, Centraal Museum, Utrecht, 1992.

—— *Gerrit Rietveld: Texten*, Impress, Utrecht, 1979.

Riley II, C.A. *The Saints of Modern Art*, University Press of New England, Hanover and London, 1998.

Rossi, A. 'Two Projects', in *Lotus*, no. 7, 1970.

—— *A Scientific Autobiography*, MIT Press, Cambridge, Mass., 1981.

—— *The Architecture of the City* (1966), MIT Press, Cambridge, Mass., 1982.

Rousseau, J.J. *Emile*, J.M. Dent & Sons, London, 1911.

—— *The Social Contract and Discourses*, J.M. Dent & Sons, London, 1913.

Rowe, C. and Koetter, F. 'Collage City', in *The Architectural Review*, vol. CLVIII, no. 942, August 1975.

Russell, B. *History of Western Philosophy*, George Allen & Unwin, London, 1961.

—— *The Problems of Philosophy*, Oxford University Press, Oxford, 1998.

Sadler, S. *The Situationist City*, MIT Press, Cambridge, Mass., 1998.

Sbriglio, J. *Le Corbusier: La Villa Savoye*, Birkhäuser, Zurich, 1999.

Schapiro, M. *Mondrian: On the Humanity of Abstract Painting*, George Brazilier, New York, 1995.

Schopenhauer, A. *The World as Will and Representation*, Dover Publications, New York, 1969.

Schulze, F. *Mies van der Rohe: A Critical Biography*, University of Chicago Press, Chicago, 1985.

Schulze, F. (ed.). *Mies van der Rohe: Critical Essays*, The Museum of Modern Art, New York and MIT Press, Cambridge, Mass., 1989.

Semper, G. *The Four Elements of Architecture and Other Writings*, Cambridge University Press, 1989.

Sennett, R. *The Fall of Public Man*, Alfred A. Knopf, New York, 1977.

Severini, G. 'La peinture d'avant-garde', in *De Stijl*, vol. I, nos. 2–10, 1917–18.

Singelenberg, P. *H P Berlage: Idea and style, the quest for modern architecture*, Haentjens Dekker & Gumbert, Utrecht, 1972.

Smithson, P. 'Rietveld, builder and furniture designer', in *Bauen und Wohnen*, vol. 19, no. 11, 1965.

Smithson, A. and P. 'The heroic period of modern architecture', in *Architectural Design*, vol. XXV, no. 12, 1965.

—— 'Mies van der Rohe', in *Architectural Design*, vol. XXXIX, no. 7, July 1969.

Straaten, E. van. *Theo van Doesburg 1883–1931*, Staatsuitgeverij, The Hague, 1983.

Summerson, J. 'Viollet-le-Duc and the rational point of view', in *Heavenly Mansions*, Cresset Press, London, 1949.

Tegethoff, W. *Mies van der Rohe, Die Villen und Landhausprojekte*, Richard Bacht, Essen, 1981.

Troy, N. *The De Stijl Environment*, MIT Press, Cambridge, Mass., 1983.

Tugendhat, G. 'Die Bewohner des Hauses Tugendhat äussern sich', in *Die Form*, November 1931.

Tummers, N.H.M. *J L Mathieu Lauweriks: zijn werk en zijn invloed*, G. van Saane, Hilversum, 1968.

Vandenberg, M. *New National Gallery, Berlin*, Phaidon Press, London, 1998.

Venturi, R. *Complexity and Contradiction in Architecture*, The Museum of Modern Art, New York, 1966.

Viollet-le-Duc, E.-E. *Discourses on Architecture*, George Allen & Unwin, London, 1959.

Walden, R. (ed.), *The Open Hand*, MIT Press, Cambridge, Mass., 1977.

Windsor, A. *Peter Behrens: Architect and Designer 1868–1940*, The Architectural Press, London, 1981.

Wölfflin, H. 'Zur Lehre den Proportionen' (1889), reprinted in *Kleine Schriften*, Basel, 1946.

Wright, F.L. *The Natural House*, Horizon Press, New York, 1954.

Zeising, A. *Neue Lehre von den Proportionen des menschlichen Körpers*, Leipzig, 1854.

Zevi, B. *Poetica dell'architettura neoplastica*, Libreria Editrice Politecnica Tamburini, Milan, 1953; 2nd, revised edition, Giulio Einaudi, Turin, 1974.

—— 'Architecture versus historic criticism', in *RIBA Transactions*, no. 5, 1984.

Zukowsky, J. (ed.), *Mies Reconsidered: His Career, Legacy and Disciples*, The Art Institute of Chicago and Rizzoli International, New York, 1986.